MORE COMMENTS ON *THE BRIDGE*...

"In the 21st Century, marketing will be the major force driving all commerce. Professor Macdonald's fascinating *The Bridge* outlines valuable tools for success in this business. The winners will pay heed."

–Peter Georgescu, Chairman Emeritus of Young & Rubicam Advertising, and author of *The Source of Success,*
Five Enduring Principles at the Heart of Real Leadership.

"Creating advertising is challenging, stimulating, rewarding and maddening. Bruce Macdonald's book on advertising is all these things - - minus the maddening part."

–Josh Tavlin, Senior Partner, Group Creative Director
Ogilvy & Mather, New York

"Whether it be the acquiescent television viewer, the detached observer of dailylife or the inattentive person witnessing world events, advertising has a way of seeping into our consciousness and persuades all of us to act in specific ways. Bruce Macdonald's admirable book *The Bridge*, offers a behind-the-scene analysis of why the techniques of marketing work and how the giants of Madison Avenue have energized the American economy by persuading the consumer to buy. Macdonald goes deeper in using history to good advantage in providing interesting perspectives of the logo as far

–Wm.T. O'Hara, President Emeritus, Bryant
Author of *"Centuries of Success."*

"More than ever, cutting edge marketing is the ultimat succeed in the fast paced digital economy. Mastering the discipline of effective marketing is the gateway to unlimited growth for your business - and is well expressed in Bruce Macdonald's book *The Bridge*."
–Andre LaCroix, CEO of Inchape, London (former CEO of EuroDisney, Paris)

The Bridge

The Role of Design in Marketing

Bruce Macdonald

with contributions from leading advertising executives,
graphic designers and college professors

New York

The Bridge

The Role of Design in Marketing

by Bruce Macdonald

ISBN: 978-1-60037-446-3 (Paperback)

Library of Congress Control Number: 2008927031

Published by:

MORGAN · JAMES
THE ENTREPRENEURIAL PUBLISHER ™
www.morganjamespublishing.com

Morgan James Publishing, LLC

1225 Franklin Ave. Ste 325

Garden City, NY 11530-1693

Toll Free 800-485-4943

www.MorganJamesPublishing.com

Habitat for Humanity®
Peninsula
Building Partner

Dedication

- To Arch Macdonald
Who was one of Leo Burnett's finest writers.
His copy was spare, strong and true.
He inspires me still.

Contents

Foreword

Preface

Acknowledgements

Section I: Bridge-Building Basics

Section III: Promotion by Design

FOREWORD

Of Bridges and Design and Life

In many ways you can understand the book in your hands because of design.
That's right, design.
The readability of the type that was chosen, the overall proportion of the page and the hierarchy of information communicated by the size and weight of the body text, the subheads and chapter headings, the margins and even the paper, are all aspects of design that helps you cross over into the information in this book.
Without design it would be chaos.
Yet you are hardly aware of any of these things

And that's a good thing.
Design is critical to all kinds of successful outcomes, whether it is launching a business, helping a package communicate while sitting on the shelf , or just aiding a thirsty consumer find the refreshment stand and quickly and clearly understand what to order.

Design works both subtly and boldly.
Successful design involves many decisions and requires important management skills from both marketers and designers.
And while no book can communicate all the variations and possibilities, this book can help both marketers, students of marketing, and designers reach across the gaps and build bridges to success: in the marketplace, in the classroom and at the drawing board.

I believe that this book will help marketers become better designers-and designers better marketers.

-Bruce Bendinger,
Advertising man, Author and Publisher,
Chicago

PREFACE

On Bridges and Knowledge

I have seen, sketched and crossed many kinds of bridges: steeply- arched stone structures like you can find in Scotland, massive steel and cable creations that can span rivers or bays to take you from San Francisco to Marin County, and modest concrete slabs that can get you and your car across the creeks near our home in the mountains of Virginia.

Big or small, impressive or modest, they all serve a single purpose-to get you from one spot to another. There are of course other kinds of bridges, the non-physical kind. I'm talking about bridges of thought, of understanding, of knowledge. This book is about all such bridges, some you see, some you don't.

The bridges we'll explore in this book are design-related visual bridges that span the gaps that too often exist between a marketing strategy and the whole range of decisions that are a part of a coordinated marketing execution. Think of all the visual decisions that are (by necessity) part of a single marketing program, like the logo that reflects the company's (and brand's) true personality, the package that reveals (and enhances) the brand's benefits, the promotional literature that sparks action and finally, the advertising that expands our thoughts and desires through artful, often humorous imagery. The end result of a carefully planned, researched marketing strategy is priceless. When marketing strategies don't take this path, in effect don't cross these bridges, the gap in their effectiveness can be prodigious; the whole effort amounting to nothing more than shooting skeet.

Concept and Framework

The concept of this book is based on why people do what they do, prefer one idea or product or service over another etc. and how art and design play the pivotal role in influencing and directing choices in the marketplace. Additionally, the book's concept will cover how market communicators (graphic designers and marketing managers) use this knowledge in the creation of logos, packages, brochures, promotions and ad campaigns.

You will encounter six bridges in this book, what I call "The Six Bridges of Marketing" Here's how they relate to each other.

The First Bridge (Chapters 2 and 3) is all about the logo from their origins in ancient times to the look and purpose of the logo in modern times as a brand or corporate identity program. This book will explore the dynamic of such brands, how they started, became part of our lives and ultimately pillars of our collective aesthetic experience.

The Second Bridge (Chapter 4) is all about people and motivation. The marketer must determine what affects his target audience and know how to do it. Research is the marketing tool required for unlocking a consumer's preferences and prejudices.

The Third Bridge (Chapter 5) is packaging, which is, perhaps, the most tangible. You can pick it up, you can even drink from it; that essential receptacle from which we all get our food, drinks or toys.

The Fourth Bridge (Chapter 6) is called placement. Here is where the package gets to show off in what I call the "Arena." I have compared the store (in particular a Supermarket) to a Roman coliseum and the packages to the gladiators fighting for brand dominance.

The Fifth Bridge (Chapter 7) is promotion, where marketing executives plan and execute compelling price-off programs or lotteries to lure customers into the arena and to their products.

The Sixth Bridge (Chapter 9) is advertising. No marketing tool has received so much attention as advertising-the stuff of movies, books and jokes. Yet for all of that it is still the main event, the center ring. Certainly it is where the most money is spent. Advertising industry figures exist for all advertising which project that almost
$250 billion dollars is spent every year in America to create, produce and place advertising. If you add Europe and Asia the total approaches a half trillion. Big bucks!

In this chapter we will examine the inside workings of a typical advertising agency and the functions of the major players and meet some memorable ad men and their famous campaigns. These are the building blocks of a modern marketing communications program.

The very first chapter, entitled "Marketing-The Essential Bridge" is a short introduction to the principles of marketing. It is, I hasten to add, a simplified intro-based on those marketing practices I encountered (often from my learned clients) related to the visual marketing goals: the logo, the package or promotional advertisement. A modern university (such as mine) will teach a more in-depth study of this subject and including analysis of a firm's current marketing strengths and weaknesses, environmental issues, market segmentation, targeting and positioning and the interrelationships between marketing and other disciplines. A serious marketing student should take advantage of such courses at their own schools.

What of the other chapters? How do they fit in? They serve in a support role, providing either colorful and instructive tales of brand warfare (The Cola Wars-Chapter 8), or the currently popular craft of public relations (Spin-chapter 10) or the under-appreciated but essential marketing tool known as the brochure (Chapter 11). The last chapter (12) is a review of where we've been and where (we think) we're going. It is called the Bridge to the Future. Design plays a major part in all six bridges, sometimes directly as in the design of a package, or logo or advertisement, sometimes indirectly, as in the research behind a successful campaign or promotion.

So, the diversity and persuasiveness of marketing communications is one subject of this book. The other subject is the critical link between design and marketing goals, the same links that comprised the "whole egg" of many years ago. The underlying truth is that all people, all consumers, will respond consciously or unconsciously to good design, where ever they encounter it.

And when that happens the marketing engine moves, and magic happens.

Making Magic

And just what exactly is marketing magic?

Since the mid 1970s advertising agencies have realized that their clients needed (and wanted) more than what they were then providing, traditional media based advertising. As a result the big agencies began buying design firms, like mine in 1976 and offering our skills in logo design, packaging etc. to their clients under one umbrella. In time they bought more affiliates, like public relations firms, direct mail agencies, retail gurus, media placement firms etc. If there is one linking factor (bridge) common to all, it is the presence of graphic design. It turns up in ads, in packages, on displays, on billboards, on bus sides, on trucks, even hot air balloons floating above football stadiums. Brands (logos) are even appearing super-sized on the facades of sports complexes, like the Staples Center in Los Angeles.

This book is designed to work on several levels. On the first level it is a straight time line laying out the development of communications from plan to man, ultimately from corporation to consumer going back to the first millennium. Professors and students will be able to trace the origins of logos, packaging and selling to their roots (perhaps for the first time), providing a deep base for understanding the marketing expressions of present day.

On a second level students will be able to read the inner thoughts and observations of active, present day practitioners of the communicative arts: graphic designers, retailers, marketing chiefs, promoters, packaging pros, writers and art directors – the advertisers from Madison Avenue.

Their stories are often colorful and what they practice is, in a way, magical. When done with skill, occasionally with brilliance, a simple but well-designed newspaper ad, a memorable TV commercial, a radio spot or a clever package can convince a total stranger, an unknown consumer in fact - to act, to open his wallet, to part with his money and make a purchase.

That's magic!

-Bruce Macdonald,
Lexington, Virginia

ACKNOWLEDGEMENTS

Many people helped in the writing, research and preparation of this book. Some are friends, some colleagues from the business world and some are colleagues from the university/teaching world. In addition I had a number of contributors, men who are still active or recently retired from advertising, graphic design or the corporate marketing world. All took the time to write short essays, anecdotes or words of wisdom for me and my readers. Their names and profiles are available to readers in the back of this book.

To be more specific, I'd like to mention and thank: Robert MacCullum, author and retired businessman who read and corrected a number of final drafts, as did my old friend Ralph Rydholm, a former agency head and worldwide creative director for J. Walter Thompson Advertising. Another advertising executive, Bruce Bendinger lent his expertise to the content of the book, supplying regular inputs of energy and new ideas throughout the process. Professor J. Bard McNulty (Trinity College, Connecticut) helped me get the ancient history of the logo right, especially that of the Bayeux Tapestry. Robert Lauterborn, Professor of Advertising at the University of North Carolina/Chapel Hill, read drafts and contributed to the book generously. An old London friend, popular writer Jay Levinson, provided unique and special material (as well as advice) for this book. Rob White, a seasoned copywriter with a major ad agency in Chicago, contributed valuable input about daily life in today's ad agency.

Two (former) prominent advertising agency chief executives have generously contributed much of their time to help my students understand the business of visual communication. They are: Ed Ney, Chairman Emeritus of Young & Rubicam Advertising in New York, and Harry Jacobs, Chairman Emeritus of the Martin Agency in Richmond, VA. Both are contributors to this book.

Because so much of the book's content was tested and sharpened by the demands of the classroom, it is appropriate to thank some of the men and women who helped me learn the craft of teaching and/or provided the opportunity to teach. These include: Alden Gordon, head of the Fine Arts Department and Gerald Gunderson, Shelby Cullom Davis Professor of

American Business – both of Trinity College, Connecticut. At Washington and Lee University in Lexington, Virginia I would like to thank Pamela Simpson, head of the Fine Arts Department, George Kester and Dean Larry C. Peppers of the Williams School of Business, Economics and Commerce at W&L, who did as much and more for me in the academic world.

Finally this book was helped to its completion by Donelle Bowman, with whom I designed all the pages and graphs through the book. Most of all I'd like to thank my wife and friend Sunny Macdonald, who read more than anyone else and gave wise counsel on many, many occasions. I am grateful to you all.

SECTION I

BRIDGE-BUILDING BASICS

Casselman Bridge, Maryland, built 1813

1

MARKETING

The Essential Bridge

Imagine a bridge.
To function a bridge must connect both sides–that's its job after all. To function well a bridge must allow efficient traffic to go both ways. Now think of that bridge as the marketing process, again allowing traffic (this time ideas) to flow both ways. Those ideas must accomplish goals–essentially to sell products, services or concepts. There are two kinds of entities carrying the ideas across; on one side are business/marketing professionals equipped with technology, research and a focused plan. On the other side we have design professionals, trained in the art of design–persuasion through art, through shape, color, words and pictures. Each thinks their side of the bridge is the most important. Regrettably few in business schools are trained in the basic principles and concepts of design, and few in design schools learn the basics of business marketing.
Yet they can't live without each other. The overall goals of the business community and the necessary and positive response of the consuming public–demands it. Marketing people must manage many projects that have critical design components–like the logo, the package, retail and advertising.
In this chapter, and indeed this book, we will teach marketing people to work more effectively with the range of design issues built into their businesses, and design people to better understand the business concerns of their clients and marketing partners. Whether you come to this book as a professional marketer, professional graphic designer or student in college or

design school, we hope that this book will help make you become better equipped to make the critical journey across the bridge between business and design.

The marketing process is made up of many parts and practices, all powerful weapons, and personified in the topics, subjects, stories and persons profiled in this book–all marketers of one sort or another. The common denominator they all share is that they all practice or utilize design of a product, of a logo, of a package, of an illustration, an advertising or public relations campaign. Each alone is a marketing technique, an essential element of the marketing process. But these techniques aren't alone. None are, or should be.

All of these marketing techniques must be interrelated. The logo must be designed so that it enhances the package, and the package must be created in such a way that it shines in the marketplace (the store), and the advertisement must introduce and reinforce (through frequency of use) an image or idea or association with one that causes the consumer to remember and want one particular brand over another. In concept it is simple–as in, "let's sell something to someone;" but marketing in the execution phase is far more complex.

Part I
What is Marketing?

All businesses anywhere need to understand and practice sound marketing principles to achieve success. Some do it grandly and some modestly.

For example, Wal-Mart, United Airlines, and Procter and Gamble practice marketing in a manner vastly different from a restaurant in Chicago, a laundry in Richmond or a florist in St. Louis, but they are all practicing some form of marketing. One group is doing it on a national, even international scale, the other group on a localized, regionally defined scale.

At any level, however, marketing is an aggressive, strategically-driven process, one which matches the company's directors, managers and designer's skills, strengths and resources (and experience) against a faceless marketplace of potential customers in a highly competitive arena, with the aim of causing an exchange of goods for money. It's not easy.

Today's marketplace is information-rich, maybe too much so.

Information proliferation has made the process of designing and implementing a realistic, effective strategy much tougher. We are in an age of competitive intensity through information bombardment (more on this in Chapter 12). It is a new deal.

The computer and the Internet contribute to it through our Blackberries, YouTube, blogs and our cell phones. Publishers provide it through daily and weekly newspapers (over $45 billion in ad revenue reaching about 60 million households) and the many and diverse magazines (there are over 11,000 magazine titles in the U.S.) on every subject from cooking to fly fishing, television provides it 24 hours a day on more than 500 channels (over 98% of all US households own one television set, 67% have two), radio provides advertising messages on over 14,000 stations, and reach 94% of all Americans over age twelve at least once a week. And finally, guerrilla marketing techniques are at work where we least expect them –through what we see and react to on our city streets, on bus sides, on taxi tops–even hot air balloons parked in the sky above football games. Some call it a tectonic shift, a new paradigm, a move from a commodity based economy to an information economy. The secret of succeeding as a marketer in such an environment is to design your appeal to the consumer through a real understanding of what pushes his/her buttons and then delivering your message through the right media and right design so that it will reach the target consumer. It sounds simple, but it isn't.

The purpose of this book then is to explore and explain the marketing basics, to help you through understanding marketing, make the complex seem as simple as the reason behind it. Essentially we will reveal:

- **What is the purpose of marketing?**
- **How did marketing start?**
- **How does marketing work?**
- **Tactics and Implementation**

What is the Purpose of Marketing?

The primary purpose of any business is to attract and secure customers–a process called "Marketing." Today most companies assign this critical task to the CMO (Chief Marketing Officer) and his or her team. Their job is both complex and important, but with a simple goal–get customers! Complexity resides in the process of identifying, analyzing and then articulating which customers their company is seeking, and then crafting the methods by which they will attract and retain them. Importance resides in reality–that some companies practice marketing well and flourish, and some practice marketing poorly. The price of "poorly" leads to mediocrity, which in turn often leads to a take-over or bankruptcy. While public companies are more vulnerable to this phenomenon than private companies, generally speaking those that practice sound, well-targeted marketing don't fail.

1. The initial phase is to establish a company philosophy or attitude that defines and then influences how the company's marketing message will be presented to the world. The goal of the company's marketing philosophy should be to gain customers through satisfaction with their product or service.
2. The other phase is the development of a set of activities that are adopted by the company

and become the tactical tools for implementing the accepted marketing philosophy. As we have seen, marketing is both complex and simple at the same time, often even down to the brand level. What makes it particularly complex is the necessity to understand and anticipate the nuances of customer behavior, a never-ending, never easy task for the modern marketing executive. What makes it deceptively simple is that marketing rests on certain fundamental precepts which carry their own logic, such as supply and demand, positioning and image. Here's an example of both aspects at work simultaneously.

Making Magic by Enhancing the Package

If a box of Ritz crackers costs twice what a box of Sunshine Saltines costs in a supermarket, the customer is likely to buy the Saltines, unless the image on the Ritz box front is particularly tempting, and he/she remembers that moment when Ritz crackers tasted so good at home with a bowl of hot tomato soup on a cold winter day, and then, maybe Ritz wins.

That is an illustration of marketing magic in action. Ritz trumped Sunshine by playing the nostalgia card—on its package and probably in its advertising. It is sometimes referred to as "marketing aesthetics."

Creating aesthetic magic is another subject of this book, and it takes many forms. As you will see the necessary ingredient is to achieve magic... marketing design magic. It is design that carries the day. Good design will always triumph over bad design, all other things being equal.

Marketing has many faces.

Marketing means various things to different people. To the housewife making her weekly trip to the supermarket it is getting the best buys for the necessary items she needs for her family. She is simply shopping, wisely and well.

To the consumer (and very much influenced by age) it may mean the fashion–driven urge of a teenage girl to compete with her peers at school by purchasing a pair of designer jeans.

To the marketing managers of large, modern consumer products corporations, it must and will involve a variety of cognitive, analytical processes.

At the most basic level, the marketing manager must accurately assess the state of the marketplace in which he is introducing his product. Are people buying? Is he launching a new product at the right time? If his is an international company, is his corporation selling its products in a free-market economy? Clearly selling designer jeans in Russia might be harder (certainly different) than in New York. The national state of economic being (the GDP, if you will) and even the political state of being can influence price, patterns, frequency–in fact everything. Consumer sales suffer in a down economy, even more in a no-growth society.

Another duty of the marketing manager is to look at marketing as a concept, with the accepted wisdom that a consumer products company must present its products from a well thought-through plan, involving strategies, tactics and a professional, well-timed execution.

The establishment and practice of a viable, realistic marketing concept is truly essential to the success of the corporation. It can become a philosophy for management to follow and the best ones are. Sam Walton's "Always low prices, always" is one such philosophy, and it has served Wal-Mart well. There are essentially two fundamental methods for attracting the customers and gaining sales.

They are known as… **Pull vs. Push**

1. Pull Marketing

Pull marketing is when the essential advertising message is the major thrust in attracting customers to the product being advertised and the store (where it must be purchased) is the quiescent recipient of this effort. All they have to do, in theory is take the money.

2. Push Marketing

Push marketing has the same goal as Pull except that the thrust is this time at the store level. The retail outlet will run promotional ads, price-off opportunities, sales contests, lotteries etc., all to bring the customer to the store-and it is the store that is the hero of this marketing technique.

Smart marketers like Pepsi and Coke work both methods skillfully and well, and they call it "Channel Marketing."

Not many years ago only advertising was king. Manufacturers of consumer products concentrated on advertising heavily to force retailers to handle their products by virtue of the fact that consumers demanded brands that were advertised, known, seen on TV. This example illustrates "Pull" marketing. The ads were able to pull the manufacturer's product through the channel of distribution, because of customer demand.

But the world has been changing. Pull-oriented marketing is now considered less effective, probably due to the fragmentation of advertising (Internet advertising, etc.).

This means that its opposite partner, Push-oriented marketing, or sales Promotion, is in the ascendancy.

Part II

The History of Marketing

A few years ago the Chair of the Marketing Division at Columbia University Business School (Noel Capon) conducted an extensive research project to determine who were the best marketing companies, and in some cases, marketing leaders in the business sphere. He and his team (probably students of his at Columbia) studied the top companies as ranked by *Fortune magazine, Forbes, Business Week, Advertising Age*, and others. Then they interviewed fifty-seven executives from organizations in businesses as diverse as banking, investment, industrial, media, entertainment, information, health-care, transportation and logistics. Most were American, but not all–business and markets being as global as they are today.

The result of all this research became a book, called *The Marketing Mavens*. In this book the author identifies what he called "The five imperatives or challenges that all companies in his best of class survey had in common." They are:

> **1. Pick markets that matter**
> **2. Select segments to dominate**
> **3. Design the market offer to create customer value**
> **4. Integrate to serve the customer**
> **5. Measure what matters**

It is the third one (design the market offer) that most precisely touches on the overall message of this book the most precisely.

The Toyota Story

Let's take Toyota. This company leads the automotive world in building high-quality vehicles on a low cost basis. In fact last year Toyota tied and possibly overtook General Motors with 9.36 million vehicles sold worldwide and a net income of $11.67 billion. How did they do it?

Back in the 1960s and 1970s when Toyota entered the US market they designed three integrated market-driven systems created to meet customer needs. They are:

> **1. A sophisticated research system**
> **2. A highly responsive, efficient manufacturing system**
> **3. A dealer management and customer service system.**

That three-tier integrated system served Toyota well and the company achieved near dominance in sales of low-cost, reliable cars for the baby-boomer and generation X markets. Toyota decided they wanted to try for something more. They reasoned that they might be able to follow this demographic (upward mobile) group with a new upscale car, a luxury car that would now be affordable thanks to their target audience's new affluence. Toyota's R&D group carefully and thoroughly analyzed this new market segment that they wanted to enter. They assigned research teams to visit upscale communities (affluent suburbs where many of the baby-boomers had moved) and talked to luxury car owners (BMWs, Audis etc.) to see why they liked these cars and, importantly, what features would turn them on. They studied more than the vehicle; they studied the whole car-owning experience. They tried to determine how the owners drove and handled their cars, how their cars reflected their lifestyles. They digested all this information and then turned the designers loose. They worked in teams and competitively at each of the five R&D studios. What resulted was the Lexus. The marketing of the new Lexus was equally well thought through. They decided to offer it as a stand-alone brand, purposefully separated from the other Toyota cars. It would have its

The new Lexus GS

own name, with little or no reference to the parent company. They then selected what they called "Primary Market Areas" (PMAs) where they knew their target audience lived and went to existing dealers in these areas or created new ones and they sold the Lexus only there. In some ways they were emulating what Honda had done when they brought out the Acura (which is an upscale Honda Accord).

In 1990 the first Lexus models were put on sale and for an initial launch year they did surprisingly well. If customers had problems they jumped right on them and fixed flaws free of charge and returned the car to the owner washed and with the gas tank full.

They were counting on word of mouth about their great service and generous warranties to help market the car.

By all measurements the Lexus has been a success. Last year they had sold over 2.4 million cars since its debut 16 years ago.

The Toyota story illustrates the benefits of intelligent marketing that also follows the five "imperatives" mentioned in Mr. Capon's book.

But, these principles (these imperatives) are not new. Successful marketers have been following these principles in one form or another for most of the second half of the twentieth century. *Advertising Age* did a survey to determine which of fifteen brands have remained popular, brand leaders over a period of 80 years. The results were impressive and a lesson in sound positioning and consistently good marketing.

Lasting Loyalty (Brands that remain popular, year in, year out)

A study of 15 popular product categories and their leading brands show that branding was an important concept 80 years ago. And all but two of the brands listed below are still dominant today (Source: Proprietary Research by Jack Trout–printed in *Advertising Age*, March 14, 2005).

Product Category	Dominant Brand in 1923	Dominant Brand in 2005
1. Bacon	Swift	Swift
2. Breakfast Cereal	Kellogg's Corn Flakes	Cheerios
3. Cameras	Kodak	Kodak
4. Canned Fruit	Del Monte	Del Monte
5. Chewing Gum	Wrigley's	Wrigley's
6. Chocolate	Hershey's	Hershey's
7. Crackers	Nabisco	Nabisco
8. Mint Candies	Life Savers	Life Savers
9. Paint	Sherwin-Williams	Sherwin-Williams
10. Razors	Gillette	Gillette
11. Soap	Ivory	Dove
12. Soft Drinks	Coca-Cola	Coca-Cola
13. Soup	**Campbell's**	**Campbell's**
14. Tires	Goodyear	Goodyear
15. Toothpaste	Colgate	Colgate

Let's examine one of these, **Campbell's Soup**–number 13.

Marketing Soup

Everyone likes soup–it is easy to prepare, it is easy to eat and it goes with almost anything. For that reason, ironically, it is hard to market. It won't stand out in a crowd. However, one company has succeeded admirably in overcoming the difficulty of marketing soup: The Campbell's Soup company of Camden, New Jersey. This company is one of America's oldest brands and has diversified since its inception. In recent years Campbell's has added numerous (non-soup) consumer food products to its line. Some of these are Franco-American, Pepperidge Farm, Prego and Godiva Chocolates. But soup still leads the way with consumers purchasing over 2.5 million cans of soup last year.

Clearly they were good marketers then, as today. In 1892 Campbell's started advertising in a serious way. They created a group of cartoon characters called "The Campbell Kids." This series became instantly popular and contained the first look at their new red and white can (more in Chapter 5), and the cute kids. Americans loved them and the firm expanded its campaign to New York streetcars and on to 372 other cities and towns–35,000 cards in all. By 1911 they were spending $400,000 per year on advertising. Today their ad budget is over $130 million. Campbell's was ahead of its time, marketing its products vigorously and imaginatively even 110 years ago.

Brooks Brothers and the Golden Fleece

ESTABLISHED 1818

Another early marketer was Brooks Brothers, the oldest surviving men's clothier in the United States. In April of 1818, Henry Sand Brooks opened his first store in lower Manhattan, near the East River and Fulton Street. Henry's vision was to make and supply a ready-made suit for gentlemen of means. As he put it, "To make and deal only in merchandise of the finest body… and deal with people who seek and appreciate it." In 1850, his four sons inherited the business and renamed it "Brooks Brothers." Their styles were always conservative, then and now, reflecting a target market that is upscale. The firm claims to have invented the first button-down dress shirt and the seersucker suit. Among their customers were such eminent men as: Abraham Lincoln, Teddy Roosevelt, John F. Kennedy, Andy Warhol and Bill Clinton.

Their logo (other than the letter-face name on the outside) is interesting and unusual. It is a sheep suspended on a ribbon. This is an ancient symbol dating from the 15th century when it was the symbol for the Knights of the Golden Fleece. It was adopted in the 19th century by British and Flemish wool merchants and way back was the prize sought by Jason and the Argonauts in an ancient Greek legend. Today, 190 years after it opened its doors, they have 170 stores in the US and 70 overseas.

Procter & Gamble Sets the Standard

Neil McElroy

In 1931 a novice employee straight out of Harvard sent a memo to his boss and in so doing changed marketing forever. The date was May 13, 1931, and the author of that memo was Neil McElroy. He had been assigned to the advertising department and while working on the advertising campaign for Camay soap, became frustrated with having to compete not only with soap brands from Lever and Palmolive but also with P&G's own brand, Ivory. His memo argued that each brand at the company should have its own person in charge (the beginning of the brand manager concept) and that a team of brand people should be created to study every aspect of how they market their product. Such a dedicated group, McElroy felt, should be rewarded by the results of their brand—and would include a brand assistant and several "check-up" people.

Furthermore, he brand would be marketed as if it were a separate business so that the qualities of every brand that P&G owned would be distinguished from those of the other. The ad campaigns of P&G's competing brands like Camay and Ivory would be targeted to different consumer groups, preceded with careful research on the target market. The result, less cannibalization of brands within the company and better and more product differentiation. It became a key element of marketing and has influenced companies in all categories to this day. In this way the modern system of brand management was born and has been widely emulated in one form or another by many consumer-product companies throughout the world.

Neil McElroy was well rewarded for his audacity and brilliance. He became President and CEO of the company in 1948 and became Secretary of Defense under President Eisenhower in the 1950s.

Brand management as a business technique was one of the most outstanding innovations of American marketing in the 20th century, typified by the theme of balancing centralized oversight with decentralized decision making of marketing strategies and tactics. Modern marketing and marketing management really began with P&G 76 years ago when they set the standard.

Part III

The Marketing Process

Marketing has two fundamental parts. The first part is a philosophy as manifested by a corporate attitude or a (collective) point of view. Usually it is aimed at satisfying a customer- with the obvious reward of selling that target customer something. The second part is the sequence of activities needed to implement the company philosophy. These two comprise the marketing process at its simplest.

Step 1: Establish Corporate Goals

A logical and common corporate goal is to create, communicate and deliver value to un- known customers in such a way that they express their agreement by purchasing the com- pany's product or service. To put it more simply: generate sales by generating customers. Sometimes these goals can be more indirect. Here's an example.

Fifteen years ago Richard Teerlink (CEO) rejuvenated a nearly bankrupt company with a storied brand into a profitable powerhouse. Because of his efforts, customers now wait months for his product, want to be part of the "team." In a world of give-away tee shirts, people pay hundreds of dollars for clothing and accessories with the company's logo on it. The brand is Harley-Davidson.

He did this through clever advertising and promotion. He and his creative people (his ad agency) built an image around HD that made it seem both dangerous and appeal- ing at the same time and it became a badge brand.

Very often the realities of the corporation's makeup strong- ly influence the organization's marketing activities and potential. The management says, "What do we do best?" Then they build their company philosophy around that. This is critical and it is important to be honest, to be realistic. Not all companies are alike, and understanding yours and that of your competition is critically important.

Companies fall into categories, have personalities like people and like people, have widely differing philosophies. Here are four kinds.

The Product Centered company: follows the philosophy that if we make and offer a really good product, and stand by it, we will get sales. Companies like these typically utilize the skills and contacts of manufacturer's representatives to make sales. In a way it is like the *Field of Dreams* (movie) concept, "build it and they will come." Examples would include: big pharmaceutical companies (like Pfizer) or tires (Firestone) or metals (Alcoa). Their products are almost commodities, necessities of life.

The Sales Centered company: depends heavily (as you might expect) on the strength of its aggressive, highly incentive-oriented sales force. Incentives usually involve the traditional one of commissions–sometimes as much as 50% in ascending stages related to volume, as well as perquisites such as trips and sales conventions to exotic places. This has been the nature of automotive marketing for years–the annual Toyota "Sale-a-thon" being a perfect example.

The Market Centered company: is most common in the highly competitive packaged goods business. Companies with products like shampoo, toothpaste, detergent, packaged food items, beverages–in short, almost everything one can find in a supermarket belong in this group. To succeed in this environment takes a lot of work. Marketers must do extensive research and analysis of their customer, who they refer to as the Target Audience (TA). Once they have determined the TA's likes and dislikes they must structure their marketing plan to attract just these people and hold them, sometimes building loyalty over many years. For

non package goods companies, as in the service business, this would be the method utilized by brokerage and financial consultancy firms like Charles Schwab or UBS Paine Webber. It is highly customized for the individual and presented that way.

The Society Centered company: is smaller, less market share measured. To companies like these, the environmental impact is most important and is part of their market strategy. They will advertise their products as being harmless to the watertable, or totally biodegradable, or environmentally friendly. It is part of their sales pitch. Toms O'Maine toothpaste and other products like this (Nabisco's SnackWells, or Turtle Wax) are founded (and marketed) on this principle It is sometimes referred to as "Green Marketing."

No matter what the product or service or marketing philosophy the corporation's marketing concept must be to create and continue to create customers, new customers.
This is bottom line basic.

How to tempt consumers into choosing to spend more money for their product (or service) over that of the competition, is always the corporation's biggest challenge.

Step 2: Create Marketing Objectives
This is usually a statement (invariably beginning with the preposition "To"). This statement will spell out what is to be specifically accomplished through specific marketing activities. Some examples:
To increase sales of Pepsi's Slice by a factor greater than 10 percent (of norm) in the market area of greater Chicago in the month of July. Or, to get 2,000 new passengers to fly on United Express between Roanoke, Virginia and Chicago O'Hare airport during the summer months ending with Labor Day. Marketing objectives should be consistent with organizational objectives, should be measurable and should be specific in time and place.

Step 3: Create a Market Strategy
This is a most important step in the marketing process. If you don't get this one right all that follows might be off-target. You must consider many aspects of the marketplace when setting your strategy.
It begins with Research & Analysis.
There are three critical building blocks in your research phase:
> **1. Understand the marketplace and the environment in general (what is hot, what is not)**
> **2. Understand your target audience**
> **3. Understand your competition.**

1. Understand the Marketplace: find out where you can gain an advantage, where your product has a chance and with the kind of customer you are seeking. It begins with knowing where opportunities lie, then analyzing where and if your product or service can create customer value in these areas. You must concentrate on those market segments and design offers that understand customer wants and needs. You must scan and interpret all the information you can gather on the environmental forces, events and relationships that could affect your product. These can be such things as: the changing role of families in which women work outside the home, the spending power of your potential customer, the economy's general health (recession or inflation), technological innovations that can affect the marketplace, that part of the nation to which you wish to sell (north or south, New England vs. southern California, urban vs. rural), and even the political climate (conservative vs. liberal). These are all forces that you cannot control but which will influence your ability to sell your particular product or service, or help you to craft your advertising/marketing message.

Howard Shultz and Starbucks

The Starbucks story is an excellent example of the value of
understanding your audience well. When Howard Schultz returned
from a business trip to Milan in 1983 he was
convinced that he had seen the future of coffee
retailing. He had seen, sampled and fallen in
love with the Italian coffee Espresso bar. What
he most loved about them was their conviviality,
as a social gathering area (frantically busy in the
morning, laid back and slow in the evening).

Howard Schultz

He returned to the US determined to try coffee-restaurants in the U.S. It took him until
1987, a lot of investors and a few false starts before he had a small chain of Starbucks coffee
restaurants up and running (the name came from the first mate of the book *Moby Dick*).
By 1989 he had 50 stores and he had learned some lessons. One of these was that he had to
control the look and the ambiance of his branch outlets. He decided early on that the equity
of the brand was closely tied to a number of non-traditional, visual and aesthetic clues, like the
overall look of the store, the senses of aroma and the sound of music playing in the background,
the design motifs of warm wood tones, greens, leather and magazines and newspapers strewn
about. He urged his customers to linger and relax. What happened next was a bit of a surprise
to him–his stores were becoming meeting places for book clubs, poetry readings, chess games
and Backgammon. They decided to support that aspect of the store by creating a game, called
"Cranium", which is now popular and widely played and enhances the brand experience of
community with its customers. The brilliant research that Schultz did was to let his **customers**
<u>define</u> what they really value and then deliver that value in an enhanced form. Shultz's vision
was to offer a new kind of community to coffee drinkers–and it became a big selling point
and a positioning advantage that is special and (was) unique. Today Starbucks serves over forty
million customers per week out of eleven thousand stores located in almost forty countries.

2. Understand your Target Audience.
The Starbucks story perfectly illustrates the benefit of studying and understanding your target
audience. The target audience should be researched along certain obvious lines.
Gender: male or female? Obviously they do not both buy the same things, or in the same way.
Also consider if your product is gender-neutral. There are some, television sets, tennis racquets,
toothpaste to name a few.

Age: teens buy on impulse and from group pressure, young mothers buy with an eye on their budget, middle-age folks with more expendable income may buy more lavishly (take great vacations, own a Lexus), the elderly living on a fixed income probably buy carefully.

Socio-Economic Level: where does your target market (TA) fit? Are they affluent, comfortable, hard-pressed or poor (not a good target). Generally, social economists divide them into four groups: A, B, C, D. Most offers are aimed at the top two categories (A&B) where the most expendable income really is.

Education: these categories somewhat mirror socio-economic (above). College educated, high school, grade school. Often the more eductated the more affluent the TA is.

Geography: where does your TA live? The buying habits and mores of potential customers in New Orleans are not likely to be the same as for those in Minneapolis, for example.

Ethnicity: Obviously those of Anglo-Saxon background have different tastes and desires than those who are Asian, or Latin, or African-American, which can affect buying trends.

There are ways to cut these groups even finer (religion, marital status, health etc.) but the six above are the biggest and most important in terms of differentiation. The bottom line is to study and get to know your TA as deeply as possible. In the end you will have to decide if your strategy can best be served by (1) trying to appeal to the entire market spectrum with a single offer, (2) concentrate on only one segment of the market or (3) attempt to appeal to more than one market but not all segments with one basic message.

3. Understand Your Competition

Competitive moves and positioning must be given careful consideration as well. No two companies observe each other more carefully than Coke and Pepsi. When one company brings out a new product the other automatically follows suit. It isn't necessary to always be as tightly connected as those two companies, but being aware of price and image and positioning of your competition is smart marketing.

Marketing Mix. This is what you will want to have when you finally go to market. As the title suggests, it is a mix of Product, Place (distribution). Promotion and Pricing strategies that all emanate from one marketing objective but that are each special in their own way. These are sometimes referred to as the four Ps (more on this in Part IV-Tactics and Implementation).

Part IV

Tactics and Implementation

This is when you will turn the marketing plan (Objectives, Research, Target Audience analysis and Strategy) into action assignments designed to accomplish your marketing goals.

This is also when you must select the markets and market segments in which you want to succeed. Your goal is to create customer value (or at least the perception of it) and to select and integrate all the action assignments (logo, brand, package, retail, advertisement, public relations and guerrilla) open to you into a cohesive, coordinated effort.

Tactics are the methods and actions that are put in place when the marketing plan is launched (or implemented) and may involve simple decisions like "in what season should I launch my new soft drink?" Answer: in the hot summer months when customers get thirsty, for example. Or more complicated and expensive questions such as "what broadcast media should I select and at what price and place?" Possible answer: in markets where you know your competition is vulnerable.

All of these actions have their roots in military science. The science of planning and the direction of large scale operations, such as battle plans, or battalions, is its genesis. The metaphor is attractive to young marketers and it is apt. The planning and pre-positioning of resources to anticipate competitor actions and customer response is what makes it both poignant and fun. Books have been written in this vein.

The Marketing Process

Step 1 | **Establish Corporate Goals**

Step 2 | **Create Market Objectives**

Step 3 | **Create Market Strategy**
Research and Analysis
The Marketplace
The Target Audience
The Competition

Step 4 | **Tactics and Implementation**
Tactical Tools
The Product
The Price
The Place
The Promotion
The People
The Package

Step 5 | **Evaluation**

Five (maybe six) Critical Tactical Decisions

Five critical decisions shape the marketing strategies and ultimately the tactical directions that marketers must face. Consider them tactical tools.

1. **Product**
2. **Price**
3. **Place (physical distribution)**
4. **Promotion (most of the marketing activities you're familiar with: design, advertising, etc.)**
5. **People (understanding the consumer–the target market).**
6. **Packaging (not always included but the sophistication and science of packaging these days is becoming a force in itself.)**

Product

Product strategies are basic and will influence all strategies that follow. The nature of the product to be sold (marketed) dictates how it is sold. Is it a cosmetic product, or a car, or a golf club? Each is different and such factors as package, warranty, brand name and image, influence its success or failure.

As we have learned in Part III, it is important (essential) to have a good product. Advertising legend Bill Bernbach (Chapter 9) put it well, "Nothing will kill a bad product faster than good advertising." What does this mean, a good product?

One criteria is functional superiority–or a useful, evident advantage over competition and that the consumer recognizes. Procter & Gamble has always held this quality high. Another criteria is design superiority.

Product Design

The market appeal of products known as "consumer durables" are heavily influenced by how they look and function. The skills of industrial designers play a very important role. What had been the role of engineers and consultants has now broadened to include the industrial designer.

1. The Herman Miller Company of Zeeland, Michigan has been an American manufacturer of outstanding office furniture and equipment by designers like Charles Eames and George Nelson since 1923. A more recent example can be found in their prize-winning (2007 International Design Excellence Awards) graceful and functionally superior lamp called the "Leaf." This achievement extends the company's brand from chairs to lighting. It is energy efficient and long lasting and it is "green," using 37% recycled materials.

2. Another is IDEO, of Palo Alto, California. They have long been considered one of the world's most influential product development companies. On average its design teams create over 90 products a year–ranging from sophisticated medical equipment to the mechanical whale used in the movie "*Free Willy.*" IDEO received a total of seven awards in this year's International Design Excellence Competition-but the most accolades went for their design of an airplane. It is called the "Eclipse 500 Very Light Jet."

The Don Sebastian Story

Don Sebastian: A New Product Success

Several years ago The General Cigar Company (of New York) set out to research, design and launch a new product in the crowded cigar marketplace. This is a market environment with two tiers, the top end (imported, hand-rolled cigars) and the bottom (cheap, fast smokes replacing cigarettes). They thought they could bridge the gap and called it appropriately, a "bridge brand."

This meant that they would offer the quality of a hand-rolled, carefully made cigar to the general public and sell them not in smoke shops or tobacconists but mass merchandisers like CVS stores or Wal-Mart. Because the company produces an impressive list of prestige brands (like Partagas and Macanudo), they already had a reputation for quality cigars. The bridge didn't have to be too long. The most critical factor was to correctly identify and reach the correct audience: cigar smoking aficionados in their 30s and 40s.

Extensive research revealed preferences for imagery that was Latin (like Cuba, the islands) and special graphic devices, colors, decorative borders etc. reminiscent of the look and "aesthetic" of the smoking world. My firm got the assignment which involved: the creation of a new name, a logo for the name (brand), several packages, sales promotion materials and some advertising. The result illustrates successful marketing as a bridge in several ways: first as a clever strategy to place a new product between the top and bottom end of the market, and secondly, the value of design to reassure existing cigar smokers that they were getting a cigar of high quality. The brand is a success and continues to sell briskly.

Price

Pricing strategies are critical. The marketer must decide what price the product will bring, based on the economic situation of the marketplace and what the competition is doing. Such

20

basic considerations as cost of manufacture, cost of distribution, cost of promotion etc. must all be dialed into the ultimate asking price. Some items (like soft drinks) have low profit margins but high volume; others (like designer clothing) have high profit margins and low volume.

Clearly the price of a product can significantly impact on the product's success in the marketplace. Many products fail when a minor increase in performance is not judged worth the price increase. Product superiority, with an accompanying price increase, must be "functional." An example is Dell computers.

The Dell Story

Michael Dell decided to sell his computers direct–it was the defining part of his strategy. Dell takes orders, manufactures and ships product direct and maintains a support system that customers can access directly. There are no wholesalers and no retailers. The result: the cost of finished inventory is eliminated and this is passed on to the customer. There were two advantages for Dell. Initially the lower cost to the customer by going direct created volume and over time contact with customers became a strategic advantage. They were able to keep in touch with their customers and move from an initial sale to a long term relationship. Dell was able to combine two of the 5 Ps to their advantage: price and place (i.e. distribution).

Place

Place (Distribution) strategies are the retail arena in which the product will be sold. If your product will be sold in a supermarket, a gourmet market, a Fifth Avenue specialty store, or on the Internet? Retail science and background will be covered in Chapter 6.

Where and how the product is sold is another critical element in marketing decision making. The cost of putting a common grocery item on the shelf can be substantial–involving transportation, warehousing, and supermarket relations. It is often called "Channel Marketing." Grocers can now track individual packages (called SKUs) and brands through the use of UPC (Universal Price Codes). They can even calculate the worth of what they carry on their shelves and may charge "slotting allowances" for products that undersell.

Getting adequate distribution is a critical part of every company's marketing and always a critical consideration in strategic marketing planning.

Two elements are important, transportation and channels.

One is the cost of moving goods from the warehouse to the store, and back if not sold. The other is channels of distribution–the cost of shelf and store maintenance. Wal-Mart has a very cost efficient system of warehouses and distributors–giving them a big advantage. Dell has gained an advantage by eliminating the middleman, as has Fed Ex.

Pepsi route truck making its daily deliveries.

For some years Pepsi and Ocean Spray have been discussing a distribution merger (if not a total merger through acquisition). Pepsi has route salesmen who visit the supermarkets every day, arrange the shelves, remove older product and conduct "due diligence" to its brands. Ocean Spray can't afford this much shelf attention but would like the shelf maintenance and they have to rely on other means for delivery and maintenance of their product. The two companies have tried pilot programs to test the waters, including a vending machine program serviced by Pepsi route salesmen (and designed by my firm in the mid 1990s), but so far, I believe, they have not done a lasting deal.

Promotion

Promotion strategies are a broad category and includes: personal selling, advertising, sales promotion and public relations, to name a few. The goal of the promotion strategy is to inform and persuade (and more on this in Chapters 4, 7 and 9).

This is an all inclusive term for all those rather familiar manifestations of visual marketing, the most recognized and memorable of which is advertising.

There are other equally effective (in their own way) methods available to the marketer. Some of these are:

Direct Marketing
Event Marketing and Trade Shows
Merchandising (display)
Packaging
Public Relations
Sales and Retail Relations
Price-Off Sales Promotion programs

Pepsi-Cola often offers prizes under the cap, instantly or through collection of letters, words or numbers.

All (or most) of these activities will be discussed in depth in subsequent chapters of this book.

Most of these activities are referred to as sales promotion. Sales promotion is almost always related to price. The opportunity to acquire a particular product at a particular location (in a supermarket, a convenience store, a department store) or more often these days, online or as advertised in newspapers, but always with a built in savings.

The price is discounted and time sensitive.

Some examples:

Airlines are using sales promotion heavily lately to promote travel during peak, or more likely off-peak travel times (Florida in summer, Europe in winter etc.). Airlines are also working with credit card companies to offer travel with a free seat for a companion by joining a particular credit card company within a certain time frame.

Here's a good definition of the promotion business:

"Sales Promotion (push) moves the product toward the buyer, while traditional advertising (pull) moves the buyer toward the product."

Albert W. Frey, Professor at the Tuck School of Business/Dartmouth.

Packaging

Sometimes included in promotion, sometimes separated, it is an increasingly important part of most marketing plans. Packages have become important vehicles for brand recognition as well as an integral part of our lives.

People

This brings us to the last, perhaps most important requisite of marketing–how to attract people as customers and retain existing customers–to build loyalty. Customers are the only true asset a marketer has. Sometimes successful companies actually have no product, per se. Companies like Ebay or Google are flourishing without any true hard assets, no machinery, no inventory. But they do have customers, thousands of them.

The science of attracting and keeping customers involves the basics of good design–as manifested in the identity (or logo) of the brand, the package's look in the marketplace and the advertising that creates and perpetuates the brand's image. It also involves the sales force, trade relations, distribution, merchandising, promotion, public relations, research and new product development.

It is critically important to investigate and understand the kind of customer you are seeking (as covered in Part III of this chapter), through sales analysis, market research and consumer insight.

Marketing Mix and Design
In the end, what you want is a good mix of the various marketing methods at your disposal. Not all will be useful but all, save one (price), will have design as its basic ingredient. Marketing–Design touches or invades the marketing mix: product, placement package, and promotion, at all levels, influencing how consumers form opinions that are crucial to the success, survival or failure of big business or small ventures alike. While marketing concepts, fundamentals and an effective strategy are essential to success, it is the creative aspect of marketing: the design, the words and images, graphics and color that actually span the space between success and failure. This is another essential bridge; these are the elements that we use to construct the soul of a brand, and a major portion of these elements is visual.

Evaluation

When the campaign is concluded you must measure it. Information is critical to the measuring of success and the learning power of a promotion, no matter what form it takes. The best, most useful information comes from evaluation of the campaign just completed, or even as various stages are completed.
For advertising campaigns one can track the consumer exposure to ads by measuring them against sales in the target area. There are services that can do this, such as A.C. Nielsen for television or Starch/INRA/Hooper Reports for print.
The results of the evaluation data should then be reported to senior management of the marketing department so that changes can be made or emphasis increased in certain strong sales areas.

Creativity

Even the most researched campaigns, or the most tracked promotions will be a non-starter if that illusive quality called "Creativity" isn't present. Creativity is a rare commodity that can give an advertising campaign buzz in the marketplace and increase sales volume in the retail arena.
Marketing craves creativity, but it must emanate from an accurate analysis of what the buyer will respond to. How do we learn about a product? How do we absorb its message. This is the duty of creativity.

At its heart, it is art and it starts with the idea that we can use words and pictures to create deep affection for something as mundane as twelve ounces of cola, or a can of soup, or a box of Ritz crackers, turning them into a moment of refreshment or a hearty pick-up on a cold winter day.

The art can be conservative or extreme, humorous or serious, but ultimately the brand will probably succeed or fail based on the relationship to a real "life-moment" that is carried in its image. Humor never works unless it is grounded in some form of reality. Consumers will grow to trust or reject a brand based in good measure on the quality of that image, as much as on the quality of the product itself. Evidence of this surrounds us every day–is reflected in the marketplace.

The Creative Person's Assessment

You, as a Creative Director, will have to make some critical decisions early in the product analysis process. Essentially you have to identify and assess and select among five key elements of your brand.

- **Experiential:** meaning, how should the customer feel when buying your product or brand, i.e. thrilled? Deeply satisfied?
- **Functional:** meaning, will your brand improve the life of your targeted customer? Will the brand/product solve problems, i.e. turn hair from gray back to brown, or whiten teeth?
- **Emotional:** meaning, how will the consumer feel about owning, wearing or bragging about owning your brand, i.e. looking great in a new Ralph Lauren Polo shirt or carrying a Chanel handbag?
- **Visual:** meaning, how should the brand appear to the customer: appealing, effective, enticing, i.e. that little alligator on my shirt pocket is so cool?
- **Narrative:** meaning, will owning your brand lead to a good life experience, perhaps a romantic connection, i.e. dress smartly, have wavy dark hair, bright teeth and an aura of confidence, meet girls (guys)?

Sounds trite but it really isn't. These emotions are at the heart of selection and persuasion to a typical consumer, for a cosmetic product, a food product, clothing or even a car.

Each of these key elements incorporates and demands marketing disciplines and strategies that mold and shape the imagery you select as well as the substance of what is brought to market. Managing imagery is one of design's core responsibilities. It is the failure to manage the design/imagery portion of the marketing strategy that most often leads to disaster.

 We respond to marketing programs by the way the brand is presented to us: the colors, the names, logos, typeface, shape, color, the package and the advertisement.

For example, the Nike Swoosh becomes an icon for doing one's best, and Coke becomes a symbol for the good life, optimism and the Harley-Davidson eagle and shield logo becomes a badge of power and of being independent (or at least thinking about it).

On Creativity
by Jay Levinson, retired advertising creative director for Leo Burnett Inc., and J. Walter Thompson, Inc.

Creativity in marketing is very much different from creativity in the arts, although marketing is as eclectic an art form as has ever been devised by humankind. Marketing embraces writing, design, photography, video, special effects, music, dancing, and acting -- and yet its purposes are not those of the arts.

Here are several insights into marketing creativity that illuminate the path for them. These insights prevent them from going over the edge, losing their way or wasting their time and money.

1. Creativity in marketing should be measured solely by how well it contributes to your overall profitability. If it helps you sell at profit, it is creative and if it doesn't, it's not creative. That makes creativity easy to measure. Awards and compliments have nothing to do with it.

2. Creativity should always be blended with its ability to withstand repetition because purchase decisions are made with the unconscious mind and repetition is the best way to access the unconscious. If your creative marketing idea can get stronger with repetition, you've got a winner.

3. Marketing is business far more than entertainment, and although it may be entertaining, that is not its prime requirement. It exists mainly to create a desire to buy and not mainly to entertain.

4. Gain awareness and a crucial share of mind by showing and saying your name creatively, helping people remember your name the next time they're in the market for what you sell.

5. Creativity in marketing is the challenge of demonstrating your benefit in a way that people will remember. It is important that your prospects remember your name and equally important to know what makes you special and why they should own what you are offering.

6. Creativity begins not with a headline, graphic idea, special effect or jingle; it begins with an idea. The idea should center around your offer, your competitive advantage or your main benefit -- and it should come singing clearly through your marketing in any medium.

Creativity in marketing should be both flexible and enduring.

One of the most creative men of the 20th Century was graphic designer Paul Rand. He was preeminent in the design of advertisements, posters, corporate identity and as a professor of design at Yale University. His influence was broad and remains relevant to this day.

Paul Rand

> *"Design can be art. Design can be aesthetics. Design is so simple, that's why it is so complicated."* — *PR 1997*

He has been called a legend, and in this case it's true. Paul Rand's brilliant career as a graphic designer centered on New York City and had three distinct phases embracing such linked media as corporate identity, trademark design, package design, posters and advertising. He was good at them all. In style, his work adhered to the principles of simplicity and recognition with the client's product or service. It was surprisingly easy to like his work and to get it right off.

He grew up in Brooklyn and was educated at some of the nation's best art schools: Pratt Institute, the Parsons School and the Art Student's League, but perhaps it was New York City that was his greatest education - with its rich mix of ideas, diversity and energy. In New York at this time (1930-1940), he came into close contact with many of the Bauhaus designers and thinkers escaping from Germany: men like George Grosz, Marcel Breuer and Moholy-Nagy In Manhattan he met and interacted with outstanding contemporary design talent of the time: Raymond Loewy, Donald Deskey and Walter Dorwin Teague. From 1941 until the mid 1950s he worked as an art director with the young copywriter Bill Bernbach, on the early, brilliant advertising campaigns for Ohrbach's, Air Wick and packages for the Consolidated Cigar Company. He designed many covers for Esquire magazine as well as posters for Disney, 20th Century Fox and The National Park Service. They were always original and fun.

The second phase of his career was as a designer of corporate and brand identities, and a number of important institutions were his clients: Westinghouse, UPS, ABC, Cummins Engine and IBM. His friendship with IBM's CEO Tom Watson Jr. in the mid 1950s led him into collaborations with industrial designers Eliot Noyes and Charles Eames and for nearly a decade the three men designed many of IBM's products, packages and displays-even films.

He loved typography, particularly some of the older, elegant faces such as Garamond and used them in modern applications. His imaginative use of space, size and color helped carry two-dimensional graphics to a new high.

The final phase of his career was as a teacher and he taught at Pratt Institute, Cooper-Union and ultimately as professor of graphic design at Yale University. His course was popular and many of his lectures got wide exposure for their logic and insight into marketing communication.

He lived a long time, dying in 1996 at age 81. His personal style was invariably simple, innovative and powerful, often humorous. Many of his logos, although decades old, are still being utilized and should be. Paul Rand set the bar high.

A sampling of Paul Rand's logos and a poster.

In the next chapter—the origins of the logo—you will learn why most of us react the way we do. We will learn how it all started… back in the mists of time.

2

A BRIDGE BACK

The History of the Logo

The logo is known by many names: a brand, a trademark, an emblem, a badge, a symbol, a heraldic device, an identity, and more. This very diversity is one of the reasons that logos are so ubiquitous, so profound and so ancient.

And they are ancient.

Logos, defined as devices with the function of identifying something, or somebody, have existed for at least 5,000 years. Their shapes and styles influence us in ways that are both subtle and obvious, consciously and subconsciously, deeply and (sometimes) instantaneously. Some consider them "short-cuts to deeper meaning" (with associations and preferences intertwined). It is curious that such a tiny graphic shape could have such influence.

The word "Logo" is in itself old, coming from the ancient Greek meaning "legend, or story-telling." The word "Logo" also appears in the New Testament (James) where he refers to the word of God appearing "infused with light/luminously as in a "logo."

We do not know when someone first demonstrated identity, ownership or creative and productive parenthood by means of a graphic device. We can, however, assert that the first attempts were made with pictures or shapes or symbols–not with letters.

Think of the cave paintings in Lascaux, France, which are at least 10,000 years old. Think of the hieroglyphics on the walls of tombs in ancient Egypt, which are at least 3000 years old. Whether from caves in France or Egyptian tombs, I believe we can attribute the motive behind the ancient logos to one of four conditions:

> To identify, a tribe, a leader or member thereof.
>> i.e. "I belong to the 'Cave on the hill' tribe."
> To identify ownership, i.e. "that cow is mine."
> To establish the origin of something,
>> i.e. "I made this sword."
> To placate a god, i.e. "I believe in (and am afraid of) Zeus."

29

Ancient Needs and Yearnings

In the middle ages, craftsmen in many trades demonstrated pride and responsibility by marking their products with their personal mark or logo of the time. That tradition continues to this day and can be found in the stores and shops of our cities and towns. In early colonial America, the physical material in which the craftsman worked influenced the shapes of makers' marks: ceramic, stone, silver or wood.

Clearly there were lots of reasons.

Some were inspired by desire or pride or by need,

> i.e. a farmer needed to establish ownership of his cow, or he'd lose it.

> i.e. a silversmith wanted to identify what he'd made to get more trade.

One thing is certain...all around us today we see symbols, logos and names created to differentiate one product from another in the marketplace. Look through any magazine, watch television at any hour or stand in Times Square and spin around 360 degrees and you will see an overwhelming proliferation of logos. Those identities, whatever the medium, have become part of our daily lives, embedding themselves deep in our subconsciousness.

For example:

> When we make a photocopy of something we tend to say, "I'm going to make a Xerox of this letter." When we send a package via courier we tend to say, I'm 'FedEx'ing a box to you." When taking a trip you might say, "I'm coming to New York on the Amtrak" (not the train). And invariably we picture each logo in our mind when we say it.

But how did it all start? When did it all start?

Symbols

There are deeper meanings underlying identity not as immediate as a neon-lit Toyota logo in Times Square. There are meanings even more visceral than tribe identity, ownership or origin. I'm referring to symbology.

Symbols are profound expressions of human nature. They have occurred in all cultures at all times, and from their first appearance in Paleolithic times (like the cave paintings of Lascaux) they have developed hand in hand with the development of civilization.

Symbols are powerful stuff, they can address us subconsciously and consciously by reaching our fears, our intellect, our emotions and our spirit. One is tempted to say "soul."

Stonehenge, in Britain, circa 500 B.C.

Part One
In our Subconscious

Modern languages (at least most of them) consist of words often combined with gestures reflecting clarity, meaning, actions or concepts in the world around us. They are (or should be) succinct and unambiguous.

Contrary to such discourse, symbolism communicates in less explicit ways, in ways that relate to our inner psychological and spiritual world—and this is the realm of the logo.

Early civilizations used the power of symbols extensively in art, in religion, myths and rituals and they are particularly intriguing. They are surprisingly consistent from area to area in appearance and meaning. Some served as calendars, some to foretell the future.

Numbers had symbolic meaning: three referred to divinity, four referred to man and wholeness, the four elements in nature, and seven was heavy with meaning and still is.

So, the number seven is the amalgam of three (Trinity) and four (mankind), representing the relationship of God to the world, to humanity, and is expressed thus. The world was created in seven days, there are seven stages of initiation and there are seven deadly sins.

But it wasn't just Christian dogma; that same number was sacred to the Greek god Apollo—and it certainly has serious meaning at the crap tables of Las Vegas!

The abstract symbols of prehistoric life are largely dismissed in the western world today, but they shouldn't be; their influence persists and is pervasive.

Deep-rooted symbols are used subliminally and cynically in advertisements and even in the images and rhetoric of political campaigns.

Examples can be found in the writings of Swiss psychologist Carl Jung, or Marshall McLuhan. or Vance Packard (His book, *The Hidden Persuaders*).

Here are some early shapes and their attendant marks or logos.

The Circle

No shape had a more pervasive influence on early man than the circle. The circle stood for The Sun–a supreme being in the heavens, one who had to be placated lest he send destruction on you, your crops or your tribe.

Target Store's logo

The circle also symbolized divinity, appearing later as the halos around the heads of angels. Since it lacks a beginning or end, it also can represent infinity, perfection and the eternal. Europe–particularly Great Britain–is dotted with Stone Circles.

Their function has never been totally revealed and may never be: sites of worship for Druids, the universal goddess symbolized by a great round eye pointing to heaven, or astronomical markers-yet it is their very circularity that defines them: alpha and omega, never ending, always beginning.

The Square

This form represents solidity and strength, total balance. The psychological connotation is: dependability, honesty and shelter, safety. The Hindus used it in their symbology–standing for order in the universe.

The Triangle

Here is the magic number three again–representing the sacred Trinity. Since it points upward the triangle stands for ascent to heaven, fire and the active male principle.

If it is reversed, it stands for grace descending from heaven, or water or the passive feminine element.

Ancient Symbols Found in Today's World

For the Circle: Target Stores, AT&T, Vodaphone, Lucent
For the Square: Home Depot Stores, American Express, H&R Block
For the Triangle: Bass Ale, Citgo Gas, Delta Airlines
For the Star: Texaco, Heineken Beer, Wal-Mart, The Texas Rangers,
    Mercedes Benz
For the Scallop shell: Shell Oil

The Scallop Shell

Shell Oil Co. logo

These, along with fishes, possess a positive meaning.
Unlike the fish, the scallop shell is universally feminine–being associated with the Birth of Venus, for birth, good fortune and resurrection.

It also was adopted by early Christians for pilgrimages, specifically for
St. James I in the Spanish city of Santiago de Compostela. St. John the Baptist used it to scoop water for baptisms. And today: Royal Dutch Petroleum, or Shell Gasoline, of course.

The Symbology of Animals in Identity

Animals are, and always have been popular with their own important foundation for symbol systems with all cultures. No other source has provided such a varied range of iconography because there are few human qualities that cannot be represented in animal form.

In early primitive societies, animals were particularly revered-they felt that they were more in touch with unseen cosmic forces than humans. Because most seemed to have superior physical and sensory power, natives were convinced that they possessed magical or spiritual powers and that they could tap into them through rituals.
Native Americans built totem poles, wore skins, furs and feathers of their most revered animals.

Early Egyptians gave their gods an animal personality–Isis or The Sphinx or The Ba had the personalities of jackals, hawks, half-lions and more.

33

The Lion

This beast was the all time favorite in medieval Europe for Heraldry. Royalty everywhere favored the lion, but particularly in Great Britain.

The lion became the emblem of valor, royalty and protective power. The Lion embodies the wisdom and energy of the animal kingdom.

Animals and Birds as Symbols

For the Lion: MGM, Harris Trust, Dreyfus
For the Tiger: EXXON Mobil, Frosted Flakes
For the Bull: Merrill Lynch
For the Horse: Texaco
For the Dog: Greyhound
For the Bird: U.S. Postal Service, Lufthansa

The Tiger

The tiger is most revered in China and India. The tiger symbolizes ferocity and protectiveness, it represents vitality and animal energy.

The Jaguar

The jaguar is a truly mystical cat in his native South America. Indians consider the jaguar a conduit to the realm of the spirits, able to foretell the future.

The Bull - represents strength and procreative power.

The Eagle - represents vision, speed, perception, ferocity.

Mythological figures

Some other popular mythological beasts came from Greek and Roman mythology.

Take for example, Pegasus: the winged horse, which symbolized courage, speed, power and nobility. Poor Pegasus, he emanated from the blood of Medusa, representing artistic inspiration, speed, strength and immortality, progressed to become the mount of Zeus, the mightiest god on Mount Olympus. And today he can be found on the side of a motor oil can where the Mobil Corporation (now ExxonMobil Inc.) put him in 1911.

Nike

Nike was the goddess of victory in Greek mythology. She had wings and was swift. She became a most appropriate symbol for runners' shoes–the Nike Corporation.

Mercury

Mercury comes out of Roman mythology, and is remembered as the speedy messenger of the gods. He turns up on many corporate logos: Interflora (florist's delivery service), also Hermes (credit insurance in Germany), and Goodyear tires, and finally, AT&T (early version).

Griffin

This beastie is an exotic creature with the body of a lion and head and wings of an eagle. The griffin head is prominent as the hood emblem on the Saab automobile.

The Influence of Early Symbols?

You may well ask, is there an enduring influence of symbols in today's world?

My answer would be definitely yes.

I have been part of design teams that created new logos and created new names for companies and products for years and I know the process always starts with an analysis of what shapes or symbols will affect the impression that the company or product wants to make. When we created the Diners Club logo in the late 1970s we were working with an existing, powerful mark, created some twenty years earlier.

The Diners Club Story

Diners Club was founded in 1950 by Scandinavian Airlines as a means of increasing travel on their airline–both business and personal travel.

At the time this would have been a good example of an "endorsed" identity.

SAS/Diners had a distinguished history:

       1952- first international charge card

       1967- first automatic air travel insurance

       1975- first corporate card program

The Competition

Their big competition was American Express, who had approximately 40 percent of all travel card business (this was before the expansion of the bank card business of today).

The strongest asset that American Express had was its name, and Lippincott & Marguiles (New York design firm) recommended that it be retained but reconfigured to fit into a new, wide-ranging nomenclature.

American Express was redesigned to fit into a small blue box, and the related services (travel, financial, etc.) would appear out of the box, in similar type, with three bold red lines to hold it together. This new logo would replace the popular Roman Centurion and color green. And it worked; it simplified the overall look of the company and provided consistency anywhere in the world.

The Challenge

With this as background, we approached a different problem–how to retain the split circle designed for Diners/SAS in 1950 by the highly regarded graphic designer Paul Rand. It was a very busy card that included no less than eight icons (one for each category of service: a key for hotel, a plane profile for travel, a glass for drinks, etc.) that sat just below the circle logo, competing for attention.

The Strategy and Process

We designed a series of graphically compatible sales kits, pamphlets, counter cards, posters, key fobs, even large twenty-four sheet outdoor billboards to show the new Diners logo to as wide an audience as possible. Simultaneously with this effort, a Young & Rubicam affiliate created advertisements and direct mail solicitations. They came up with a catchy headline, "Suddenly, it's The Obvious Choice" and another, "More Card Than You've Ever Had."

The visuals showed two cards in hand, one for business expenses, one for personal expenses, with double invoicing, separate and easy to allocate.

All of the advertising copy, or collateral copy emphasized the advantage of Diners over American Express, and these advantages were:

     -Lower rate of discount to restaurant

     -Faster pay back

     -Access to a large and affluent membership (21 percent CEOs, etc.)

     -Well designed (we thought) tip trays, signs, counter cards, etc.

Finally, because Diners had to reach retailers and restaurant owners, as well as attract new customer/members, we designed a sales presentation kit to be used by the DC sales staff in "pitching" these establishments.

This kit featured a series of smart, affluent looking couples eating, buying or enjoying travel in restaurants, airline counters, hotel lobbies, and in the smartest, most expensive shops on Fifth Avenue. The ideas were presented in San Diego at a national sales meeting, approved with some refinements and launched the following spring across the country. It was an immediate success.

Reflections on Symbology
Essentially our final design retained the split circle, reminiscent of the "Tai Chi" symbol–more popularly known as Yin Yang. It is an ancient Eastern symbol representing balance between opposing forces: good and bad, male and female, right and left–each dependent on the other for definition.

When we added the dark shape to the right of the split circle some observed that we had created "The Waxing Moon" which symbolizes creativity, regeneration and fertility. In European cultures it was believed that sowing seeds by a waxing moon would stimulate improved germination.

I must confess that none of this occurred to us in our design planning meetings. But did it subconsciously? And more important, do present and future clients respond positively because of this association?

Aftermath
A decade later Diners Club was acquired by Citicorp, merged with Carte Blanche, and remains financially viable around the world. While I am certain most of our collateral materials have been replaced, I am happy to say that the logo and the card, remain virtually unchanged in twenty-five years.

Greek Vase, circa 300 B.C.

Part Two
On the Battlefield

The view from the beach on that October morning... must have been stunning.

What would have caught your eye first would have been the flags, thousands of them: some furled, some flapping; then the knights' bright tunics and pennants and stacks of shields – each bearing a colorful pattern or symbol: red and green checks, yellow suns on an orange background, blue triangles on white, black diamonds on yellow, eagles, lions, boar's heads, Griffins, crowns and helmets with plumes, and occasionally, a blue banner that displayed the graceful golden arms of the Fleur de Lis. You were witnessing, for the first time, the most massive display of logos ever in one place–more than a coronation, grander in scale than imperial Rome 500 years earlier.
The year was 1066 and things were about to pop.

When I began this study of the logo and its origins, I went looking for any early examples that showed a logo on display, in print or in a tapestry, a vase, or a fresco. The best one I found was a beauty – The Bayeux Tapestry.

The Bayeux Tapestry
This tapestry was commissioned ten years after the Battle of Hastings (in 1066 AD), by William the Conqueror's half brother Odo, Bishop of Bayeux and Earl of Kent. Odo had aspirations of succeeding William to the throne of England and he conceived of the tapestry

as a piece of political propaganda, like perhaps an early political poster.

As a political statement it failed, as a piece of art, it is effective, as history, it is invaluable. (Professor J. Bard McNulty of Trinity College, wrote a popular book on the tapestry and its meaning. He described the Bayeux Tapestry as well-conceived depiction of the conquest of England). It is altogether two hundred and thirty feet long, and about twenty inches wide. It was embroidered on bleached linen and was probably made in a number of separate pieces by a team of women (Anglo-Saxon nuns living in Normandy) who stitched over drawings that had been made directly on the linen by an unknown artist.

The main story runs through the center, as in a comic strip. In the border at top and bottom are mythological and symbolic beasts and birds.

The tale it tells is of the Battle of Hastings, when William, Duke of Normandy and bastard son of Robert, the former Duke of Normandy, attacked the British (known then as the Saxons) at Hastings, and defeated them in a day-long, bloody battle.

Why did he do this?

The reason is interesting and tricky. Evidently King Edward (known as "The Confessor") promised the throne to both William (a cousin through his mother) and also to Harold II (the Earl of Wessex). Harold was related only as a brother in law to the king. In any case when Edward died in the spring of 1066 Harold claimed that Edward had given him the throne in a deathbed declaration and had had himself crowned in Westminster Abbey without delay.

Needless to say, William was furious and he immediately started to raise an army to set things straight!

Fleur de Lis

The battle occurred on October 14, 1066, and the outcome changed the course of British history forever. William crossed the channel with 750 ships, and anchored offshore at Pevensey (Sussex). He had approximately fourteen thousand men, some knights with cavalry, some yeomen, and a lot of foot soldiers.

He landed unopposed. Even though Harold knew of his coming he had had to march north to York to put down an invasion of Norsemen.

After doing this he turned his army around and began a forced march south to meet William on the coast. The actual battle site is a few miles north of Pevensey, at Hastings, in a large field. Harold occupied the high ground and set his defenses along a ridge south of the village of Hastings. Over the ranks of foot soldiers he flew his flag (logo), a single red dragon on a white or yellow field. The backbone of his army were the "Housecarls"–big men armed with long battle-axes. They had the reputation of "never giving ground" and of being deadly with the axes–able to bring down a horse with one blow. The battle began in the morning–medieval armies almost never fought at night, for some reason.

William's archers advanced and fired a volley of arrows. Then he sent in his infantry, with no apparent effect. Next he tried his cavalry which also was repulsed by the Housecarls.

The battlefield, like all battlefields, was chaos, with men locked in combat and only the symbols (logos) on their tunics helped identify friend from foe. Harold's flag carried a single winged lion. William's army, made up of many free-lancing knights from all over France and parts of Europe, was less cohesive. The banners they carried would have reflected many family crests. William would have carried the flag of the Roman catholic church, the Pope having endorsed this movement, and possibly a pennant with the Fleur de Lis on it (an ancient symbol representing three white lilies, and soon the logo of the royal house of Bourbon), and some say a winged lion logo.

This chaotic scene of two armies at stalemate, lasted all afternoon.

Finally the Normans tried an ancient strategy—that of the feigned retreat.

Here's how a contemporary described the battle, "Through this device the closed body of the English opened for the purpose of cutting down the straggling enemy, and brought upon itself swift destruction, for the Normans facing about, attacked them thus disordered and compelled them to fly... in this manner they (the English) met an honorable death." (Chronicle of William of Malmesbury, 1096).

Bayeux Tapestry

Harold is reputed to have died from an arrow in the eye, but this fact is disputed.

In any event, one brief, bloody conflict on one October day changed the course of English history and won the throne for a new line of kings. William was no longer called "The Bastard, or Duke of Normandy." He became forever after known as "William the Conqueror."

After the battle, William consolidated his foothold on the island and then marched north to London. He entered the city unopposed, on Christmas Day, 1066. That same day he had himself crowned King of England. He also adapted the flag (logo) of Harold by making the dragon into a lion and adding one more lion, to demonstrate consistency and (perhaps) leniency. It stayed that way until the time of Henry V in the twelfth century, when he added a third lion.

The Essential Logo

This is the first recorded example of the initiation of a logo in ancient times, and of its modification from outside influences. The importance of the Bayeux tapestry is that it is (a) old, (b) represents an historical moment with (more or less) accuracy and (c) shows the importance of logos on the battlefield. Confusion on a battlefield in the middle ages (or any time for that matter) would have been dominant and frightening. The importance of knowing friend from foe or where the front line was can't be over emphasized. In fact, at one point in the Battle of Hastings, William went down and the Norman line wavered, thinking their leader was slain. It wasn't until he climbed back on his horse and raised his helmet for all to see that their line restrengthened. The logo, as displayed on a helmet, or shield or pennant, was essential, vital even.

In the intervening years, warfare raged, almost as a sport. England prospered, and the Norman influence was good for the country. The Normans organized the country in a more orderly way, introduced taxation, and established teams of knights throughout the country to keep order. William built large fortresses, including Durham and The Tower of London. He expanded England's borders, pushing all the way north to the edge of Scotland and west to the tip of Cornwall. Even though the

First logo of Great Britain, 1066 A.D.

years which followed were far from peaceful, the royal lineage stayed in place. For the next 333 years all the English kings were either Normans or the war-like Plantagenets.

An (Almost) Thousand-Year-Old Logo
Observations of Dr. J. Bard McNulty, author of Visual Meaning in the Bayeux Tapestry, Professor Emeritus, Trinity College, Hartford, CT

"There is no doubt that the Bayeux Tapestry is full of symbolism and allegory. It is evident in the main figures, in the borders and most recently in the type of animals on which certain soldiers and knights are mounted," so says Bard McNulty. Professor David Bernstein, in his book, *The Mystery of the Bayeux Tapestry,* (pp.127-169) notes that winged lions in the Tapestry's borders are associated in particular with the triumphs of the Conqueror, soon to become King William. Professor McNulty suggests that, on this basis, one may reasonably infer that the Tapestry's winged lions, closely associated as they are with William, may be considered among the earliest in terms of the development of heraldic emblems and logos.

The British Royal coat of arms is in itself a logo, one that provides a perfect example of the evolution of this identity as affected by history and royal lineage. The three lions logo of Henry II in 1154 remained so for almost 200 years, until Edward III decided to start the 100 Years War with France in 1337. His new logo displayed the Shield of Britain quartered with the French Fleur de Lis upper left and lower right, and the familiar three lions of England upper right and lower left. This of course infuriated the French and guaranteed action on the battlefield. Two battles involving logos and men at arms highlighted this war, The Battle of Crecy in 1346 (where the English long bow dominated the field of battle) and the Battle of Agincourt in 1415, where again the long bow helped Henry V defeat French forces twice his size.

The Coat of Arms of Henry II

The Battle of Agincourt

What were the prominent logos on the battlefield that day in France?
The French knights would have displayed the heraldic crests and patterns of their families, but the dominant flag was three white Fleur de Lis on a blue field, now officially the royal standard of France. The flag and shield that flew above the English king that day was a slender red cross on a white field, known as the "Cross of St. George."

The Cross of St. George carried by Henry V in 1415.

The French knights riding to battle. (from the movie "Henry V")

The Royal Standard of France carried by the knights in 1415.

Henry V would have also carried another logo on his breastplate. This logo, which from 1337 contained the French Fleur de Lis and the three English lions, remained unchanged for 266 years. It reflected the French properties subjugated by Britain in War and through marriage (Normandy, Brittany, Acquitane and Gascony) and was called the "Angevin Empire." In many ways it was one of the root causes of the 100 Years War.

Their Coat of Arms (logo) now contained the Fleur de Lis and stayed that way.

The Stubborn Scots

The only holdouts were the Scots, who still hadn't been pacified. Their clan system supported them–providing them with warriors when needed. They were well led, at times, by such chiefs as William Wallace and Robert the Bruce. Their logo was the clan tartan, which they wore as a kilt, or a sash (plaid) over one shoulder. Their family crests (logos) were also displayed on intricate Celtic badges, and on coats of arms. These crests carried such devices as an armored fist holding a Celtic cross or short sword, or a boar's head, lion's head or stag's head. No white lilies for these folks!

A series of battles over two hundred years accomplished little–stalemate ensued. The major cities were subdued (Edinburgh and Glasgow) but not the highlands. And it stayed this way, for the most part, until 1314 when Robert defeated Edward II at the battle of Bannockburn. Robert was declared King of Scotland, and England, through the Declaration of Arbroath, was forced to recognize Scotland as a sovereign nation. The other Celtic nation, Ireland, was subdued and by 1603 the British coat of arms (logo) now carried three British lions, upper left and lower right, one Scottish lion upper right, and the Irish Harp, lower left. And it remains that way to this day.

The Coat of Arms (logo) from 1603 to today.

By the end of the reign of Elizabeth I (1558-1603) and her successor James I, a "Pax Britannia" existed. Only Spain challenged England and that was settled in 1588 with the defeat of the Spanish Armada in the English Channel.

England now turned its attention to exploration and colonization.

Jamestown was founded in Virginia in 1607, and early logos reflected the merchants and inns and products of early Williamsburg in Virginia, Plymouth Plantation in Massachusetts and Charlestown in South Carolina.

Peace and Exploration

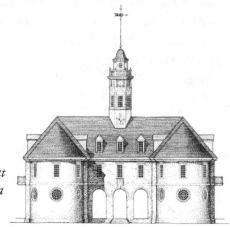

The Capital building at Williamsburg, Virginia

The Colonies

Williamsburg was the capital of eighteenth century Virginia, but this didn't happen until the early settlers grew tired of the climate in Jamestown, a few miles away on the James River. In 1698, after the Jamestown statehouse burned for the fourth time, the royal governor urged a move of the capital inland about five miles, to a site known as Middle Plantation. There were a few houses and stores in Middle Plantation and from 1695, a new college: William and Mary. The decision was made in 1699 and it was to be named Williamsburg in honor of the king of England, William III.

The architect for the new town was the governor, Francis Nicholson. He laid out the town with a typical central square, around which the Powder Magazine is located, and the Courthouse. Finally he placed a wide, central street across the middle of Market Square. This was Duke of Gloucester Street. At one end sat the college of William and Mary, at the western end, the Capital building. It was (is) ninety-nine feet wide and approximately one mile long.

The homes of residents and the Parish Church sit well back from this street. But what of the presence of logos in this eighteenth century setting?

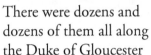

There were dozens and dozens of them all along the Duke of Gloucester Street in Williamsburg, on stores, pubs and shops.

New England

Farther north in New England, in the colony of Connecticut, Mystic Seaport developed along similar lines but with a different emphasis and look.

Mystic was a coastal shipbuilding village. Warships were built here as well as whalers. Here the logos reflected the trades practiced and products sold, just as in Williamsburg, except that they all centered on ship or nautical themes.

New England logos defined their way of life and their religious preferences for plain, unadorned dress. Many were Quakers or Pilgrims and their chosen mode of dress and practice was somber and simple.

There was the sail maker, the rope maker, the blacksmith, the barrel maker, and the maker of chronometers, of compasses, of sextants and their logos often depicted an illustration of these devices.

Mystic Seaport in Connecticut

In Europe

The Napoleonic Wars (1800-1814) notwithstanding, trade flourished in Europe at this time as well. Trade unions adopted symbols for their ships and crafts: bakeries in Denmark, beer in Germany, pottery makers in Holland, book publishers in Italy. Family dynasties, both royal and common, continued to seek and display logos in the form of crests, badges, banners and coats of arms–some as far away as Istanbul, Turkey.

With commerce came the need for identification (logos). Logos were created reflecting the trades and they included branding for livestock, ceramic marks for pottery, stonemason marks on cathedrals, hallmarks on precious metals, printer's marks on books, watermarks on paper and furniture marks on chairs. A number of companies were started in America and Europe at this time, offering products as widely different as a book is to beer. Here are some examples of logos that began (mostly) in the mid-nineteenth century on both sides of the Atlantic

1. Hofbrauhaus Brewery in Munich, Germany, started in 1589 as the royal brewery of Bavaria and became open to the public in 1828. Their logo reflects its royal roots with a crown above the monogram "HB."
2. The Bikuben Bank (which means "Beehive Bank") was established in 1857 in Copenhagen, Denmark, and they flourish today. **3. The Opel** manufacturing company of Germany was founded in 1862, initially producing sewing machines, then bicycles and ultimately automobiles. **4. Shaker Furniture** designed and built slender, beautiful tables and chairs that carried this logo in 1873. **5.** The happy fatso **Michelin Man** was established in France in 1898. Back then he was referred to as "Monsieur Bibendum." **6.** The logo **"4711"** was created in 1881 to mark the establishment of the "House of Cologne" in Cologne, Germany. **7.** The American detergent giant **Procter & Gamble** created and used this "man in the moon" logo in 1882. **8. Shell** was the name of a British transport and trading company in 1897, later merging with a Dutch firm and concentrating on oil refining and marketing. This logo-mark has undergone many changes.

Summary

As you can see from this brief history of the early logo, the necessity to identify oneself or one's craft or property had real (sometimes life and death) circumstances. On the battlefield, a confused medieval battlefield, thousands of men had to keep track of their front lines and the location of their leader and this often was nothing more complicated than following the logo displayed on the flag.

And off the battlefield, these early logos were sources of pride, of earlier triumphs and achievements.

When the world became more peaceful (relatively), the early logos were developed out of early heraldic marks and family lineage was spelled out on the coat of arms, with additions as prominent families merged through marriage.

And a peaceful world led to the expansion of trade. Commerce became a pacifying force, as it often is and the craftsmen and guilds and great merchants wanted recognition for monetary means. This period, of a logo or mark from the house of a beer maker, a publisher, a silver-smith lasted right up to the end of the nineteenth century.

The Spread of Logos for Commerce

America was getting richer, more powerful as a world trader and with it, logos were proliferating. Real growth in logos began with the invention of packaging.

The old world was ending-taking with it a colorful, energetic style. The narrow, twisting streets of lower Manhattan in 1890 would have been exciting and full of signs (logos). You would have seen logos for shops, for banks, for grocers, for haberdashers, for hats, for shoes, for money-lenders; along South Street near Maiden Lane there would have been shipping agents, freight handlers, the Fulton Fish Market (with all its smells) and the prows of hundreds and hundreds of sail and steam ships soaring over the busy cobbled street. And even the ships carried a logo of sorts on their bowsprits. Fierce Indians, bare-breasted ladies, pirates or ancient Greek or Roman gods and goddesses were carved out of wood and loomed over the heads of the shoppers and workers passing below. America was bursting with activity. Commerce was on the move. *Logos led the way.*

3

THE BRIDGE FORWARD

The Logo Today

At the beginning of the twentieth century the modern logo was developing along two fronts: displayed on products being offered to consumers in stores, mostly food products, and a few years later, on consumer durables (like cars) and service companies (like banks). But the early growth was in food packaging and as it developed, branding followed.

A Logo is Born at a Football Game

In 1898 a company executive named Herberton Williams attended the traditional football game between rivals Cornell University and the University of Pennsylvania. For Williams, the game was not as exciting as Cornell's brilliant new red and white uniforms. Unable to shake the striking image they made on him on the football field that day, he convinced the company to adopt the Cornell colors as their own by changing the labels on cans of Campbell's soups.
All they added was the flavor name and a single gold medallion that their food products had won at the Paris Expositon Universelle in 1900.
- **Beth Jolly, Manager of Brand Communications, The Campbell's Soup Company**

Corporate identity for non-food companies took a little longer–their products being either industrial design oriented (like cars) or service oriented (like banks). For both kinds of companies, however, the quarter century between 1901 and 1925 was a period of growing material comfort for many Americans, and growing confidence. In the early '20s, right before the Great Depression, advertisers and manufacturers began to realize that styling or changing the appearance and presentation of products could encourage consumer demand and lead to more sales.

New models with different colors, forms and materials began to appear. Color printing on labels was improving, packaging companies were forming, like American Can in Connecticut. There were many new companies wanting to can food products for grocery store shelves and competition was in full swing. A fast moving, colorful and lively marketplace was developing.

Three early logos for three popular food companies.

The Growth of Stores

There were no grocery chains in 1900. The neighborhood grocer was still the source for all food stuffs, and remained a trusted, generally friendly advisor to the shopper. But times were changing and by the mid 1930s he was only around to help.

Popular products of the time were Mennen toiletries, which came in a tinplate can with a baby picture on the front to attract mothers, and his (Mr. Mennen's) portrait on the cap for reassurance. A British firm named Lyon pioneered tooth powder, first offered in cans, later in tubes. Mid-nineteenth century cans were often handmade with simple labels.

Coca-Cola put its script logo on a contour-shaped bottle and introduced it to the marketplace in 1915. It grew slowly, not reaching critical mass for another sixty-some years. A&P started as a single store in New York and sold only tea and a few other high-end products. Even as late as 1911 it did not carry the full range of products that most grocery stores carried. However, thanks to John A. Hartford, son of the store's founder, it began to wake up, and from 1914 to 1916, the store opened 7500 new outlets. By 1925 there were 25,000 A&P stores.

Design Program

That part of a company's corporate logo/identity or family of packages that is visual is usually referred to as the visual identity. All companies have one, even though they may not realize it. In most cases the visual identity was created for them by a graphic design firm, and becomes part of the marketing effort. It is usually referred to as a design program.

The goal of a design program and the resulting visual identity is to provide the company with the tools to inform people inside and outside the organization.

The creative effort for the design program is usually undertaken by a graphic design firm.

The Target Groups

All large corporations have two target groups: external (customers, extant and future) and internal (employees).

External: A design program should increase the company's visibility–both for the public in general, but the target audience in particular. Take, for example, GAP stores, and its goal to reach young housewives, young mothers or young working gals, even teenagers. Their identity must fit comfortably with that target audience. But GAP's audience is even wider than that: business partners, investors, journalists and public authorities, are also part of GAP's audience.

To reach its three diverse market audiences, GAP has created three logos, three looks, three names: GAP itself, Banana Republic and Old Navy. Each logo is designed to reflect a different audience.

The image for GAP then has got to be the sum of all perceptions of the company held by external groups, in other words, consumers and potential consumers.

Internal: A design program should contribute to the company's self-understanding and in this way, increase motivation and loyalty. It is often called "Esprit de Corps."

Internal communication is critical to maintaining customer loyalty and attitude. The attitude of the top management is also critical.

Every year companies are rated for their friendliness by their employees. Often it is a direct reflection of the kind of personality that the CEO has, and maintains in the workplace. GAP usually scores high.

Whether internal or external, the over all business goal of a design program should result in low employee turn over, and increased sales.

Image vs. Identity

There is a definite distinction between image and identity. They are not the same thing. Many people confuse these terms and use them interchangeably.

A corporation's image is:

What is perceived by its various audiences–how it appears to outsiders such as the financial

community or to potential consumers of its products or services.
A corporation's identity is what it chooses to use to shape those perceptions.
Images affect us whether we want them to or not.

TIFFANY & CO.

A key ring from Tiffany's will add prestige to your feelings about how you contain your keys-
A Mercedes, BMW or Audi will make your heart quicken faster than a ride in a Subaru.
Right?
A Latte Grande from Starbucks beats coffee from 7-Eleven.
Given that images exist whether we want them to or not, the problem in business is how to make conscious decisions about image rather than letting such decisions be made by default-and perhaps in a detrimental way.
It helps to think of an image as the sum of a corporation's conversations with society.
Graphic design companies who specialize in identity design (like LPK or Landor & Associates) are sometimes hired to analyze the image of the corporation and to improve it.

Three logos for three classy cars.

The Design Brief

When a corporation retains a graphic design firm, like Landor & Associates, they will prepare and issue to them a Design Brief.
Simply put, a Design Brief is a set of criteria that are used to guide the creative effort.
All major (and minor) companies seeking to utilize the skills, knowledge and experience of a graphic design firm will begin the process by preparing a Design Brief.
In this Design Brief key subjects will be questioned, stated and challenges expressed.
This is a typical corporate design brief template.

There are three stages to this process: Research, Analysis and Execution.

LMS DESIGN, INC

Design Brief

Project name_____

Brand name_____

Corporate parent_____

Part One - Research

1. Brand
    a. What is the background of this project, why is it being undertaken?
    b. What is the condition of the brand at this time?
    c. What has the competition been doing?
    d. What is the brand's market share position?
    e. How long has the brand been in the marketplace?
2. Target Audience
    a. Who is the target audience (TA)?
    b. Identify by: age, gender, socio-economic background, education, geographic location.
    c. Is there any unique aspect to the TA?
3. Retail Situation
    a. How is the product being marketed, retailed?
        i. In stores, direct mail, Internet?
        ii. What kind of stores?
    b. What is the brand's relationship with the retail community?
    c. Is the product seasonally sensitive?

Part Two - Analysis

1. What is the Objective of this design project?
    a. To improve sales?
    b. To increase market share?
    c. To change the brand character? Positioning?
    d. To penetrate a new market, store system or category?
2. What is the Design Strategy?
    a. What package sizes will be utilized?
    b. Is the product a new entry into a brand family?
    c. How many colors are possible for reproduction?
    d. What are budget restrictions?

3. Priorities?

    a. What are the most important aspects of the design project?

Part Three - Execution

1. How will you launch your marketing program?

    a. Advertising: broadcast, print, nontraditional?

    b. Packaging

    c. Timing: Spring, Summer, Fall, Winter?

2. Post Launch

    a. How will you maintain awareness?

    b. Media exposure?

    c. Timing

3. How will you measure success?

    a. By sales increases?

    b. By market share increases?

And this brief is usually delivered in person, by the corporate brand manager or his team to the selected design firm and signed off on (both parties). If the firm is new to the corporation they may ask for a proposal, based on this type of design brief, with relative costs for each stage.

All companies must do certain things:

Here's how Lippincott & Marguiles (a recent major graphic design firm in New York) described the criteria of a design project.

1. The company must have a foundation on which to build–a cultural foundation that takes into account the company's own history and strengths.

2. Linked to one above, the company must have a clear mission, preferably one that has been expressed in writing and widely disseminated.

They must ask themselves:

    a. What business are we in?

    b. What are our priorities?

    c. Where are we going?

3. Adopt identity practices to align the audiences' perceptions of the company, with what the company believes itself to be, and the goals it hopes to accomplish.

Clive Chajet (CEO of L&M) in his book *Image by Design*, 1991

The first priority–follow the money

Graphic design firms must go (and be) where the clients are, and fifty percent of the Fortune 500 companies are located within the tri-state area: New Jersey, New York and Connecticut. So, while there are good design firms outside the northeast, the bulk are within an hour's drive from Manhattan.

The corporation has priorities too. Their primary focus must be on its ability to control the visual identity of the company. Without it, chaos results, opportunities are lost, sales and market share suffer.

And that involves a thorough understanding of: who we are, what we do, what we stand for.

Design Standards Manual

Usually the last act of the design program is to write and illustrate a rule book for the new identity's usage. In such a book (and some are large) all the applications of the new logo are shown, old applications abandoned, even color chips are provided so that the corporation and its subsidiaries will present a consistent, professional look to the consumer world.

This rule book is called the *Design Standards Manual* and it will include:

Trademarks
     Letter marks or picture marks
     Typefaces
     Colors
The common applications of a design program are:
     Correspondence (a stationery system)
     Sales literature
     Advertising
     Products
     Packaging
     Vehicles
     Signage
     Stores
     Store interiors
     Uniforms

From the *Design Standards Manual*
for the new logo for Pepsi-Cola
and its associated brands in the mid 1990s.

" This is the standard Pepsi-Cola logo. As the symbol of the brand, it's a valuable asset that is recognized around the world as a symbol of quality refreshment. Strict logo control is the key to maintaining the integrity of the logo. This chapter gives you broad guidelines that will help you reproduce the Pepsi logo consistently and effectively in a variety of situations. Consult the chapters that follow for specific applications for logo usage on: signs, trucks, cans, bottles, uniforms, caps, cups, sun umbrellas, folding chairs, vending machines and in selected foreign languages."
***Pepsi Look Book*, Pepsi-Cola Incorporated**

Designer Tools

What are the tools that a graphic design firm has to create a new logo for a client? Essentially there are four: symbols, color, shape and type.

Symbols: heraldic crests are now largely irrelevant. Except for some cigarette packages, fine and venerated whiskies and a few celebrated stores in London (Fortnam and Mason for instance), they have become passé. But there are still symbols, lots of them. Here's a partial list:

Mouse ears for Disney
Red star in a circle for Texaco
A split circle for Diners Club
Golden arches for McDonald's
A swoosh for Nike
A triangle for CITGO gas, or Bass Ale
When examining symbols, it is interesting to refer to the basic and important symbols of the ancient world to see which ones still resonate with people (Chapter 2).

NON SANZ DROICT

The Armorial Bearings of
WILLIAM SHAKESPEARE
of Stratford-upon-Avon.

Color: color was never a minor manner, even in the middle ages, but only in the early twentieth century could printers reproduce it with accuracy and consistency. Color has become a means of identification as well.

Consider:
IBM and blue
Kodak and yellow
Coca-Cola and red
Campbell's soup and red with white
United Parcel and brown

Shape: this is a little harder to define, but it is a powerful tool in the hands of a skilled graphic designer. Shape has two dimensions (in the printed-graphic world) outside shape and inside shape. This means the space outside the central image-moving to the edge of the package or page. An example would be the circular shape of the Pepsi globe in its logo and its relationship to the space at the edge of a sixteen ounce can of soda; this is a critical dimension. Too much space makes the logo look diminutive, too little makes the logo look overlarge, or too aggressive. The right balance is critical and influences the personality of the logo (the aesthetic reaction of the consumer). Inside shape must adhere to the same criteria as outside shape, but with some subtle differences. Target's circular logo, with its interior ring maintains a spacing that is in perfect balance–symmetrical, powerful and reassuring. The circular motif of the British telephone service, Vodaphone, is asymmetrical, the circular symbol (in the shape of a quotation mark) is skewed to the left of the overall logo, which gives it a dynamic strength. Both Pepsi and Vodaphone were created by highly skilled graphic designers who knew exactly what they were doing.

Typeface: the selection of the typeface helps to communicate powerfully the personality of the company and its customers. The history and use of typography in communications is interesting and ancient. Obviously we all know that the first use of moveable type was the Gutenberg Bible in 1457, but the first appearance of an organized alphabet (with upper and lower case letters) goes back even earlier, to around 800 AD. It is believed that the capital letters (upper case) were copied off Roman monuments, smaller letters (lower case) from handwriting. The first true portable book made its appearance in Venice in 1501. There were some wonderful type designers back then, like Claude Garamond (France) in 1561, William Caslon (English) in 1692-1750, and Frederic William Goudy (American) from 1863-1947. Typefaces come in essentially two styles, Serif and Sans Serif. Sans serif communicates modernity, serif communicates conservative, traditional character. One typeface usually comes in 228 characters, including the twenty-six letters of the English alphabet, plus upper and lower case, accents, numerals, commercial signs (dollar, euro, etc.) punctuation marks, ampersands and asterisks. Furthermore, it will also be available upright (called Roman) or slanted (called Italic), and finally, bold and plain. Each has a personality, and a good graphic designer will utilize the appropriate typeface to create the intended personality for his product/client.

Consider:

- Sony and serif type face–dignified
- ExxonMobil and the use of (sans serif) Helvetica type–action
- American Greetings Cards–traditional
- Brooks Brothers and its script (cursive) typeface–elegant
- Perrier and old fashioned Gothic typeface–old Europe

The weapons that a modern graphic design firm works with to achieve a favorable personality for a client company.

1. Uniqueness
The basic task of the logo is to distinguish the communication, property or products of the company. In short, it must be different from the competition–like Altria.

2. Value
It has attention value–gets noticed and remembered–like Xerox

3. Holding Power
It has the ability to stick in your head–like "Starbucks"

4. Description
It looks like its product–like the Michelin Man

5. Character
The type, or the use of shapes can communicate a lot about the product/company–like Harley Davidson.

6. Graphic Excellence
Sometimes it just looks good-and this can communicate a message from the originator–like Movado watches.

7. Reputation
When a trademark gets known, really well, and with a favorable association, it gains added value. Swiss Army products (Victorinox) have worked this field well, with pocket knives, compasses, watches and lately, backpacks.

8. Repetition
Any trademark will gain through repeated use. Recognition by repetition is the goal behind all design programs.

Three Types of Corporate and Brand Identity
While generalities can be deceptive, most identities fall into one of three categories. There is crossover and areas of gray where one identity may fall into two categories, but usage should not define or corrupt the original intent of the designer.

Monolithic

As the name would indicate, companies that use the same name and style on all logos, displays, letterheads, packages, advertising message, trucks, billboards and uniforms, are monolithic. This is the type of logo that doesn't change, whether or not the product or service is displayed at corporate headquarters, or in a store or office.
The organization is the brand.
They may, and probably have, divisions in similar businesses, but the parent organization and its subsidiaries will all use the same identity. This type is common for industrial conglomerates or business service companies. The advantage of the monolithic look is strength in singleness of message and look. Ironically, that can become its weakness, too. An overused, unchanging logo can become too common, and eventually boring and predictable. Some examples are:

> Xerox Corporation
> IBM
> General Electric

If product names exist, they are usually nothing but model designations and are never marketed without the corporate (parent) name.

Branded

Branded identities are common on packaged consumer products and found most often in supermarkets. They have become (almost) intimate friends to the consumer and usually forge aesthetic bonds with young consumers. Companies like Coke and Pepsi work hard to achieve (and maintain) these type of relationships. Often the parent company is unknown, or known only casually. Sometimes the corporate parent wants it that way.
Take Philip Morris.
This venerated company decided to change its name. Their reasons were understandable. They felt the need to create a "firewall" between itself and some of its non-tobacco brand products (like Nabisco, Kraft foods etc.). Their greatest concern was that their large tobacco product businesses and popular brands (Marlboro, Parliament, etc.) would become targets for lawsuits. Today, the parent company is doing business under the enigmatic name, "Altria"

and it shows its face publicly once a year on their annual report. Another case in point is Procter & Gamble, although not for the same reasons. P&G has acquired many companies, including foods like Pringles and Folgers, fabric and home care products like Tide, Swiffer and Mr. Clean, healthcare like Crest toothpaste, cosmetics (Pantene) and Gillette. The parent company wants a separate identity to prevent confusion, so P&G makes its appearance once a year also–on the annual report.

This is the type of logo that is a bit schizophrenic. It has one look for its stockholders, another for its customers. A characteristic of this category is the presence of two names, a supporting name and a supported name.

Consider:

> PepsiCo and Quaker Oats   P&G and Downy, Pringles, Duracell
> Ford and Mustang
> McDonald's and Big Mac

Essentially, a branded identity implies that the company has its own organizational identity, but owns a class of products that receive support from the company's organizational identity.

Endorsed

This type of identity strives to have the best of both categories (monolithic and branded). With an endorsed identity the company benefits from the brand identity-and the brand gains through association with the company. General Electric straddles the fence this way, linking itself to its more popular, ubiquitous products, like light bulbs and refrigerators.

A more common, more obvious illustration occurs in the fashion and cosmetics industry.

When an endorsed identity is present, it always reflects the person most responsible, and is inseparably linked to the product, and inevitably, the designer.

Consider:

> Ralph Lauren and Polo
> Donna Karen and DKNY
> Estee Lauder and Pure White Linen.
> Nabisco and Chips Ahoy

Almost all of the old line classic fashion houses have brought out trendy looks, prêt-a-port items and accessories, like sunglasses. The endorsed look is handy for them because they can adopt a high style, Milan or Paris persona, or become common and comfortable with apparel for the average working gal.

And, not all are in fashion. Sometimes an image-based advertising campaign has made a hero of the chief executive officer.

Consider: Charles Schwab and his brokerage business.

Naming

There is another aspect of identity design that involves all types: monolithic, branded or endorsed. It is when a company brings out a totally new product that is not a line extension, but one with a new name. The creation of a new logo often involves naming the new entity. Naming is a process, one of the most difficult and controversial in the business of creating identity.

This involves a totally different approach. It is tricky but interesting.

Many companies attack problems of identity by changing their name, or by altering the company's logo in hopes that this will change public perception. The reasoning may be thus: because we are visibly doing something different, the company takes on a new aura of being aggressive, modern, on the edge. There are reasons to change a company's name, and logo with it, but change for change sake isn't a good reason. Too often this type of action is viewed as "cosmetic."

The Altria Story

Sometimes it makes great sense. Take Philip Morris for example.
$90 billion in sales from five operation units:
Kraft Foods, Miller Brewing Company, Philip Morris/USA, Philip Morris International and Philip Morris Capital.
They are one of the largest advertisers in the country–over $2.5 billion last year.

They have thirteen national/international brands, from Marlboro to Maxwell House, that top $1 billion in sales, each.

Even though tobacco revenues are 57 percent of total, and 61 percent of operating income, generating the highest margins, with all the negative publicity that surrounds tobacco use, they are risking a lot of potential image exposure.

For that very sound reason they decided to change their name.
The decision to change the company name is a smart one because it distances non-tobacco units from their controversial cigarette sibling.

Y&R's Landor Associates created the new name and logo.
But what does it mean?
Obviously the meaning isn't immediately clear, and that was intentional. It has a fuzzy, un-defined association, one that is reminiscent of "high places." That is just what the company needs.

Spokespersons for the company call it an abstraction, and not an obvious abstraction.
Any name for Philip Morris is a lightning rod for negative publicity–unlike their non-tobacco businesses.

Creating new Names
"Of all the services we provide, the most difficult to accomplish, and to accomplish well, is the creation of a new corporate or brand name...The prime difficulty with naming derives from the fact that the subject is emotional. People form attachments to things (like old names) that are familiar, and they have a fear of the new and unknown."
Clive Chajet, *Image by Design*, 1991

It is important to remember that no name works right out of the box. There is always resistance. Even though the public expects that it will turn them on straight away- few do. Names themselves are really word symbols for what they identify. Few names have inherent magic–it is how it is used that makes it work.
Certain names work well from the start, however.

Phonetics and familiarity are a big factor. People unconsciously sound out a new name in their heads and then react to it.

Specific types of names:

Proper Names: Anne Klein, Brooks Brothers, J. Crew, J.P. MorganChase

Descriptive: Tasters Choice, Intel,

Metaphoric: White Rock, Smuckers,

Artificial: Aveeno, Dasani, Aquafina, Xerox, Altria, Haagen-Daz, Excedrin and Brillo

Adapter names that link the entity to a logical feature of the product, or brand: Tropicana, Jell-O, Gleem, Pampers, Downey, Chock-Full-O'Nuts (coffee).

Names that identify a benefit inherent in the product: Duracell, Eveready, Band-Aid, Sweet 'n Low, Taster's Choice, All Bran.

Liquor or wine names that are intentionally mysterious: Grey Goose, Absolut, Four Roses, Clos du Bois, Stag Leap, Yellow Tail

All these product's are best sellers and all their names were made up.

The Naming Process

Name consultants must follow a process, which helps them get to a happy conclusion. Before they begin generating names they will do a background study to include: competitive names, social mores and idiosyncrasies.

They will look for any distinguishing feature of the product or company they are naming that can be adapted to the new name.

Step one: evaluate the name by how it sounds and how it looks in print.

Step two: what does it stand for?

Step three: be willing to think outside the box.

Reference materials can be useful:

Dictionaries, Thesaurus, foreign language dictionaries, rhyming guides.

Making long lists of names that occur to you while "brainstorming."

International Sensitivities

Most companies are global these days and their branding and distribution makes them vulnerable to interpretation, or language subtleties.

Nova for Chevrolet didn't work in Mexico or any Spanish-speaking country because it sounded like "No-va" or "doesn't go."

The Sonoco Story
(A naming case study)

In 1986 my company was asked to undertake a total new identity for
a firm that was about to split off from Sonoco Products (a $1 billion
company in the building business). The firm had an independent divi-
sion that made metal buildings–used most often for warehouses or large self-standing shel-
ters. The project involved a total makeover: name initiation, graphics, application to signage,
vehicles, letterhead etc.

A condition of the split off and our taking the project, was that we accomplish the entire
project in six months. That was a tall order and it was not easy.

Step One: Background Study

We immersed ourselves in the company culture-interviewing all persons involved or affected
by the new company. This included corporate officers, shop foremen, sales staff, and install-
ers. We also interviewed previous or existing customers. In all cases we prepared written
questions for them to answer and conducted one on one interviews wherever we could.

Next we analyzed their competition, looking for any unusual quirks about which we could
build an advantage.

With all background research completed we prepared a list of criteria, with stated assumptions about the type of name that would be most appropriate.

These criteria were divided into two categories:

Image Criteria: how should it look?

Copy Criteria: what should it say?

Step Two: Name Generation

We got top management to review our criteria and sign off on agreed statements.

Now, and only now did we start to generate names. We did this in as much of a controlled
manner as possible.

We made lists, each headed by a letter of the alphabet.

Everyone was included: designers, officers of the company, secretaries, wives, children of
employees.

We referred to dictionaries, language books and the thesaurus.

All lists were turned in to one person, compiled in alphabetical order and grouped by name
type (Metaphorical, Descriptive, etc.)

Step Three: Names with Designs
Finally we called a meeting at their corporate headquarters in Milwaukee to present the complete list of names. These names were merged with design ideas and mounted on cards and pinned on the wall of their conference room. We filled the conference room with names.
First we presented the full list.
Then we presented the short list (our preferences)
And finally we presented three favorites.

Naturally much discussion followed, votes were taken, and we adjourned for lunch and agreed not to talk about it over our meal.

Then we reconvened, and held another vote and two finalists emerged in a tie.
We agreed to develop both finalist logos for a modest increase in the agreed fee-and we returned to New York to continue the design process.
This step went somewhat faster, and with graphic solutions overlaying the names; they began to take on personalities.

Step Four: Execution
Two months had elapsed from initiation of the project, and we now had only four months to do the execution of the final design(s) to the many outlets that needed the new logo.
In the last weeks we scrambled to apply the chosen design to:
a stationery system, billing and invoicing system, on site signage, truck panel signs, business cards, sales support materials, a brochure and some simple advertising.
The final design meeting was in our offices in New York and they signed off on our two favorite candidates. Still, one had to be selected, and they did so independently from us.

The firm adopted and has been doing business with this new name and logo, for the past sixteen years. Their sales are in the $150 million/year range today.

The new name and identity for Sonoco buildings

Restyling Logos in Mainstream America
By Arthur Congdon - President, CEO of Congdon & Company, LLC

Question: What do the Prudential Rock, the CBS Eye, and Mickey Mouse have in common? Answer: They are all well-known icons that remain as graphically fresh, relevant and effective today as they were when they were born. Now, we all know that "time marches on" and that "today is tomorrow's yesterday" and how quickly current styles become "old hat" (and that some logos out there are really old). So how do they do it? How do these icons fight back the ravages of time and continue to work effectively to represent their companies, products and services even today? They do it through subtle and repeated graphic updating over time by designers who know how difficult it is for a logo to become a familiar and valuable business asset – designers who wisely resist the temptation to satisfy their egos with radical change and recognize a situation where subtle evolution is the best solution. Not all design challenges are like this, but many are. Here are some examples.

The Big Rock. Since 1896, Prudential's Rock of Gibraltar logo has been an integral expression of the insurance company's image of strength. This symbol has undergone sixteen graphic changes since its initial introduction as a "complete advertisement" for the then revolutionary practice of providing affordable insurance to the American public rather than only to the wealthy. Each carefully crafted evolutionary design change has kept The Rock design fresh and relevant for the next generation of insurance buyers (with the exception of the 1984 stylized version that was perceived as so abstract that it lost the "essence" of The Rock. The most recent logo returns to the more recognizable Gibraltar shape. (Designers take note).

The Big Eye. The CBS Eye, designed by William Golden, was first seen on the air on Saturday, October 20, 1951, during a station break. This well-known icon has maintained its vitality and relevance for over half a century. How is it kept up to date? With only slight changes in its basic form that you probably haven't even noticed and through the careful use of photos and other graphic images of "today" (and even "tomorrow") inside and around the symbol. This risky but effective technique requires sophisticated graphic thinking and respect for the symbol by the designer.

The Big Mouse. On September 19, 1928, Walt Disney's Steamboat Willie (Mickey Mouse before he changed his name) was introduced to the world in his first cartoon, which opened at Manhattan's Colony Theatre. A global icon was born. Said the sculptor Ernst Trova, "Along with the swastika and the Coca-Cola bottle, Mickey Mouse is the most powerful graphic image of the 20th Century." Since his debut, Mickey has experienced several facelifts and tummy tucks, voice coaches, psychiatrists and wardrobes to help him maintain his essence and vigor into the twenty-first century with a following that, like Mickey, remains eternally youthful.

These three examples represent "generations" of savvy designers who concluded that subtle change is better than the clean sweep. They also represent scores of other logos that will "live" for a long, long time, again thanks to talented and experienced designers.

1896

1940

1988

The "Look" of a company

How a company appears–the visual expressions of its identity–determine in large measure how the company and its products are valued by its customers and audiences.

The public sees logos every day and while we may pay them little heed, they do pick them up. Sometimes a logo takes on a life of its own, going beyond its function as a symbol–it becomes the heart and soul of a company.

There are many examples, some already mentioned: Coke, Marlboro, IBM, etc.

So, to recap, we have:

Logos defined by symbols, or symbols with words

Shell Oil, Westinghouse, US Postal, NBC, McDonald's, American Greetings, Texaco etc.

Sometimes logos that are proper names (Merrill Lynch, L.L.Bean), or descriptive names (Krispy Kreme), or Metaphoric names (Mountain Dew).

Sometimes logos are created out of thin air: Exxon, Altria, Xerox

Sometimes logos that are descriptive (NorthFace) and sometimes logos that are so cute, so appealing, that a company is created to keep up with them.

An excellent example is the next case study.

The Black Dog Cafe
This is the story of a logo that made a company

Black Dog Cafe is on the island of Martha's Vineyard. It began in the 1970s when the captain and owner of the sailing schooner Shenandoah, Robert S. Douglas, bought a small house offshore from his mooring in Vineyard Haven harbor.

He lived in the house when he wasn't taking people on cruises and started preparing lunches for his customers to take on the cruises.

He had a pet dog–a black Lab named, of course, "Black Dog."

Word spread, the dog loved the attention, and the customers loved the dog.

The Captain started cooking ever more meals for sailing customers and non-sailing customers. He had to hire help. He got married and started a family.

He had a marine craftsman carve a replica of his dog out of wood, which now stands on a pole fifteen feet in the air–and this, of course, attracted even more attention and more customers. Soon the café was out-billing the boat.

He started tying a red bandanna around his dog's neck. The effect was good, and people wanted a red bandanna. He had one printed up, with the black dog in profile on one corner. Then he tried baseball caps–also a runaway success. Everyone wanted that dog, *on something*. He hired more help; a corporation was formed. Other items were designed and created-tee shirts, beach towels, tote bags, sweat shirts. All carried only one symbol, the profile of his black dog with a red bandanna or red collar around his neck.

They designed and brought out a catalog and direct mail sales surged.

Now the accessory business out-billed the café, which in turn, out-billed the boat business. Today the Black Dog Cafe is thriving, with annual gross revenues of over $15 million, and has 55 employees in the winter, 300 in the summer. Robert Douglas's family grew up and now help run the enterprise. Son Jamie manages the retail business (caps, shirts, etc.) and son Morgan runs the tavern (the meals, the bakery).When celebrities come to the island they have to eat one time at The Black Dog; it's the thing to do. Regular customers include: President Bill Clinton, actor Kevin Costner, Senator Ted Kennedy and many not famous (including myself).

One could say that this is a case where the "dog wags the tale."

Logos That Work

Sometimes something clicks in the subconscious of the public that turns a logo into a hero, a long-range success. This can happen anywhere or anytime for a product or service of any sort. Here are some examples.

Coca-Cola in 1887, designed by Frank M. Robinson

Ford in 1903. The logo designed by its chief automotive engineer Childe Harold Wills and has remained unchanged since 1928.

KLM, the symbol of Dutch Airlines, was designed in 1919 and modified to its present look in 1961 by designer F.H.K. Henrion

CBS in 1951, designed by William Golden

Playboy in 1953, by Arthur Paul

Marlboro in 1956, by Frank Gianninoto

McDonald's in 1962, modified in 1968 by Jim Schindler

Chase Manhattan Bank in 1960 by Tom Geismar

Absolut Vodka in the 1970s by Gunnar Broman and Hans Brindfors

Logos became brands or trademarks for the most part in the nineteenth century and some grew popular and some (many) faded from memory. The reasons for success vs. failure are diverse.Some grew popular based on good design, some on outside events like a humorous character associated with the logo or the product, etc. Logos have always had to play a dual role: identification (recognition) vs. the capacity for variation. Recognition grows out of repetition as it develops into a theme. Excessive repetition can degrade the logo's image, its sense of worth. The graphic designer must strive to achieve both recognition and room for variation. All the best ones, those with the longest life spans, have these qualities.

Sometimes it is a marriage of the logo with a clever ad campaign. A perfect example of this is Absolut Vodka. The shape of its bottle, as featured in the variety of its many off-beat witty ads, has carried this once little-known brand to new heights of recognition and popularity. Are all logos good just because they get well known, popular?

Most definitely not!
So, how do you judge the effectiveness of a logo?

Criteria for Judging the Effectiveness/Value of a New Logo

1. **Visibility**–How will it be used? Will the trademark stand out in a dark store interior, on a hillside alongside the Interstate, by a motorist going by at 70 mph?
2. **Simplicity**–Is the trademark easy to understand?
3. **Application**–If the logo is to appear at ringside in the US Tennis Open, will it be discernable to TV viewers? Distracting to players?
4. **Competition**–Does it stand out from others?
5. **Legal**–Can it be protected? If it is too close to a generic look, or word it might not be. And sometimes a mark can become so familiar that it borders on being a generic–Xerox for photocopying, for instance.
6. **Application**
   a. How will it work in color, on an ad?
   b. How will it work in black and white, in a newspaper?
   c. How will it work in the Yellow Pages?
   d. How will it work on vehicles?
   e. Will it work on/or in a television commercial?
7. **Color**
Logos, and packages, use color a great deal these days to distinguish themselves in the marketplace. Some colors are considered in bad taste in certain countries-yellow in Japan, for instance.
8. **Timelessness**
   a. Is the new trademark timeless, durable? Nothing is but will it stay current, not look too dated, in a reasonable time frame?
   b. Contrary to that, is the trademark nostalgic? Sometimes it is desirable to look old fashioned–recalling the "good old days," etc. "Johnny Rocket's" (chain of hamburger, snack food stores) is a good example of this.
9. **Pronunciation**–Can the trademark, or name, be easily pronounced? Does it have phonetic problems?
10. **Likeability**–Is it likeable? Appeal is highly subjective and hard to measure but worthwhile.

Summary

Reflections from the past—

The original designation of the logo back in time (see Chapter 2) was derived from one of four motivations: need, ownership, origin and pride.

It is still true today.

The only difference between original motivation and today, called "branded identification" is that with wider usage, branded trademarks (logos) become pseudonyms for the originator, in modern times, the company.

The trademark identifies the company as communicator, owner and manufacturer, respectively.

Success has a lot to do with where the viewer is coming from.

1. Need application

The trademark identifies the sender and becomes the shortest type of company communication, this is IBM, and all it represents (as on letterhead, for example).

2. Ownership application

The trademark identifies the company as the owner of its property. A delivery truck from United Parcel Service, for example.

3. Origin application

The trademark identifies the company as the provider of products and services. The trademark on a box of Pringles from Procter & Gamble is a good example.

4. Pride application

The Texaco star (logo) stands for quality and assurance of good driving.

The Goal of an Identity

Louis Sullivan once said, "Form follows function," and quarreled with Mies Van der Rohe over its application. Frank Lloyd Wright agreed with Sullivan, and both men's buildings reflected it. The same could be said of the use of identity in the workplace.

The double task of a trademark is to allow immediate identification while evoking important values of the organization, company or product presenting it. While this is still true, the applications and executions of logos is changing in the twenty-first century. We are now seeing huge logos on the sides of football stadiums and concert halls. It is sponsorship on a big, big scale. There is the Staples Center for sports and concerts in Los Angeles, the Home Depot Center for conventions in Carson, California, The Coca-Cola Space Center in Columbus, Georgia, the

Sony Center in Berlin, the Disney Concert Hall in Los Angeles–and many more. The logo is becoming the main event–super-sized!

The Many Faces (and logos) of AT&T

Perhaps no corporation has spawned so many names and logo changes as AT&T (American Telephone and Telegraph). The company was founded in 1879 as American Bell Telephone in an agreement with Alexander Graham Bell and his financiers. In 1880 American Bell created AT&T Long Lines with the stated goal of creating a nationwide long distance network of telephone lines. This was finally achieved in 1915. The United States government quickly nationalized the new trans-American telecommunications industry in 1918 (for national defense reasons) but paid AT&T a nice percentage of all revenues from it. In 1925 AT&T created Bell Labs in partnership with Western Electric as the firm that would own (and rent) the actual telephones customers used. No other devices were permitted on their lines, thus creating a monopoly. At this point there were twenty-two Bell operating companies owned by AT&T.

The consent decree of 1984 (between AT&T and the US Supreme Court) essentially broke away the twenty-two Bell operating companies, resulting in the creation of the "seven baby Bells." Each of these new operating companies (with its own logo) divided up 160 regional markets across the United States parent AT&T reorganized into Bell Labs, Western Electric (which became Lucent Technologies) and AT&T Communications.

In the next ten years, Southwestern Bell (one of the seven baby Bells) acquired three former baby bells (Ameritech, SNET and Pacific Telesis) and changed its name to SBC Communications. In 2005 SBC announced they would acquire former parent AT&T and change their name back to AT&T, Inc. Finally in 1996 they acquired Bellsouth, so that of the original twenty-two Bell operating companies which AT&T owned prior to the 1984 breakup, eleven have returned as part of the new entity, AT&T Inc.

The lion's share of the logo designs have gone to graphic designer Saul Bass and Associates. It is said that when he did the first corporate logo (in 1969) he had to create nine sets of design standards manuals covering every expression of the mark from stationery to uniforms to signage. He revised his design again in 1984 (after the breakup).

Today there is yet another design in use–a modification of the globe concept.

1969

1984

1993

2006

SECTION II
PRODUCT AND PLACE

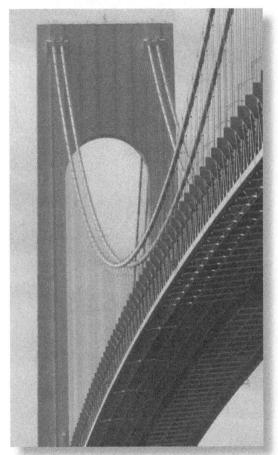

The Verrazano Narrows Bridge,
New York, New York

Completed: 1965

The longest suspension span in the world.

4

PEOPLE

Preferences, Prejudices and Persuasion

Choices. Commerce is all about choices, but...
how do we choose and when do we choose?
Choices are a direct function of what and who we are, what we like and do not like. It might
be as serious as hating something or as light as having a bias.
A more fundamental question might be, why do people buy ?

Here's how the *Chicago Tribune* put it last year as the Christmas shopping season was just
beginning.

> *"People buy because they're alive and want to stay that way. We venture that for
> many, the act of buying something, either by impulse or through long desire, is one
> of the most satisfying moments in life. You're never more alive than when you put
> your signature to the credit card slip for something you've been needing. What else
> can match the thrill, for instance, of buying a new car? At its core, the act of buying
> something to be used in the future is profoundly optimistic. It says, I'm planning to
> be here to use this. It's a celebration of life."*

"A season of desire," Editorial page, *Chicago Tribune*

The important thing is that smart marketers know how to influence our preferences and
prejudices and lead us to a buy decision, sometimes without our even realizing it.
It is a process called "persuasion" and the primary tool used to persuade... is aesthetics.

From the moment we wake up to the end of each day, we are impressed by what we see, hear,
taste, smell and feel. Our personal tastes guide our decisions in choosing our community,
our houses, how we decorate a room, how we select our clothing, beverages, automobiles.
For the average teenager in a middle class family the urge is relentless; they are constantly on

the vigil for new stuff. It's like a wheel of desire that turns and turns; a spigot that is always on. And they are very brand aware.

Polo, North Face, Kate Spade, Lacoste (and many more) drive the wheel.

Brands, per se do not alter our lives, but they are a big part of what influences us.

And brand preference, coupled with a well-focused marketing campaign can be powerful and long term.

But without aesthetics, in hasn't got much of a chance.

Aesthetics and its influence on our Preferences and Prejudices

Aesthetics is a funny word, another Greek word ("aisthetikos") but in terms of persuading a potential customer, it is an important word. It's meaning is tied to perception and feeling and is closely related to Style. It is why we like one thing over another–how we choose, what makes us tick. For the purposes of the commercial world, and the point of this chapter, we must consider Aesthetics as another (powerful) marketing tool.

Marketing Aesthetics generally reveals its influence in three areas and each with its own opposite reaction.

Product Design: Form vs. Function: the packaging (form: beauty, appeal) of the product or service vs. the utilitarian (function: how it works) benefits of the product. Consider the new Motorola.

Motorola Razr V3

Communications Design: a successful aesthetic reaction depends on two kinds of messages: the central message (What does the product do, and how) vs. the peripheral message (What does the presenter look like, what does the room, or kitchen, look like? Do I like it, can I associate with the presenter?)

Spatial design: Structure vs. Symbolism: aesthetics is revealed in how people react to the environment (i.e. the store–can I find my way, understand where things are?), vs. does this store please me? Think of shopping at Wal-Mart vs. shopping at Saks Fifth Avenue. Both communicate, but in a vastly different manner.

The best designed buildings, as well as stores, function in this way.

Think of the impression you get in St. Patrick's Cathedral in NY and contrast that with the impression you get in a modern house by Philip Johnson. The soaring height of the cathedral's Nave carries your eye and spirit up with it. You become inspired.

By contrast think of the horizontal feeling you get in Johnson's Glass House, or any by Frank Lloyd Wright–and your vision expands, feels wider, connected to the earth, its movement, its richness.

These may be two extreme contrasts, but that is the exact way a building works to provide us with an aesthetic experience.

Closer to the point, the interior space of Tiffany's is geared to communicate expensive good taste, at a price. It might communicate, "I am special just because I am in here."

Philip Johnson - Glass House

And by the same token, the robin's egg blue of the box that your Tiffany's purchase comes in tells the world out on Fifth Avenue that you are special, you're worth it.

Aesthetics cuts across all of these three categories. Good marketers can skillfully direct customer's reactions and influence buy decisions in Wal-Mart or Saks by addressing the two dichotomies within each preceding category (form vs. function, etc.). In order to be a clever marketer you have to be able to manage the public face of the organization and its brands. This is done through various corporate identities (logos): business cards, invoices, uniforms, vehicles, showrooms, websites, print and TV ads, the headquarters building and its signage, sales kits, packaging, point-of-purchase displays, etc. Because it is such a large and diverse universe, it is necessary to group them and attend to them as pieces of a group

The expression of the marketing aesthetic emanates from three product attributes: Benefits, Branding and Sensory reaction–which will be covered later in this chapter.

Let's take an example, Absolut Vodka.

The Absolut Story

When this vodka arrived on the American scene-in the late 1970s, it had little going for it. It faced formidable competition from Stolichnaya (the only true Russian vodka), which had a market share of over 80 percent.

To make matters more difficult, its brand name was not distinctive, it had no history, it was unfamiliar and the bottle was fat and had a stumpy neck.

Absolut marketers adopted a bold strategy that was closely tied to giving the product and its image a powerful, unique and memorable aesthetic personality.

Like the originators of the Volkswagen campaign (Bill Bernbach and Helmut Krone) in the 1950s, the Absolut marketers decided to concentrate on the very awkwardness of the name and the bottle, and turn them into an advantage.

They redesigned the bottle graphics in silver and blue, reinforcing the product look–one that is streamlined, straightforward and sophisticated.

They gave it an urban image.

They made it cool.

All the ads featured the bottle, dead center, and incorporated a trendy, two-word headline that always starts with the word "Absolut." So far, nothing special, but what they did next was make it "hip." What still makes the ad campaign cool, what gives it a trendy, sassy, edgy personality, is the placement of the familiar bottle in an unexpected and constantly changing setting. For example, "Absolut Perfection" features the crystal-clear bottle depicted as jewelry topped by a halo. "Absolut Original" features a stone bottle with cracks in it, as if it had just been excavated from a prehistoric site. Absolut Manhattan features an aerial photo of Park Avenue with heavy traffic and the roofs of the yellow cabs are positioned to show the shape of a yellow Absolut bottle.

In short, Absolut's cocky image was created through a sophisticated strategy that mixed consistent, simple refinement with planned and controlled unconventional executions. And they only did their advertising in print–no TV.

The sales show it. In the last ten years Absolut sales in the US have grown from 5,000 cases per year to 2.5 million cases.

It has been the first or second best-selling imported brand with a market share of nearly 60 percent among imported vodkas.

This campaign, which is an aesthetic blitz, is the work of the top management and creative talent of TBWA (Ted Bates Worldwide Advertising).

They achieved this position by:

> —studying and correctly understanding their target audience (upscale urban consumers)
> —utilizing a gentle, slightly mocking humor

And they focused on the three key attributes of marketing aesthetics: **benefits, branding, and sensory reaction.**

They knew their approach wouldn't appeal to everyone and that in itself was part of this campaign's appeal. It became a kind of "in-joke" defining the choice of Absolut (over Stolichnaya for example) as driven by refined good taste coupled with sophistication and wry humor.

It must be emphasized, however, that the product (any product) has to be good–no clever campaign can build a lasting aesthetic without delivering on taste or quality. Any company that has done this has found a powerful point of differentiation through the use of aesthetics–to create a positive overall customer impression.

Elements of Association

Not Russian (The American Vodka)

Quirky (Chunky Bottle)

Quality (Smooth Taste)

Clarity (Honest)

Comfortable (Easy Lifestyle)

Witty (Clever Ads)

Most customers, bombarded as they are with advertising and sales pitches, are not impressed by benefits alone. The customer of today makes choices based on whether or not a product fits into his or her lifestyle. Brands can provide an image. Good ones can assure us of quality, providing a long-term value through their names and associations. The best ones have something called "style."

Creating a Marketing Plan

The traditional way to establish a marketing plan is to focus on the benefits that the product's attributes will give those who buy it and use it. An example: for white teeth, use Crest toothpaste with brightener.

The communications strategy usually goes something like this: "If we develop a unique competitive advantage, and communicate it believably and well, we'll gain market share and high margin." This used to work in spades. Not so easily today. The very proliferation of competing messages, each making similar claims, has hardened the typical consumer. There seems to be an overall trend away from product attributes towards lifestyle or value systems. Clutter has killed the pure benefits message.

The trend now is toward style. Style can make the difference – unclutter the landscape. If the targeted consumer can identify with the product – perhaps by the style of the person/model shown using it, he'll be more inclined to buy the product.

Brand Characteristics

The 1990s could be called "the brand age." A maturing marketplace, more expensive media costs and the growth of alternative marketing communications laid the groundwork. Also individual ads were starting to have less impact. This caused marketers to refocus on the brand itself. Brand building became the rallying cry of the day and Y&R now calls itself a "Branding Company." In many ways the brand is the organizing concept of the business–the parent company's most valuable asset (i.e. P&G's twenty-two brands each worth one billion dollars annually).

Brands provide identity, and when linked with an advertising image, assure us of quality-offering solutions. David Aaker (Professor of Marketing Strategy at the University of California/Berkley) put it this way.

> "Brands provide long-term values through their names and associations", [because] its equity is a set of assets and liabilities linked to a brand, its name and symbol. If the brand's name or symbol is changed, some or all of the assets or liabilities could be affected–even lost. The assets differ from product to product, context to context.
> **Managing Brand Equity, by David A. Aaker, 1991.**

They usually fall into five categories:

1. Brand Loyalty
It is harder to gain new customers (and expensive) than to retain existing ones. And generally speaking , customers don't like to switch. A loyal customer base reduces vulnerability to competitive action.

2. Name awareness
A recognized brand will often be selected over an unknown brand because people are comfortable with the familiar.

3. Perceived quality
Perceived quality will directly influence purchase decisions and brand loyalty. Brand quality will support a premium price and become a basis for line extensions.
When my firm did the new product extension for Nabisco's Grey Poupon specialty foods, it was made much easier because Grey Poupon already had a favorable, high quality image.

4. Brand associations
The brand name will take on a set of associations depending on how it is introduced and maintained. Take L.L.Bean. The company enjoys a set of aesthetic associations that communicate quality, "we stand behind our product, always have always will." Competitors have a hard time attacking Bean directly.

The Singer Story

Some years ago I was the account manager for Young & Rubicam on the Singer account. We needed a spokesperson, one who was the right age (our target market was mature and female), sewed, and was probably a mother. We were certain that our ideal customer was discerning and would pay for a quality sewing machine (and they weren't cheap). The Singer electronic sewing machines were an engineering marvel–could make buttonholes in a flash, do frog stitching, you name it. I became an expert, as long as I stayed away from the machine!

We searched high and low for the right woman. The final selection was Polly Bergen. She was in her late fifties, she was pretty but not exquisite, she had style, she had been a creditable jazz singer and she had done some acting–mostly TV. She was good.

I watched her captivate a room of noisy salesmen at a sales convention, and by contrast, I saw her gain the respect of a roomful of savvy housewives. In short, she had credability. We got her and she was perfect. That was a case of Brand-by-Association benefit.

The advertising and promotion programs we created all featured Ms. Bergen as capable, concerned and committed to beauty and craftsmanship. We, and she, portrayed her as the personification of all things quality and handcrafted. Polly was totally convincing - yet to the best of my knowledge sewed very little.

Polly Bergen

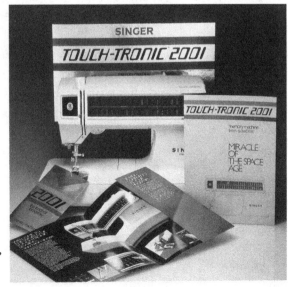

*The Singer Touch-Tronic 2001
was a "state-of-the-art"
electronic sewing machine.*

Part I
Crossing a Bridge Called "Style"

Count Marcello said, "How do you see a bridge?"
"Pardon me," I replied, "a bridge?"
"Do you see a bridge as an obstacle, a set of steps to climb to get from one side of a canal to the other?"
"I don't know."
"We Venetians see bridges as transitions. We go over them slowly. They (the bridges) are the links between two parts of a theatre, and our role changes as we go over bridges. We cross from one reality, to another."
From *The City of Falling Angels*, by John Berendt, 2005.

Count Marcello is implying that Venetians have a sense of theatre, weave drama into their daily lives. Drama and theatrics are often inherent in style, especially when used as a tool to make a point. And Venice truly has style, a style that is evident in its bridges, its architecture, its canals, its lagoons, its history, and in its people. It can't be easily duplicated, although Las Vegas has tried.

What is style? It's an elusive term, and a highly subjective one. What passes for style in Des Moines, Iowa, won't pass for style on Fifth Avenue in Manhattan, or Venice for that matter. Wherever and whatever, it is a vital component of the marketing aesthetic you want to create for your product.

No matter where we live, when we speak of style we mean a distinctive quality or form, a manner of expression. Styles have a number of important functions for organizations. They can create brand awareness, they can create associations, they can differentiate products and services, help consumers categorize products or services, they can beautify our surroundings, reduce stress–make us feel good, bond.

Styles are composed of primary elements: color, shape, line and pattern are key visual elements. Volume, pitch, pace are key elements of auditory style (Bach vs. The Rolling Stones) The process of buying, and of consuming in retail spaces is very dependent on: background music, fragrances, tastes and materials, textures etc. However, in other retail areas, the most basic is visual.

Elements of Style

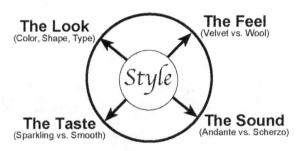

The Look (Color, Shape, Type)

The Feel (Velvet vs. Wool)

Style

The Taste (Sparkling vs. Smooth)

The Sound (Andante vs. Scherzo)

Narrative: The Essential Ingredient of Ralph Lauren
By Laurence Vincent, Legendary Brands,
Dearborn Trade Publishing, Chicago, 2002

Style requires "Narrative," the ingredient that tells the story. The story is the living proof of the idea, the means by which you, the marketer, can express and then prove your idea.

Consider Ralph Lauren and the Polo brand of fragrances and apparel. Through the narrative of its advertising, fashion shows and product design, the brand links a desirable social culture to the consumer's belief that fashion and style is both active, and refined. The brand follows two story lines: one is Ralph himself, as seen in elegant surroundings, with famous people at upscale social affairs. The other connects the social culture (of Ralph) to the brand's beliefs. Typical advertisements show attractive young people racing yachts, visiting exotic places or playing polo. And the conclusion, that Polo Brand is an agent of the refined elite, and that you (the consumer) can acquire this level of style through wearing and owning Ralph Lauren's Polo brand clothing.

Synesthesia

Synesthesia is the stimulation of one sense by another sense (and yet again an old Greek word). Synesthesia creates "a balanced integration of the primary elements of color, shape, scent and materials, into a system of attributes–that express brand aesthetic style." The authors Schmitt and Simonson (Marketing Aesthetics, 1997) cite Gillette and its new razor model, Sensor, as an example. The Sensor is a lovely design, a nice combination of visual and tactile qualities. Gillette (now part of Procter and Gamble) practices "synesthesia" with its total family of shaving products: razors, deodorants, shaving creams, and aftershaves and from a marketing design standpoint, it is a total success.

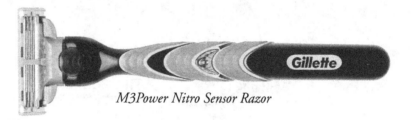

M3Power Nitro Sensor Razor

Gillette is also a good example of the importance of paying meticulous attention to all the parts that make up the whole-especially in launching a new product like the Sensor razor. Two distinguished design firms combined to make this razor a quick success and to allow Gillette to capture brand share from S.C. Johnson's Edge brand gel. Ansbach, Grossman and Portugal created the identity system for the razor and its accessories, while Desgrippes Gobe and Associates developed a line of fourteen toiletry products for men, which Gillette launched in the U.S. and Europe simultaneously. The effect was powerful.

Here is the way they describe (the package/razor) its colors: "blue communicates the cleanliness of shaving, black a universality and gutsy masculine style, silver–with its metallic sheen and industrial presence–reflect the performance of the razor..., the structural design is proportional to fit a man's hand, and is slick and cylindrical, or ribbed and reminiscent of a man's broad shoulders."

What they are saying, more simply, is that the new Gillette Sensor has style.

The Dimensions of Shape

Products such as the new Gillette razor, or the Absolut vodka bottle, mentioned earlier in this chapter, can be analyzed further by looking at how the elements of shape affect our impressions of the product inside, or the brand on the outside. Shape trumps everything in the fashion and fragrance industry. The mere shape of a bottle can have dramatic marketing effects: consider Calvin Klein's fragrance CK ONE, or SOUSON, a private label line of bath and body products designed by my firm (LMS Design) in the late 1990s for Federated Department Stores (sold in Macys). Each feature a custom designed bottle that uses clear, translucent and light metallic surfaces to highlight the natural rainbow of the product's color. Dimensions of shape aren't so diverse as one would think. There are four key dimensions of shape.

Influence of Shape

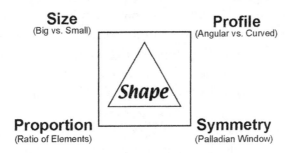

Size: Large means strong; small, short or thin means delicate; one's reaction may have a lot to do with where you come from.

Angularity: shapes with angles, like triangles, squares, and rounded forms-all have associations. Angularity means dynamism, masculinity; roundness evokes harmony, softness, feminine.

Proportion: Long shapes evoke vision, the broad view; short shapes evoke timidness, weakness.

Symmetry: creates balance, and pleasure. For interest, symmetry is often juxtaposed against asymmetry, to provide a sense of balance with a touch of excitement and movement.

Fine Tuning

Beyond identification and association color can be used to create experiences or influence a mood. Kodak's yellow, Tiffany's blue, IBM's darker blue, Mary Kay's pink, Coke's red, all become symbols, shorthand for the identity of the product. The important thing, the Aesthetic thing is, what does color mean to customers?

Color

Color can be judged by: **Saturation:** saturation means the purity of the color, not diluted with white, **Brightness:** brightness has to do with intensity of the color and hue; *hue* means shades, bold vs. subtle, etc. The more saturated the color the greater the impression that the object is moving. The brighter the color, the greater the impression that the object is closer than it really is. Hues of one extreme of light tend to be perceived as more energetic and extroverted, while those at the other end (blues, purples) appear calmer and more introverted. Reds often mean adventurous, popular with sports cars, yellows often imply cheerful, jovial, exciting and impulsive, greens and tans are viewed as calm, restful, soothing.

For years, purple communicated royalty—for obvious reasons.

Black and white represented extremes of saturation and often brightness. The color white was perceived as sunny (along with yellow), happy, active and often, pure and innocent. It is tailor-made for laundry detergent.

Black is often perceived as dark and mysterious, sometimes impure or evil. Metallic colors such as gold or silver have lustrous images, and they convey, invariably, luxury and elegance.

Sound: in retail spaces they enhance the shopping experience. Pottery Barn has found this effective and had so much favorable customer reaction, that they now sell CDs of medleys of music played in their stores with clever names like "Stir it up" (music of Stan Getz, Tito Puente, etc.).

Touch: materials can create a certain "feel" of a product. Glossy vs. matte paper for brochures, marble vs. Corian at the checkout counter—all have communicative strengths, and are integral to building style.

The Container Corporation used to design and publish a thick book that contained great art, or clever design, printed on different kinds of paper. So did Mead Paper—they called it the Mead Library of Ideas. So did International Paper. All were a vehicle for showing off their variety of paper stocks and the printability on each.

Taste and Smell: Taste is linked to smell, and smell is one of the most powerful of the senses. Scents are everywhere, and some stores make use of them—stores like Crabtree & Evelyn or The Body Shop. Even supermarkets have learned to use smell to their advantage. Usually when you enter a supermarket you turn right, and this is where smart grocery store management place the bakery. With luck, the lovely smell of fresh baked bread permeates the atmosphere as you pass by, and you get hungry.

Dimensions of Style

Even dimension plays a role in style. There are four perceptual differences.

1. **Complexity** (minimal vs. ornamental): Minimalism strives for simplicity of structure and form, while ornamentals love complexity, multiple motifs and meanings. Think of a (slim and minimalist) Kate Spade handbag vs. a Laura Ashley (highly decorative) frock.

2. **Representation** (realism vs. abstraction): Usually realism is expressed with an association to their logo or advertising to objects in the real world, while abstraction only hints at this world. Think of the American Airlines logo (eagle) vs. the Delta Airlines logo (triangle).

3. **Movement** (dynamic vs. static): This is harder to express because movement, unless one uses blurred images and speed lines, can only be suggested. The Nike Swoosh communicates

movement, however, through its association with the god Mercury, while the logo for Home Depot is purposefully static.

4. **Potency** (loud/strong vs. soft/weak): This is also hard to express. Potency is expressed in many modern marks, like Target Stores. The bulls eye is a universally powerful, focused symbol—and they do it in red! Contrast that with the identity for American Greetings, which utilizes a heart-shaped rose and simple, serif type. Achieving style in your product or brand is a start, but only a start.

Now you have to get the message out, and this requires turning it into a theme.

American Greetings logo

Part II
The Importance of Theme
Getting the message out

On Themes
By Bruce Bendinger, Former Creative Director
J. Walter Thompson, Chicago

"We Try Harder (Avis)," what a wonderful theme! It communicated the benefit of being better without over-promise. And it motivated personnel – an important and often overlooked function of advertising. This was one of the first modern "positioning" campaigns. A marvelous piece of logic. It made you believe you got a better deal and better service. It is an excellent example of "60s style-copywriting" by Paula Green, with help from Helmut Krone. Tight and delightful.

To be effective, styles must be combined with themes that express an organization's/brand's personality. Themes are the key building blocks in forming an identity—a brand position. Themes infuse meaning into style because, by their very nature, they repeat the image or brand. In other words, tell the style theme widely and purposefully until it sticks in the consumer's mind.

There is a delicate balance between repetition that grooves into a person's memory bank, and one that does it to the point of irritation. We all have had experiences with jingles that turn us off through either their banality, or loudness, or poor taste.

Symbols as Themes

It is generally better to use a prototypical figure (not a real person) than the reverse. Prototypical figures can be shaped, altered, adapted to the current scene (i.e. Betty Crocker). There are pitfalls to using real people, and the most disastrous examples might have been when Hertz used O. J. Simpson or Pepsi used Michael Jackson as spokespersons for their brands. As they and their images changed, the reflection could have been very negative on their sponsors. The Absolut campaign, to refer to it again, is a wonderful example of themed advertising that is balanced. The network of associations that their advertising agency has created around the brand is all positive. People think of Absolut in terms of: good quality, trendy, interesting bottle, clear and tasty. By contrast Stolichnaya, the brand leader (until recently), has only one associative message, it is Russian. That's not much to go on.

Image in Wine Bottles
New Yorker, September 6, 2004

A popular Pinot Noir from Villalta, Trento, Italy, evokes the pleasure of an Italian evening.

Consider the imagery which is contained in the simple, often elegant graphics of wine bottles and their labels. Some of the best packaging in the nation has been by designers of packaging for wine. Certainly the graphics found on the labels deserve special praise.

Bottle shapes vary widely, from the typical slender, long necked bottle to shorter or wider packages. The imagery of life in Simi Valley, or Napa Valley helps to establish image for the wines–it is a kind of combination of Tuscany, mixed with California healthy-laid back lifestyle. It starts with the rhetoric, as expressed in the ads and in the wine magazine write-ups. Here's an example: "In the aroma of a bottle of Krug 'intense empyreumatic fragrances of toasted milk bread, fresh butter, café au lait, and afterthoughts of linden join in a harmonious chorus with generous notes of acacia honey, mocha, and vanilla." Wine writer Eric Glatre is climbing a Mount Everest of words.

And then there is ritual. Evidently wine has always had certain mystic qualities in certain societies. It related to the drinking vessel, and even to the sacraments, as in the communion service.

Finally, as stated, it is reflected in the package (bottle), in the ads about the wines, and in the attitude that the wine marketers want the consumers to assimilate when thinking of their particular wine.

1994

The Xerox Story

2007

It isn't surprising that compact, well-shaped logos (and short names) become the most memorable. Think of Alcoa or 3M or BMW. They must do more, however, to retain attention. They should say something about the product and its benefits. A good example is the highly successful Xerox brand. The original name was Haloid-Xerox and they were headquartered in Rochester, NY. The prominent design firm Lippincott & Marguiles created the logo for the name in the late 1960s, back when they had basically one product–a photocopy machine. It was one of the first and it was wonderfully popular. In fact the name became so popular (after they dropped the Haloid part) that it became the generic expression for making a photocopy. People would say, " Let's Xerox this," using it as a verb.

In the 1970s they decided to expand their product line to include personal computers, printers and even financial services. It wasn't a big success so in 1994 they returned to their core business–photocopy machines. Two new design firms coordinated the new design effort for the new logo, Siegal & Gale (head designer Don Ervin) and Landor Associates, headquartered in San Francisco on a ferry boat called "The Klamath." One of the most effective parts of the new identity was the tag line, " The Document Company." It was a wise, strategic move and today the company is doing very well with annual revenues of over $15 billion.

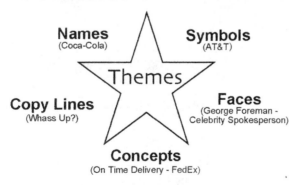

Themes as symbols

Symbols are highly subjective and hard to own. They usually don't carry over to the product itself. Sometimes, as in the case of Col. Sanders for KFC, it does work. A life-sized statue of Col. Sanders is often used out in front of stores as an attention-getter. Lately, Quaker Oats has been doing the same thing with its statue of the smiling Quaker.

Colonial Sanders did exist, but not so the Quaker. The Quaker Oats gentlemen is pure symbol: an idealized version of the Quaker image of Philadelphia–embodying simple, honest values (and food). Another is Betty Crocker who was created by General Mills as a symbol of the idealized American housewife/cook. She has been described as a paragon of white middle America-created in 1936 and updated every 10 years (or so). Conversely, Aunt Jemima is the idealized African-American servant/cook/family retainer (and not too PC these days)

The Marlboro Cowboy: idealized figure of the American independent, action-oriented," honest as the land," male figure. All of the previous examples (except Col. Sanders) are fictitious. Sometimes these images are based on real people.

Charles Schwab Associates – on Charles Schwab
Virgin Air–on Richard Branson
Donald Trump and anything large and showy
Lipton Tea–Sir Thomas Lipton (heritage)
Tom's of Maine (toothpaste)–Tom Chappel–the green movement
Jell-O–Bill Cosby (warm and comfortable)–family values
Martha Stewart–clever, craft-oriented (for K-mart) or her magazine
Oprah Winfrey–tasteful, genuine, for her magazine.

Themes as narratives

The Disney Stores, and the Warner Brothers Stores utilize their cartoon characters as narratives for a themed identity. The only one that works consistently is the mouse ears of Mickey.

Themes as slogans or jingles

The cola companies have done this particularly well.

Coke's "Things go better with Coke" has worked for a long time. Their current one: "Coke Now."

Pepsi's "You've got a lot to live and Pepsi's got a lot to give" also worked well, and endures. Currently their slogan is "Generation Next."

Marlboro's "Come to where the flavor is. Come to Marlboro country," does, also.

But while these have endured, some don't and have to be abandoned or adapted. The ones that last are strong because they are playing off the aesthetic image associated with each.

Themes Evoke Impressions

Mickey Mouse - cute and happy
Coke - the good life, I feel good about me
Pepsi - on the edge, I'm energetic, a risk taker
Marlboro - I'm my own man

Theme changes are fed by cultural images and a theme can become tired or outdated. Changes can also be brought about internally, from within the client organization. Customer demographics and lifestyles are also constantly changing-particularly in food or in clothing. Banana Republic originally had a safari and rainforest, third world image-which proved limiting and a little non-PC, so today the chain (owned by GAP) has an upscale, modern image.

Competition can dictate change. Companies must always keep an eye on the advertising of the competition, and be ready to change it if they see that they are losing their uniqueness. Circuit City advertising appears to be getting copied in style by Best Buy.

Making an Impression

Overall impressions are formed from mental pictures of a brand's aesthetic, through a process called "interpretation."

How do individuals integrate the many pieces of information that they are exposed to daily–into a clear impression? Can it even be done? The best marketers do it in one of two ways.

The Centrality Effect. Consumers form overall impressions, based on the biggest element of a corporation's, or brands entity. For a bank it might be the bank's building or its logo. The Harris Trust Bank of Chicago adopted the lion as its symbol, giving the impression of nobility, strength and reliability.

The Primacy Effect. This states the obvious; that first impressions last–usually dominate other impressions. Once a negative first impression roots in-it is hard to shake. A good example is the current P&G acronym and philosophy explained in Chapter 3: called "FMOT" (first moment of truth).

There are attitudes that work in both situations (Centrality or Primacy Effects).

1. Inferences: These are conclusions that customers draw based on the identity elements that they perceive–in which they fill in missing information based on their personal experiences. Here color can play a big part (red is exciting) and shape (angularity is tension), etc.

2. Attitudes: Attitudes are the effective evaluations of customer impressions. They are usually definitive: positive, neutral, or regrettably, negative.

3. Time Factor: Where is your product in history? All people are affected by time. We think of things, events, and products as being in the past, present or future. This, too, is a factor in the effectiveness of an ad campaign or a product or logo.

4. The Past: Customers often judge an identity to be traditional if it uses elements, styles and themes that are strongly identified with past periods. And this reference can be valuable for some products, negative for others–Brooks Brothers clothing vs. Donna Karen clothing–both reflected in their respective logos and advertisements. Elements that communicate past are: black and white photos, soft focus, Roman columns, serif type, etc. Here are two excellent examples of utilizing the past as the theme of a product or ad campaign.

Nostalgia

Sometimes advertisers or identity managers will intentionally want to achieve a "retro" effect. Nostalgia for the good old days can be persuasive and appealing. Some restaurants try to achieve the look of a fifties diner-like Johnny Rockets, with its shiny chromium counters and wall-mounted juke box machines. The Converse "One Star" sneaker is another example of a popular retro look.

Johnny Rockets Diner

Elegance

A very successful example is in the advertisements for Longine's watches, featuring Audrey Hepburn, or sometimes, Humphrey Bogart. For Audrey they utilize a picture of her in an evening gown, holding a long cigarette holder, next to the headline "Elegance is an attitude." The association with this popular, classic star, with the movie "*Breakfast at Tiffany's,*" and the watch and its curving strap, make a powerful argument for the benefit of Retro and Legacy combined.

Contemporary: An overall impression that is deemed contemporary uses styles and themes of the present. The packaging of two of the leading water brands are good examples of this: Aquafina (Pepsi owned) and Dasani (Coke owned) use simple type, blue background, no frills, a spiritual and "pure"aesthetic. The same is true for the packaging of the leading energy drinks: Powerade, Gatorade, or Red Bull.

Futuristic (Avant-Garde): A representation that is futuristic usually uses avant-garde design, new materials, and modernistic typefaces. The logo of the French bullet train-TGV, fits this representation, as does the logo for NASA, or Sony's logo for their laptop computer.

National Aeronautics and Space Administration

The architecture of Frank Gehry (the Guggenheim in Bilbao, Spain, for example) is very avant-garde.

Legacy and Contrasts. This is an impression rendered with a little of both past and present. Usually products that have a sense of history, are known to their public, and projected into the future-use this approach. The "We've been making Dewars Scotch since the 1870s" approach.

Other considerations:
Space: City vs. Country. It is often a lifestyle statement, urban sophistication and energy, as opposed to simple pleasures, honesty and directness. L.L.Bean uses this method admirably, as does Donna Karan (DKNY) at the other extreme.
East vs. West: New England seashore (Nantucket) as opposed to Southern California (say Malibu–the broad Pacific). The imagery used so well by Marlboro is clearly the Teton Range of Wyoming, and the clear, high mountain air, while the imagery of Arizona and New Mexico and its utilization of Indian blankets, teal blue and green evoke some of Sobee soda's packaging, or some of the fragrances of Estee Lauder.
Authenticity: impressions of an identity are often based on whether it seems authentic and original, or derivative and/or an imitation.

National Broadcasting Corporation

The Rango Story

Sometimes we misread the style clues.
Some years ago my firm won the assignment
to create a new packaging system for the large
cosmetics and toiletries company, Alberto Culver.
We flew to Chicago for the briefing.
They planned a new entry in the men's aftershave
market, one with a western theme. The product
was to be an aftershave and lotion based on the
image of the High Sierras, the music of John Denver and the popularity of Aspen, Colorado.
We went through many name candidates, packaging concepts and advertising slogans. The
name the client passionately wanted was "Rocky Mountain High" and it might have worked
until it was pointed out that the name strongly suggested the young hippy culture, as in "getting high" (a clear reference to a drug high). This was also the time of Woodstock and hippy
communities in San Francisco. Alberto got the point and the name was changed in favor of
"Rango."

With the name established we then designed an attractive square-sided bottle and package,
sales promotion literature, premiums with the name etched in wood and a sixty-second TV
commercial that was shot on location. Our "TV cowboy" (selected by the marketing manager) was in fact a well-known football player from the Chicago Bears. The client seemed most
pleased and felt it all had the connotation of rugged masculinity and the atmosphere of New
Mexico or West Texas. We weren't so sure; some of us felt that Rango evoked the image of
dust, thirst, and sweat, but by then we had a tight launch date and were running out of time.
It was wrong from conception and we all knew it at the launch party held in the ballroom of
a downtown Chicago hotel. After a buffet lunch, a few speeches for the business press by the
marketing director, we had the big presentation. Curtains parted and out rode our "cowboy"
on a black horse and everyone immediately recognized him (thus shattering any pretense at
authenticity).

Then the horse, unaccustomed to the ballroom, the noise and the people, "misbehaved," to
the hilarity of all present. It was a total disaster.

Rango didn't last long in the marketplace, partly because the name didn't seem authentic to
the image (the well-known football player) and partly because the product had an offensive,
pungent odor. At least the horse took care of that problem.

That was a lesson learned and not soon forgotten. The lesson had many parts (The investment was around one million dollars) but underlying all was, "know your target audience" and then structure your package and advertising to fit the interests and preferences (and prejudices) of your target audience. Good things happen when a customer processes his/her impressions into an overall pleasing and authentic brand personality.

A brand manager can only hope that they have selected well and are receiving a favorable representation. Research conducted before introducing a name, logo, package or an ad campaign almost always prevents costly mistakes like the ones we made with Rango.

Sometimes, however, the cowboy image rings true, right from the start. One such example follows.

The Marlboro Story

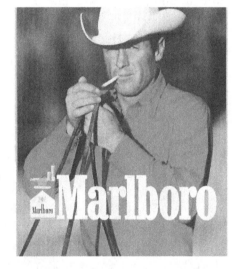

Marlboro worked because it was authentic and well designed. Before 1956, the Marlboro cigarette was red and ivory-tipped, long and slender and aimed at a female user. Because the client wanted to appeal to the larger male-smoking audience, they decided to do a sexual about face. First the ad agency (Leo Burnett, Inc.) redesigned the package to a hard pack with a flip-top lid and printed the name in bold colors of red and white. In the ads, they featured rugged, virile-looking men deep in their work. As a capper, all the men featured in their work: firemen, fishermen, skiers or writers, had a tattoo on the back of their hands. This, of course, showed prominently as they held their cigarettes, and the message was that the Marlboro smoker, the Marlboro man, was rugged and had had an interesting past. The final promotional touch was when Marlboro began distributing transfer pictures of tattoos. It was called "a man's cigarette that women like too."

To their delight, women weren't turned off by this new macho approach. Later they abandoned the tattoo theme in favor of all cowboys.

Next the agency president Leo Burnett changed the advertising to match the package. In meetings of the agency he asked "What is the most masculine image in America?" The answer was not long in coming.

The Cowboy

Movies have honed our love of the cowboy-his resolute sense of duty, and as a free-spirit sitting on a fast horse. We all carried the image of Gary Cooper, Jimmy Stewart or Clint Eastwood in our heads. And the agency picked their cowboys well.

By 1955 the Leo Burnett Agency (in Chicago) was running ads that featured an attractive, intelligent looking cowboy, always in a white hat, riding the range, opening gates, enjoying the scene, always with a long white cigarette in his mouth. He was the perfect type, ruggedly authentic and yet discerning and sensitive. I was once told by a friend who owns a dude ranch, that he had met some of the men in the ads, and that they were genuine cowboys from around Jackson, Wyoming.

Marlboro has succeeded so well that the brand has become a symbol for a number of (non-smoking) brand name products. At the end of twentieth century it joined the pantheon of classics like Coca-Cola and Levi's blue jeans as a worldwide icon of American-ness.

The Components of Brand Equity

The assets and liabilities of brand equity will differ from situation to situation-largely depending on the type of product and the type of retail environment, even seasonality. There are essentially five influencing categories:

> Brand Loyalty
> Name Awareness
> Perceived Quality
> Brand Associations
> Identity

All of these qualities are inherent in the Marlboro and Absolut image and package and it is a success story for both repositioning of an image, and a success story because one (Marlboro) has remained consistent for almost fifty years, the other has kept its top share of market and position for twenty-five years. No easy feat.

A colleague of mine at the University of North Carolina discovered some methods that one of the most creative advertising agencies uses to help understand the target audience.

Doing Research on the Target Audience
By Robert Lauterborn, Professor of Advertising,
University of North Carolina at Chapel Hill

DDB Needham uses a method for analyzing how a potential consumer (TA) reacts. It tracks how a person spends his or her day, from eyes popping open in the morning to the last blink of the lids at night, and using that behavioral insight to develop a pattern of lifestyle, and potential media exposures. Does he or she awaken to a clock radio? Tuned to what station? Does the person turn on TV while eating breakfast? For that matter, what does he or she have for breakfast? Milk and cereal, perhaps? There are two little billboards (the cereal boxes), right there on the breakfast table. Another contribution to media thinking and TA analysis from DDB Needham is the concept of "aperture" – the moment when the prospect will be most receptive to a particular message. Fast-food ads run just when people are beginning to feel hungry. Goodyear knows people won't think about snow tires until it actually snows, so they have commercials standing by at radio stations in northern states with a release schedule tied to weather predictions. On a more sophisticated level, planners for one agency created a "media map" showing how a prospective car buyer uses media over a three-year period from the moment the thought strikes – "I need to start thinking about a new car" – through the several stages of the buying decision down to the moment of signing. It won't surprise anyone to hear that the media used at different stages for different purposes are quite different.

The Hidden Persuaders

Perhaps one of the most controversial persuasion methods was one which secretly inserted subliminal messages into movies. They would flash a half second message on a movie screen, such as "Drink Coke" and "Eat Popcorn" and see what would happen. This was part of the subject of a popular and much discussed book by Vance Packard, called *The Hidden Persuaders* in 1957. A market researcher named James Vicary claimed he had done just this and increased sales of Coke and popcorn in a movie theater by inserting hidden messages into the theater's feature film. The phrases were not consciously recorded in the viewer's mind–but the impulse to buy remained. Vicary's claim caused a stir but he never was able to prove it. In the 1970s several books were written on the subject, but Vance Packard's got the most notoriety. It was never widely practiced, and was considered lacking in morality.

Other than the subliminal issue the book was a good in-depth discussion of how consumers react to advertising, based on certain basic psychological reactions. According to Vance Packard, there are eight hidden needs shared by all customers and prospective customers. These certainly reside in our subconscious.

1. The need for emotional security
2. The need for reassurance of worth
3. The need for ego gratification
4. The need for creative outlets
5. The need for love objects

6. The need to have a sense of power

7. The need for finding one's roots

8. The need for immortality

The book discusses research conducted by two Columbia University professors, on consumers and human behavior. They called it, "*The Depth Approach.*"

The Depth Approach attempts to reach the unconscious or subconscious mind-and in so doing, to stimulate preferences or prejudices that are determined by inherent factors of which the individual is not aware. The advertising industry noticed and decided that they could make use of such persuasion techniques to help sell their client's products.

In the hands of ad men, soap became more than a cleansing agent, it became an agent of beauty enhancement. Cosmetic makers decided they weren't selling lotion and creams; they were selling hope. Oranges became vitality, automobiles transcended transportation to become agents of prestige. Teeth-brushing (and its associated products) became the means of acquiring a bright smile, fresh breath and attracting the opposite sex-romance in a tube.

The social scientists, the depth motivators, identified three mental states, or levels of awareness in most Americans. The first level was the rational, conscious level-where the consumer is in control. At the second level the subconscious is in charge and the consumer is only dimly aware of his urges, prejudices and assumptions and feelings. At the third level there is no awareness. Naturally, the motivational researcher works on levels two and three.

This method was probably the beginning of the popular method of qualitative research in which a group of consumers are brought together and asked to respond to personal questions, like laxative use, cold tablets, alcohol use, athletes foot, etc. and they are observed through one-way glass by psychologists and product makers in an adjacent darkened room. The conclusion results in an analysis of the product to be introduced, or advertised, with clues to indicate what will work, will push "psychic buttons" of the consumer in the target group, and sell the product. Here are a few case studies.

P&G's Ivory soap is presented in the context of a mother and

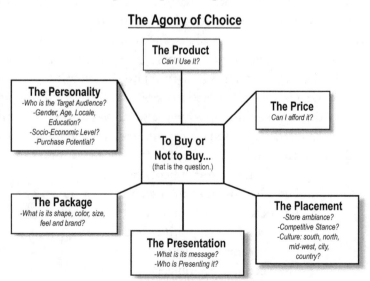

The Agony of Choice

The Product
Can I Use It?

The Personality
-Who is the Target Audience?
-Gender, Age, Locale, Education?
-Socio-Economic Level?
-Purchase Potential?

The Price
Can I afford it?

To Buy or Not to Buy...
(that is the question.)

The Package
-What is its shape, color, size, feel and brand?

The Placement
-Store ambiance?
-Competitive Stance?
-Culture: south, north, mid-west, city, country?

The Presentation
-What is its message?
-Who is Presenting it?

daughter represented purity and wholesomeness. Camay soap is presented as the path to glamour; Hathaway shirt ads that depict an interesting looking man wearing an eye patch connotated that this is the shirt for a sophisticated person, one who is experienced and a little mysterious. Sometimes the appeal is to class consciousness. Cadillac is presented as the vehicle for the totally successful man, proud, responsible. Ford is presented as the car of the young, on the way up; Mercury is presented as the car for the assertive, flashy owner. Today it might be Cadillac/Lexus or Jaguar, Ford/Volkswagen or Mini Cooper, Mercury/BMW or Audi reflecting the invasion and acceptance, and status, of foreign cars. Sometimes the persuader is on a guilt trip and fears and anxieties must be overcome. Smoking is one of the biggest. One of the psychologists in the book explored the reasons for smoking: to relieve tension, to express sociability, to reward for effort, as an aid to

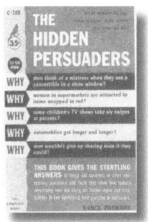

The Hidden Persuaders by Vance Packard - 1957.

poise, as a proof of daring, etc. Sometimes it is simplicity itself. Young people smoke to look older, older people smoke to try to look younger. The anecdote to all this is to emphasize the anxiety-fixer qualities of smoking. Many of the messages and observations of *The Hidden Persuaders* are true today, one of the reasons why the book is still popular. We live in an acquisitive society and our mores are known and manipulated by the psychologist, modern marketer, advertising executive or public relations practitioner. Vance Packard's book was (possibly) ahead of its time. The techniques he described in the Depth Approach are very much in practice today.

Finding 'Our Place'
By James Stengel, Procter & Gamble's Global Marketing Officer

We have a very different process of building a brand than we did five years ago. If you were the consumer who I wanted to engage today it would begin with a pretty open discussion about your life. We're developing very different communication programs that are much more varied... Look at our portfolio now: we're into fine fragrances, prestige skin care, car washes, pet care, pharmaceuticals–and all of them are going to have different consumers who have different habits–and they're going to be different in the U.S., Venezuela, Turkey and Russia. We need to be there and to organize our communication programs around that.

Then the creative work follows.

From the *Wall Street Journal*

5

PACKAGE

The Brand Bridge

Packages understand people much better than people understand packages, so said Thomas Hine in his book *The Total Package.*

An odd statement, to attach intellectual powers to an inanimate object like a package, yet it's true.

As consumers we take packages for granted, ignore them. The reverse is not true.

Packages have the ability to relate to us as consumers both logically and emotionally, employing techniques that are both aesthetic and deep-seated. Those who design packages and those who run marketing operations for packaged-goods companies know this and utilize shape, graphics, color and style to enhance their power and allure. For the consumer, all this is below the radar, a subconscious reaction.

Vance Packard knew it too and talked of this in his book *The Hidden Persuaders,* which we just explored in the previous chapter. Packard cites a Dupont study from the 1950s which concludes that seven out of ten purchases in a supermarket are decided in the store, and that most shoppers buy on impulse. This is where and when packaging plays a vital role in influencing the impulse moment.

One hundred years ago (prior to supermarkets and self-serve shopping) this couldn't have happened. Product information was conveyed to the consumer by a man or woman behind the counter. In those days (late nineteenth century) a package was considered merely a container for the safe delivery of products from the grower to the manufacturer to the ultimate purchaser/user. It was a time of neighborhood grocery stores, a shop for meat (the butcher), a shop for greens (the Greengrocer), a shop for baked good(the bakery-obviously), a shop for general merchandise (often called "The Market"). The same was the case for non-consumable goods, like hardware. And items like nails or screws were sold by the ounce or gram, poured into a metal hopper attached to a counter-weight.

Purchases were based mostly, on need. The nineteenth century housewife would go to market to purchase just what she needed, like flour or yeast for baking. Occasionally, perhaps if she had her daughter with her she might buy her little girl a piece of stick candy or licorice. This introduced the second and now much more compelling buying stimulus–desire.

So even then there were two stimuli for shopping:

Need

Desire

But sometimes, even back then, packaging could alter the equation.

The package has the ability to bypass the intellect and induce a consuming forgetfulness, and (sometimes) a consumer will buy a product just for the compelling graphics or beauty or copy promise written on the outside of the package.

The Package as a Nuisance

Packaging is ubiquitous, part of our daily lives in ways that can be hard on the economy. I live on a country road in Virginia and I spend a lot of time walking the road picking up discarded items: soda cups from Burger King, Styrofoam boxes from McDonald's, empty beer bottles from the grocery store.

When I am doing road cleanup I am dealing with the dark side of packaging – the pervasive commonality of packaging.

Too many consumers hold the package in little regard–a convenience for transport but of little value afterward. Litter is the unhappy result.

Despite the fact that many consumer surveys have been conducted on the problem of solid waste disposal, little has happened. A 1993 poll conducted by Opinion Research Corporation for the Gerstman + Meyers design firm, revealed that the single most important environmental issue was solid waste. Yet it has made little headway with the government. Few regulations have resulted.

Recycling programs have worked in most areas and I have even seen and purchased socks, and once a casual throw rug that I was told was made from recycled plastic bottles. And surprisingly, they were comfortable and attractive.

The main point, however, is that food packaging can and does lead to less spoilage because of its protective ability. Because it cuts down on spoilage, especially when going from farm to market or processing plant, it translates into less energy (and attendant air pollution) needed to produce food products. The net result is positive, an example of environmental conservation.

The package, when viewed as a whole in America, is an entity of great worth in annual gross revenue.

Packaging also taps into many industries in this country, as well as Europe. The paper industry, the canning industry, the bottling industry, the fiber-board industry, the folding carton industry, the plastic industry (molded and extruded and vacuum formed).

It can be wasteful, it can be misleading sometimes, but it can also be clever, inventive, colorful and lively.

And it is indispensable. It allows food to be distributed more widely and efficiently. It helps make consumption predictable.

The package has but two criteria.

> It must *protect* the contents of the item contained therein.
>
> It must *glorify* the contents of the item contained therein.

How does it accomplish this?

That will be the subject of this chapter.

In The Beginning

How did packaging start?

The earliest package has been identified as beer, from a mountain village in western Iran, estimated as being more than seven-thousand years old.

In this same area they also found ancient wine bottles, made with round bottoms so they had to lie on their sides, thus preventing sediment in the wine from settling and congealing on the bottom.

Another old and well-known type of packaging came from the Mediterranean region, known as the Canaanite Jar. It was called an "amphora," a vessel that took on its classic form around 1800 B.C. There were many amphora back then and they all looked relatively the same. They were usually made from clay, had a bell-shaped body, handles near the narrow neck and a round or pointed bottom. The theory behind the shaped bottom (making it impossible to stand on its own) was that it distributed the pressure of the contents, necessary and common, with fermented and fermenting liquids. Vessels like these have been found in the holds of ancient ships in the eastern Mediterranean. The contents were invariably wine, oil or even water. And some were even labeled. Wine jars from ancient Egypt have been found with the name of the reigning pharaoh stamped into the jar-date, type of grape, where grown and designation such as sweet or dry.

Was this a form of early branding? Absolutely!

Perfume and cosmetics come in packages, and the packaging is sometimes among the most glorious, most decorative and inventive in the pantheon of the packaging universe. This category provides one of the most direct connections between the ancient world and the invention of modern packaging in Europe and the U.S.

Glass–the packaging medium of choice

It was the beauty, the relative simplicity and the flexibility of glass that made it so popular 7000 years ago.

There were three critical developments that led to glassmaking. First was around 5000 B.C., when the process of melting sand (silica), soda/lime and potash (to make glass) was discovered. The second was the invention of the blowpipe about 300 B.C. and third and finally,the automatic bottle-making machine at the beginning of the twentieth century.

The Golden Age

The first four centuries of the Christian era were a "golden age" of glassmaking and the center of this activity was Rome. This was due in part to the invention of the blowpipe and partly to the political stability of the Roman Empire. The Egyptians (during the Roman Era) are credited with making glass of quality and variety, from plates to goblets to bottles to jewelry.

Venice

Medieval Venice took glassmaking to an even higher plane. They developed the art of "spun glass," a very delicate method of spinning rods of glass in diverse colors and shapes, resulting in beakers and stem glasses of delicacy and great beauty. As one can imagine, they guarded their glassmaking techniques as if they were state secrets, passing from father to son. To help guard the secrets, all glassmaking was carried out on one island in the Venetian lagoon–the island of Murano.

Fifteenth century Venetian Glass

Inevitably of course, the secret leaked out, thanks to the Medicis of Florence. Through one Venetian glassmaker, they introduced Venetian techniques to the French court in the sixteenth century. From there it went on to Spain and Queen Isabella. It seemed to move with the affluent, the privileged upper classes–certainly in the royal courts of Europe.

The only country that didn't get into the glassmaking business was England, although Elizabeth I imported much perfume (in glass packages) from France. But the English did make one massive contribution. They invented the coal burning glass furnace in 1611.

This allowed for much more heat and as a result, a better glass–purer, harder and of greater clarity.

Branding on Packages

By the eighteenth century people were beginning to think for themselves, the result of the writers, teachers and philosophers in the Age of Enlightenment. This age (which was widespread throughout Europe and eventually the American Colonies) marked the beginning of the questioning of traditional doctrines and values and led to a trend toward individualism, the free use of reason and the concept of choice. Certain religions like Puritanism echoed this position as well. Individual thinking led to the idea of a consumer who can make up his or her own mind. That led inevitably to packaging, packaging that could (through art or design) *persuade.* Throughout the 1700s, packaging was becoming more and more common. Some was crude and basic, some elegant: simple wooden casks for ale, earthenware pots for wine, glass bottles for emulsions or medicinal potions, paper wrappings for candy. Because their contents were for sale, and competitive, they had to be identified–through branding. Commerce and personal choice (particularly in cities like London or Paris) had arrived.

First Brands: 18th Century

The first identifiable packages appeared in London in the eighteenth century, a large majority of which were patent medicines. Some of the early brands were:

1710: Stoughton's Drops (a big seller in Colonial Williamsburg)

1745: Turlington's Original Balsam

1780: Daffy's Elixir (30 percent gin content)

All the containers were hand-blown glass bottles. These were all patent medicines to make one feel better-and the inclusion of alcohol usually did the trick. They used grain alcohol freely and without restriction and it might have been a way to get around the community's and church's objection to the use of liquor. Results were quickly evident and received fulsome praise.

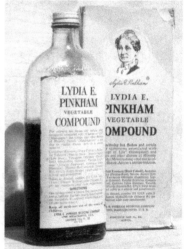

Popular nineteenth century medicine

In the American colonies at this time, similar patent medicines were being made, packaged and sold. Many of them (before the Revolution) came from Britain.

Some of these were:

1796: Lee's Bilious Pills (the earliest big success) came from Connecticut.

1800: Colgate's toiletries

1850: Smith Brothers Cough Drops

1870: Lydia Pinkham's Vegetable Compound (5 percent gin)

1880: Kikapoo Indian Sagwa

The Kikapoo

Kikapoo Indian Sagwa had a particularly colorful history. Representatives of the product traveled to circuses and minstrel shows with a small entourage made up of the "pitch man" and four "red Indians" in full warpaint. They put on a little show in which the Indians danced in a circle, looking possessed and very fierce, and scaring the audience. At some point the pitch man would feed some Indian Sagwa to one of the most frantic of the Indians, who would immediately become calm. He would, in turn, feed Sagwa to his three brothers, and all would become normal. It usually ended with the Indians passing out (selling) Sagwa juice to the gathered crowd.

By 1857 there were approximately 1,500 different patent medicines being sold in the United States. They were often sold out of wagons (along with iron pots, cloth, spices etc.), driven by Yankee peddlers–the original traveling salesman (more on this in Chapter 6).

Packaging Comes to the Marketplace

Up to now there really was no marketplace. Food products were purchased either directly from the farmer or farmers markets on certain days of the week, or from emerging grocery stores. The emergence of the general store began (slowly) in the middle of the nineteenth century and blossomed when the Civil War ended.

Inevitably a bond developed between the grocer and the housewife. There was a state of trust between them. She wanted assurance that perishable items like crackers, sugar, salt, rice and flour would come to her fresh and unsullied by insects, mold or rodents. He wanted to maintain the same thing–but most of all, her trust (i.e. loyalty).

When crackers or flour was doled out by the pound from a barrel, freshness was hard to maintain.

Then Along Came Uneeda.

In 1890 The Uneeda biscuit company introduced a breakthrough package which featured a sealed paper bag inside a folding box. They called it the "In-er-seal"package, and they took out a patent on it. For the first time grocers could offer their customers a package that contained crisp, uncontaminated crackers. It was the beginning of a new era–the grocery store that didn't need consultation with the grocer, the beginning of self-serve shopping (i.e. the supermarket). It changed the grocery store for all time. This package supplanted the cracker barrel with the box, and it led to other packages that protected their contents: like rice (Comet) and cornstarch (Argo).

What is also curious is that the logo that Uneeda adopted for their famous 1890 package has never changed to this day, even though the name of the company has (it is now known as Nabisco).

The logo contained a somewhat mysterious symbol, an orb and cross with a double horizontal bar above it. This logo was adapted from a fifteenth century Venetian printer's mark. The story goes that he had taken it from the ancient symbol for Christ's redemption of the world, which is also known as the Cross of Lorraine (adopted by Charles de Gaulle as his logo during and after World War II).

Uneeda also ran a series of advertisements featuring a little boy in a yellow rain slicker coming home in the rain with a Uneeda package under his arm.

So, the Uneeda story represents an early, maybe the earliest example of IMC (Integrated Marketing Communications) in action. It also represents packaging which provided the grocer's guarantee of freshness, the advertiser's support of the manufacturer's promise of freshness and the brand/logo's promise of consistent quality(as in- wherever you see this logo).

Early Nabisco Packaging

As packaging began to catch on (and it took decades), it brought with it the proliferation of a single look on a package (a theme), and with that naturally came the proliferation of logos. So while the birth of the modern logo preceded packaging, it also accompanied this staggered but inexorable movement toward package systems and branding systems.

The dawn of the twentieth century was also the dawn of modern packaging, advertising and logo/brand usage–on a very wide stage.

Early Packages

By the late nineteenth century, American and British companies were becoming established, and they were producing products for the home: cleaning, decorating and cooking. All of these were competitive and led to colorful and inventive packaging.

Ivory Soap (from the newly formed Procter & Gamble in Cincinnati). The advertising motto for this product was "It floats."

Quaker Oats (from the American Cereal Company in Chicago)

Morton's Salt (Their advertising slogan was, "When it rains, it pours.")

Early Morton's Packaging

Smuckers

In 1890 a man named Jerome Monroe Smucker began bottling fruit jams and jellies that he made at his cider mill in Orrin, Ohio. He also sold apple butter from the back of a horse-drawn wagon throughout the Midwest. Today, that company does over $2.5 billion in annual sales, with a large family of products. The products range from Smuckers jellies and jams, to Crisco, to Jif peanut butter. They are the market leader in fruit spreads, ice cream topping, health and natural food beverages.

Modern Smucker's Packaging

Arm & Hammer

In 1846 Austin Church and John Dwight started a company to manufacture and sell sodium bicarbonate. This product was popular at the time as a treatment for indigestion, and for baking. The company did reasonably well until the 1860s when they created a more modern (for the time) package and introduced their new logo, the hammer-wielding arm of the Norse god Vulcan (god of fire). The company grew but it wasn't until the 1950s that it started offering Arm & Hammer products as household cleaners and air fresheners. In 1972 the concept of putting Arm & Hammer baking soda in the refrigerator caught on, then a carpet deodorizer, detergents and most recently, Arm and Hammer toothpaste. Today it is a public company, traded on the NYSE with annual revenues in the $1.8 billion range.

The Quaker Oats Story

In 1870 oatmeal was considered fit for only horses and a few mad Scots. Thirty years later this "animal feed" was known as the "delicacy for the epicure, a delight for children" and given the brand name, "Quaker Oats."

Two men launched this brand: Ferdinand Schumacher and Henry Parsons Crowell. Schumacher came to the U.S. from Germany and built one of the largest mills in America in Akron, Ohio.

Henry Parsons Crowell was native born and lived in Ohio also. Sharing a mutual love of oatmeal made it inevitable that they got together. In 1890 Schumacher and Crowell formed a marketing and manufacturing consortium called The American Cereal Company.

Crowell was a zealot for Oatmeal. He believed it was God's food and he was a superb marketer. He was the first to use the round cardboard box and to put the figure of the Quaker on the outside. In addition Crowell was a consummate promoter and in 1891 he pulled off one of his grandest promotions. He chartered a special fifteen-car freight train that he ran from Cedar Rapids, Iowa, to Portland, Oregon, stopping frequently for the distribution of miniature packages of Quaker Oats off the back of the train. And just for good measure, he had sign painters on board his train and while the train was stopped they painted giant pictures of the smiling Quaker on the sides of barns! He created much demand from this method of distribution. And it got better!

A few days after he had chugged on west a team of salesmen arrived. Their job was to sell Quaker Oatmeal to the grocers and fledgling grocery chains in the wake of Crowell's visit.

In the space of a few years Quaker Oats became the most promoted product of its time. Packaging (and smart promotion programs) played a major role in making this product popular.

Today, Quaker is part of the Pepsi-Cola Corporation (purchased in 2000) and had net revenues in 2007 of over $1.5 billion.

Let's explore some important inventions, necessary for the further growth of packaging.

The Tin Can

The Tin Can was developed as the direct result of British government intervention. The long term preservation of fresh food was seen as a necessity, and a means of growing the national economy and of providing the military with preserved food. This was the mindset in Britain in early eighteenth century. It became a top priority.

By 1818 the British Royal Navy was buying and using about 24,000 large cans of canned foods on its ships. Generally, the foods canned were meat with gravy, or meat with vegetables, and they did much to improve life at sea over long voyages. The mindset then and now was that "an army travels on its stomach." The absence of a well-fed army can lead to defeat or surrender, as it did for General Lee's army in 1865.

The Tin-Can went to the North Pole - *Twice*

There was even a famous four-pound tin of roasted veal that went on two voyages (first in 1824 to the north pole with Admiral Parry) and was never opened. It was put in a museum after Parry's second voyage to the Pole, and still not opened. Finally in 1938, after 100 years and two round trips to the top of the globe, it was opened. It was tasted and declared "fit for eating."

One of the first large markets for tin packages in Colonial America came from England with the biscuits from the firm of Huntley & Palmer. Their crackers and biscuits were delicious and much sought after in Virginia, so the firm crafted tin boxes (packages) for a dozen biscuits and put them on ships to the United States and then stagecoaches for distribution throughout the country.

The Challenge of Preservation

In 1795 a Frenchman named Nicolas Appert experimented and developed early techniques for preserving food in bottles. More serious canning efforts were being made 25 years later in Scotland at the fish canneries. Two Scots Thomas Kensett and William Underwood) were among the best and took their knowledge of canning to the United States with them in the early nineteenth century. Both men preserved food in tin containers, which included hermetically sealed oysters, meats, fruits, and vegetables. Underwood specialized in packaging pickles and fruits in glass jars.

One must remember that these tins were heavy, thick cans because that is what metal workers knew how to make, with tops and bottoms soldered on, using lead solder–a bit hazardous to one's health. In 1859, the Baltimore firm of Wilson, Green and Wilson invented and patented a lightweight tinplate container that had interlocking sheets, eliminating the need for solder on the main seam or the tops and bottoms. This became the method of manufacture for the double-seam can and is still in use today.

The Pressure Cooker

The final advance was the invention of "The Retort" or pressure cooker in 1874. Now the canning industry was really humming, so much so that by 1890 semiautomatic processes increased production to 2,500 cans per hour and then years after that, to 6,000 per hour. Such companies as Campbell's, Hormel, Swift and Stokely Van Camp, were established because of this invention.

In 1900 America's first canning company was formed. A financial syndicate purchased 123 can companies, (about 90 percent of American production) and formed the American Can Company, which "shaped the daily life of man in the United States" (according to *Fortune Magazine* in a 1941 article).

Canning, the ability to preserve food and make it portable and palatable, was probably the most influential advance in packaging in the world, yet other inventions had to happen also.

Necessary Inventions That Made Packaging Possible

1706 – The Tin Can in Britain
1798 – Lithography (printing on a plane surface) in Germany
1807 – Paper Making (mass manufacture) in Britain
1808 – The Canning Process in France
1850 – The Box (folded paperboard) in America
1852 – The Paper Bag in America
1890 – First Fully Automatic Glass Bottle Making Machine
1892 – The Sealing Bottle Cap (vital for soft drinks and beer)
1892 - The Metal Tube (which led to packaging for toothpaste).
1900 – Automatic Glass Blowing in America

These inventions opened opportunities for enterprising businesses, like Anheuser-Busch in St. Louis to create a nationally distributed bottled beer that kept its head until opened or Colgate to package its ointments and creams (as well as toothpaste) in a hygienically safe manner for its customers.

There were two other inventions that must be included, but they came much later, after packaging was an accepted tool. They are aluminum and plastic.

1935-63 – Aluminum became fully operational and a substitute for steel or tin in cans, especially soda and beer cans and grows in usage every year.

1930-1945 – Plastic, was initially developed as a substitute for rubber during WWII. Then in 1978, with the development of polyethylene it turned to the form used in modern packaging.

What is the mix of packaging materials in a modern grocery store today?

Metal (tin and aluminum) – 16 percent
Paper (bags and boxes) – 26 percent
Plastic (bags, bottles, tubs and cartons) – 30 percent
Glass – 28 percent

Borden's Foods

A man named G. Borden advanced the cause of canning milk. Borden, using a vacuum pan he found in a Shaker colony in New Lebanon, NY, was able to evaporate much of the water from milk and then "can" a product that the general public found palatable.

Borden started a cannery in Connecticut which targeted the New York market, which he ad-

Elsie The Cow is still a popular Borden's logo.

vertised as "cleaner, purer, fresher" than anything else available. His package label used pictures of sun-drenched fields and contented cows munching on clover. But it wasn't the clever advertising and attractive packaging that launched Borden–it was the Civil War. By 1862 Borden found it impossible to keep up with the demands for his portable milk for the Union Army. The war increased demand for canned vegetables, fruits and other food stuffs as well and American output of canned food grew from about five million cans per year in 1860, to thirty million by 1968. It was the beginning of the Borden Food Corporation.

Once products could be safely stored in packages, designers began to create innovative ways of dispensing the product within. The package was the original user interface for consumers long before the modern technology industry coined the term.

The Campbell's Soup Story

Shortly after the end of the Civil War two men started a business. One was Abraham Anderson, an icebox manufacturer, the other was Joseph Campbell, a fruit merchant from Camden, New Jersey. Their concept was to buy agricultural products from south Jersey farms, package them (in cans) and sell across the river in Philadelphia.

They called their new firm the Joseph A. Campbell Preserve Company

Circa 1875

and they produced and sold canned: tomatoes, vegetables, jellies, soups, condiments and minced meats. It was a promising start but they were by no means unique with their product line.

Then along came a man named Dr. John T. Dorrance, a young chemist who had just returned from study in Europe. He was determined and persuasive and finally (reluctantly it seems) his father (Arthur Dorrance-General Manager for Campbell's) hired him to help at the new company. It was a fortuitous hire because within a year young Dorrance had invented the concept

Circa 2008

of condensing food products, principally soup. He did so by creating a process which eliminated the water, which in turn lowered the costs of packaging, shipping and storage. The Campbell Preserve Company now had the ability to seriously undercut its competition by offering a 10 ounce can of Campbell's condensed soup for a dime, versus more than 30 cents for a typical 32 ounce can of (whole) soup. Campbell and Abraham and the senior Dorrance knew they had a winner and even renamed their company to "Campbell's Soup." They were one of the first companies to utilize a package to establish a brand identity.

The Modern Package
Many modern packages derive from basic geometric shapes – and some from nature herself. I am referring, of course, to the egg.
Here are some memorable and prominent inheritors of the basic forms of geometry and nature found in the marketplace today.

The Egg   = Hanes L'Eggs panty hose
The Cube   = Tiffany's robin's egg blue box
The Triangle = Toblerone Swiss chocolate bar
The Cylinder = Pringles Chips from Procter and Gamble
The Hexagon = Spalding Sports Basketball package
The Clamshell = The Revlon Compact face powder package

Packaging Characteristics
Whatever the shape, packages have certain characteristics that make them unique in the marketing arsenal of weapons.

They are long-lasting.
Because of the investment required for a new package, whether from a stock container or a custom designed container, it is important that they have "shelf-life." This often used term means exactly what it says. Shelf life is dependent on a successful combination of shape, color, placement, correct type face, and feel.

They are handled.
For example: if the package is a shampoo and it is likely to be used in the shower, it should be made from a non-breakable product such as plastic. It should also be shaped so that it doesn't easily slip from a wet, soapy hand.
If the package is a toothpaste it is important that it dispense its prod-

uct easily, in small amounts-probably onto the end of a toothbrush. Additionally, if it is a toothpaste, it must fit into the retail environment in which it is placed (in the store). Except for certain (uncommon) stand-up dispensers, it is usually a long flat rectangular box with a tube inside and it must stack on the shelf in a horizontal position.

If the package is a bottle, and contains beer or a soft drink, it must stand on its bottom, have a prominent (but not too wide) front panel and probably (but not always) a long neck.

If the package is a can, it also has a vertical configuration, also stands on its bottom, and has a front and a back.

If the package is a box, all configurations are possible–vertical facing or horizontal. Cereals invariably are vertically positioned, with the exception of Quaker Oats Oatmeal, which is round. If the product is tissue (like Kleenex), it is likely to be contained in a rectangular solid, or a square solid.

And finally there are those products that are simply wrapped in flexible polyethylene. This includes bathroom toilet tissue, paper towels, and even bread. These are usually printed by the flexographic method, which until recently had severe limitations regarding colors and registration.

A new and growing packaging category is the plastic box-which can retain a premolded shape. These are handy for baked goods items which are fragile. They are made out of molded polystyrene and can be opaque (an egg carton for instance) or clear (cookies, cakes etc.). For both, the only method of identification is on a printed, applied label. Plastic packages get their shape by one of two processes: molding or vacuum forming.

But no matter what the material or shape of the package, all must adhere to two rules:

Rule One: the package must *protect* the product inside

Rule Two: the package must *glorify* the product inside.

Packaging Design
To create the ideal package the designer must:

Design a package that will have the potential to reach the correct TA (Target Audience).

Design a package that will fit into the retail area where it can (reach) attract the attention of the potential customer (again the TA).

Design a package that stands apart from the competition.

Design a package that may have to join a family of other packages with the same brand name.

Design and Business
By Paul Rand, from a lecture at Yale University in 1987

"Good design is good business," said Tom Watson (founder and CEO of IBM). But it is equally true that design, or even bad design, can be good business. An article in the *New York Times* described how a package for cheese was redesigned in order to improve product identity. The result was not worth the effort. Not only were all the good features of the previous design abandoned, such as an old horse and carriage mark and an elegant typeface, but type designs of many different weights, sizes and colors, were substituted. The client was happy, I assume.

But if this new design means more sales, how much might a more distinctive design, one in which good type and imaginative ideas, were present?

A badly designed product that works is no less ethical than is a beautiful product that doesn't. The former trivializes the consumer, the latter deceives him.

Successful packages must employ, to a varying degree, the following characteristics.
Image (that quality that allows a package to become memorable through associated imagery).
Identity (the ability to immediately identify its product).
Mobility (the ability to contain the product, effectively and with easy transport).

Here's an example of one package design case study.

The Nabisco Story

A few years ago we pitched and won a significant packaging project from Nabisco Foods (a division of Altria). The brand we were expanding was Grey Poupon and it required a totally new package configuration.

Background. Grey Poupon was a French (gray) mustard from the Dijon district and not widely known in the United States in the 1970s. Thanks to a very clever TV commercial involving two white Rolls Royce cars, the brand was beginning to get known and capture some market share. Their parent organization in the United States (Nabisco foods) decided to expand on its growing awareness and image with a line extension. Twelve products were planned, each carrying the Grey Poupon brand,

and each an item necessary for the preparation of gourmet meals.  **The Target Audience** was determined to be young married couples who had a desire to prepare gourmet meals and invite friends over. It was decidedly urban, upscale and somewhat sophisticated, a clever extension of the English approach (i.e. the Rolls TV campaign) with an American twist. The products would be sold in upscale (city or suburban) gourmet food stores like: Zabars, Dean & Deluca, Foods of All Nations, The Fresh Market or Harris Teeter chains. The resulting package look involved (maybe for the first time) a series of paintings on the labels by the major French impressionist painters: Monet, Manet, Cezanne, Van Gogh, etc. The advertising and promotional imagery which accompanied the launch incorporated the white Rolls Royce again, this time painted to look like a French impressionist painting. The car and the product line toured the U.S. in the spring of 1995, attracting curious and favorable attention at the same time it was introduced into the various gourmet grocery chains.

Achieving Brand Equity
Grey Poupon had little brand equity at the time. They hoped to achieve it in the first five years. It is never an easy task.

What is Brand Equity?

Brand equity is a set of (visual) assets and sometimes (unfortunately) liabilities linked to a brand, its name and symbol (logo). All together they will add or subtract from the value provided by the product in the minds of the brand's customers.
Brand equity is a frequently used word and usually applies to a product that has been a marketing triumph for some years.
The following are examples of brands whose equity has rooted so deeply in the minds of consumers that they have led their product categories for more than thirty years.

> Nabisco's Oreo cookies
>
> Procter & Gamble's Tide
>
> Hershey's chocolate bar (with or without almonds)
>
> Anheuser Bush's Bud beer
>
> Coca-Cola's Coke
>
> and of course...
>
> Philip Morris's (Altria), Marlboro cigarettes

The Marlboro Package

The king of brand equity is Marlboro and it is strongly represented in its package.

No package more comfortably adopts the cowboy image than this package—

Its package echoes the shape of snow-clad mountains

Its advertising makes ample use of western scenery

It plays off America's (indeed the world's) love of the cowboy mystique: independence, determination, physical prowess.

The package designer was Frank Gianninoto, who created the bold, red and white package and the cardboard box that flipped open. The advertising agency (Leo Burnett & Co.) liked this innovation and quickly created a slogan for it, "filter, flavor, flip-top box."

The Pepperidge Farm Package

A superb illustration of distinctive packaging can be found with the brands of Pepperidge Farm.

The cookie market is large, competitive and dominated by Nabisco. Nabisco's share of supermarket sales is estimated at nearly 50 percent of the market. Their brand leaders are: Snack Wells, Oreo, Chips Ahoy and Fig Newtons–all are heavy hitters.

Pepperidge Farm is not a big player, but because of distinctive packaging and clever positioning, they have acquired an increasing share of the market category, somewhere near 10 percent, up from 4 percent just fifteen years ago. They have done this by achieving recognition for five key product lines, which they call "collections."

They use imagery, and they use it as a metaphor for life-associations from Europe.

The collection is called "Lido, Geneva, Bordeaux, Milano and Brussels."

Some packages highlight a photograph of their cookie superimposed onto a map of Europe.

> Each cookie is styled differently-as if it were the cookie of the region-baked in regional, small bakeries.
> They keep the imagery going with evocative copy on the back.
> *"Imagine strolling down a cobblestone street toward your favorite European bake shop (like we all have one!). The aroma of Old World baking fills the air [and you realize that it's been a long time since lunch]..."* and so it goes.

The advertising, largely restricted to the back of the package, plays on the themes of tradition, quality and home goodness.

The campaign is brilliant in the way it utilizes associations we tend to assign to old world values. And it is exclusive (the TA probably has to have some knowledge–even experience–with European travel to get it/like it). In the same way the Absolut campaign really resonates for those who "get it."

In 1985 Pepperidge Farm introduced an American collection, which played on regional (USA) themes. The cookies were lumpier and larger as if made in your grandmother's kitchen.

They named them after well-known, upscale watering holes in the US: Nantucket, Chesapeake, Sausalito, Santa Fe, and Tahoe.

Sales for the American collection reached $50 million by 1994–just nine years after launch. This campaign shows the simple economic value of packaging with imagery.

Today the company (founded in 1937 by a woman named Margaret Rudkin–a Connecticut housewife who loved to bake) is part of the Campbell Soup Company. They are nationwide, with eight manufacturing facilities, over 4,000 employees and $1 billion in annual sales.

Outside Influencers
By Barbara Crawford
Professor and Director of Fine Arts at Southern Virginia University

I have often noticed the interesting contribution that fine art makes to the world of advertising and marketing communication. There are many examples-particularly in packaging. The shampoo and conditioner offered by L'Oreal is clearly influenced by the severe geometric designs in the paintings of Piet Mondrian (1872-1944), Gustav Klimt's painting "The Kiss" turns up regularly in posters and ads, and of course Rembrandt's famous painting "Syndicates of the Cloth Guild" dominates the packages of Dutch Masters Cigars.

In an interesting twist, impressionist painter Edouard Manet (1832-1883) painted two bottles of Bass Ale very clearly into the corners of his famous painting, " The Bar at the Folies Bergere," and Andy Warhol used *all the* flavors of Campbell's Soup in his popular silk screen paintings, now hanging together in the Museum of Modern Art in New York.

Finally, the artist Barbara Kruger uses advertising slogans to make powerful points in her collages on contemporary life. Savvy advertisers, package designers and even fine artists use any and all the items around them in our world to stimulate recognition, sometimes humor and ultimately pleasure - the necessary ingredients of commercial persuasion. The influence of the fine art world should never be underestimated.

Color

Like all visual entities, color in packaging plays a big role. It is subjective and it is often a trigger for rejection or acceptance. Certain brands are associated with colors as much as with their shape or logo or product line. For example:

Kodak is **yellow**. This color has been found on their packages of film around the world, and to find a package of film that is other than yellow, makes one pause for just a moment in contemplation of whether or not this film pack is up to the Kodak standard.

However sometimes yellow is a negative, as in Japan. Yellow is associated with unpleasant experiences to the average Japanese and so, in that country, Fuji film is in a green pack.

Brown is now the color of **United Parcel Service**, thanks to the color of their clever and nostalgic trucks and a clever advertising campaign by the Martin Agency of Richmond, Virginia.

Red is the color of **Coca-Cola**, thanks to consistent use on their cans and bottles. The presence of a red sun umbrella in a city square, or in a large waiting room, immediately signifies a café selling Coke.

By the same token, **Pepsi** has adopted **blue** as its identifying color. Their packages reflect lots of blue, as do their signs and trucks and billboards.

Green is found on **Perrier** bottles and sun umbrellas in European squares.

Blue, dark blue, is also **IBM's** color.

Gold as in golden arches, has become the symbol for **McDonald's** and with consistency, they can carry the image in the more than 28,000 restaurants they have worldwide.

Coke and Packaging at the end of the twentieth century

In the 1970s the Coca Cola company abandoned one of the greatest, most beloved packages ever invented, and hardly anyone noticed. One reason is that Coke called little attention to it. To abandon their contour shaped bottle (never totally) was a shift of strategy of major proportions. They lessened the shock by maintaining their ribbon, a ribbon like shape that has appeared horizontally or vertically on all Coke packaging since the mid 1970s. Now we see it on a straight- sided bottle or can, and while it is a far cry from the old curvy bottle, it does provide a certain echo of the past. It also helps keep the memory alive. In 1993 Coke reintroduced the bottle as part of the company's logo, along with the tag line "Always Coca-Cola," partially in response to the debacle of the formula-changing episode in April of 1985 when Coke brought out the "New Coke" (see Chapter 8). As many now know, the new Coke lasted only four months and was abandoned and the old formula reintroduced and repackaged as "Classic Coke."

Packaging Innovations

Two innovations had a big influence on the retail space. One was the invention of the aerosol can. This was a container that came directly out of the war. It was invented to dispense insect repellent in the South Pacific. In 1945 it came home from the war and got launched into thousands of new products. Cleaning products offered the simplicity of spraying the dirt and wiping it clean like spray-on furniture polish. In addition we have spray dessert toppings, spray-on first aid antiseptic, spray garlic, and still, insecticide.

Aseptic Packaging

Another and perhaps the most innovative was aseptic packaging.
This method of packaging has been familiar in Europe since the early 1960s, but was slow to win acceptance in the United States. It is essentially a variation on the canning process. Aseptic packaging sterilizes the containers separately from their contents and fills them in a sterile environment. The process works ideally for the packaging of foods with ingredients that can't survive the rigors of normal canning (the retort-pressure cooker). This is particularly true for milk and eggs. It also allows the use of containers made of plastic or plastic layered with paper or foil, which are lighter and easier to ship and handle.
Aseptic packaging allows fresh pasteurized milk to be kept for long periods in sealed cartons without refrigeration.
Even though it was first introduced at the world's fair in Knoxville, TN, in 1982, it is only

now catching on. The first applications of this package to be generally accepted are portable juice boxes-handy for children's lunch boxes. Another are single serving puddings or yogurt packages. Obviously, psychology enters into the picture. Milk, which is one of the most profitable items in a supermarket, is assumed to always be cold and fresh. To offer milk in other ways, warm and small, goes against the grain (although it is common and popular in Italy). In many ways the refrigerator is part of the package. The packaging does not have to end at the container's edge.

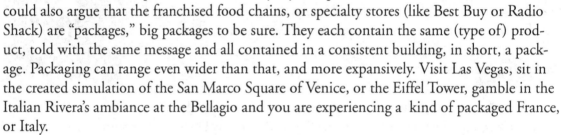

The Biggest Packages

One could argue that the whole supermarket is a package–conditioned and controlled to create a set of sensations, expectations and satisfactions tailored to promote customer loyalty and profit. One could also argue that the franchised food chains, or specialty stores (like Best Buy or Radio Shack) are "packages," big packages to be sure. They each contain the same (type of) product, told with the same message and all contained in a consistent building, in short, a package. Packaging can range even wider than that, and more expansively. Visit Las Vegas, sit in the created simulation of the San Marco Square of Venice, or the Eiffel Tower, gamble in the Italian Rivera's ambiance at the Bellagio and you are experiencing a kind of packaged France, or Italy.

Packaging's Retail Roles
By Richard Shear, CEO of LMS Design Inc.

The consumer product package now plays four roles on the retail stage. The first three are natural outgrowths of the package function; to protect, dispense and identify the product within. The fourth and perhaps most interesting is the role a package plays in the lives of the consumer. The package has become the visual reflection of the brand. Consumers now relate to packages the way they might to the cars they buy, the jewelry they wear, or the houses they live in. The package represents a lifestyle choice.

The First Role: Product Protection, A Can of Soup and The Model T

An early step in the development of modern packaging was established in the 1850s in France with the development of canning to protect foods. This innovation was the first of many package improvements that protected the product, reduced spoilage, and helped to make product distribution much more efficient. Joseph Campbell started canning foods in 1869 and introduced his first canned soups in 1898 with simple typography and clear descriptive language to identify the product within the can.

This first can of soup is much like the early auto industry. One of the first steps in the establishment of this industry was the introduction of the Model T by Henry Ford. Just like a can of soup, this auto allowed its occupant to have safe affordable transportation from one place to the next protected from the elements. Packaging has been transformed since these early days. The simple black utilitarian Model T and the can of soup both demonstrate how a product and an industry can evolve from a strictly functional utilitarian object to the object of desire.

We have come a long way since the Model T and the first Campbell's Soup can. The early innovations in the packaging and automotive created the basis for major industries that have become part of the culture.

The Second Role: Package as User Interface
The Coke and Heinz Ketchup Bottles

Once products could be safely stored in packages, designers began to create innovative ways of dispensing the product within. The package was the original user interface for consumers long before the modern technology industry coined the term.

In 1876 John Heinz began to bottle ketchup, and in 1894 Dr. John Pemberton, an Atlanta pharmacist, began to bottle Coca-Cola. While the packages were somewhat unique for their time, it's certain that the original designers of these two products would be amazed that they have become such important visual icons of product marketing. These two packages are unique in three respects.

–They protect and display the product in clear glass, something that in the late 18th century was still somewhat unique.

–The bottles have become a physical embodiment and the distinctive characteristic of the brand. The shape of the two bottles is still unique and recognizable even without graphics.

–The bottle shape created a unique dispensing method for the brands that is closely tied to the product's enjoyment. Chugging a Coke out of the bottle or tapping the bottom of a ketchup bottle to dispense the product have become intrinsic to both brand's heritage.

There are many other examples of contemporary packages that combine product storage with unique dispensing approaches including the Kleenex tissue box, the Crest toothpaste tube, or the Gillette shaving cream can. Each of these packages have become icons for the way they combine the basic storage necessities of the product with a unique user interface.

Third Role: The Package as Brand Identity

The late nineteenth and early twentieth centuries saw the establishment of the design industry as a key player in the development of packaging that protected the product and gave the consumers a simple and sometimes unique way of dispensing the product. The third phase of package design evolution was signaled by marketers' recognition that the creation of memorable structure and graphics play a key role in attracting and creating loyalty with customers. In a day when advertising was limited exclusively to the print media, marketers began to understand the impact of package design and its role in marketing. Often the first time a consumer would come in contact with a brand was at retail. Packaging had to be unique and it had to make a clear statement about the product because in the early twentieth century there were few of the media outlets we now take for granted.

This shift to clear unique brand identity represents the third major phase in product packaging. As the package began to take its place in the growing retail industry of the early twentieth century, the sense of a brand was created. The growth of brands and unique package design solutions mirrored the growth of national retailers like A&P, Sears & Roebuck and Macy's. Additionally, as the transportation system improved from trains to cars to airplanes, and the consumer became more mobile, brands were becoming nationally and even internationally recognized.

The Fourth Role: The Package becomes a reflection of lifestyle.

The last and final role was when the package became a reflection of the consumer's lifestyle and is examined in the last chapter of this book, Chapter 12.

Packaging today

Consumers now shop for products with the same level of interest as they plan a vacation, or select a vehicle, or pursue a hobby. Today, each package and each product makes a contribution to the way a person chooses to live his life. Whether that contribution is large or small a package makes a lasting bond with a person in ways that we are only beginning to measure. Packages promise predictable, reliable satisfaction—in food that is germ free; in consumer durables—say compact music discs, the promise of convenience, sound fidelity and portability. It's a promise that they must keep or lose customer loyalty.

We are all packages

"A group of related things, offered as a whole" is the (Webster's) dictionary definition of a package. This is a pretty broad definition with wide application. If you consider packaging in a wider arena (the common denominator being "consistency") then KFC stores with their 6,890 identical stores worldwide are packaged, or McDonald's with its 27,707, or all the banks with their Greek columns out front in order to look solid, dependable and conservative, or students with their jeans and Polo shirts, or professors with corduroy jackets and leather elbow patches, or the biggest bunch of packages, politicians with their packaged persona and packaged opinions.

To some extent we are all packaged.

Lobby of a typical Manhattan bank

6

The Arena

Even if the logo is imaginative, appeals to the correct target audience; even if the package glorifies the product inside in a way that is compelling and interesting; even if the advertising campaign which serves the product is clever, memorable, growing out of an exciting theme and has rooted in the mind of the consumer (like Absolut, for example)... if it doesn't work in the store, all of the foregoing marketing tools fail.

The store is the moment of truth. Where the tire meets the road–crunch time. The make-or-break moment.

The store is where it has to happen.

It's all about retailing, one of the most important activities of the American economy.

The U.S. economy is very dependent on retailing. According to Standard & Poor's Industry Surveys, retailers bring in over $3.18 trillion in sales annually, about a third of the gross domestic product (GDP) for our country. Furthermore, retailers are the biggest employers in the nation, employing one out of every five workers (U.S. Census Bureau).

Think of the store as a retail arena, an arena that is not unlike the Roman Coliseum where Gladiators fought for their lives, where combat, mano-a-mano, happens.

Think of the Gladiators as the brands or packages who are fighting each other for shelf space, for category dominance.

And the price of failure may be death, market-share death.

Who, and what, are the major arenas where this daily drama takes place?

This chapter will explore them all as well as the origins of retailing in America.

Part One
The Supermarket as the Bridge

Supermarkets are ubiquitous, found in the smallest towns and in the crowded canyons of Manhattan. They are part of the American (and indeed the European and Asian) scene and have been for a long time. They are where economists project Americans spend about 10 to 12 percent of their disposable income. Supermarkets are usually big–30-50,000 square feet of selling space (on average), very diverse, selling anything from milk to socks to plants and operate on a surprisingly low (average) profit margin, 1 to 2 percent of sales. Clearly they count on volume to offset low margin.

For the past thirty years, however, supermarket sales (volume) have actually been declining, probably the result of more dual income families in America. In twenty-first century America we have busy, working housewives who have less time for shopping and cooking and a willingness (indeed the need) to eat out more often.

Another lifestyle factor is the need for one-stop shopping-a retail center where one can buy not only food items but flowers; pharmaceutical items; videos; shoe repair; dry cleaning services; optical shops; salad bars; in-store bakeries; in-store takeout of prepared meals; even sit-down restaurants. They aren't everywhere yet, but the trend is growing. There is even a new term for this new kind of superstore, "scrambled merchandising."

The Origin of the Supermarket

The self-service grocery store (the concept at the core of the super-market experience) began in Memphis in 1916. Clarence Saunders is credited with creating this concept which he put to work in his small group of stores called "Piggly Wiggly." He even patented it in 1917, wisely, because it caught on and his competitors (like Kroger and Safeway) wanted to copy it. In his stores, customers entered the store, passed through a turnstile and walked through four aisles to view the store's 605 items – all packaged and organized into departments. It influenced and hastened the proliferation of packaged product. Another supermarket pioneer was Michael J. Cullen who founded (in 1937) what many consider the first "true supermarket." He called it "King Kullen" the name influenced by the movie *"King Kong."* His stores were larger, up to 6,000 square feet and sold dry goods and packaged goods as well as wrapped fresh meats.

Probably the real impetus to growth was the natural effect of the post WWII era when expansion out of the cities began. The desire for a home of one's own in the suburbs, low interest loans and the beginning of the modern highway system in the 1950s stimulated store growth. Shopping could now leave the city centers and housewives could drive to the market, park with ease, load up with ease and return to their homes to unload in the driveway. Grocery shopping has become big business in the years since it began. The U.S. Labor Department calculates that food items purchased by the average family of four was $450 per month, or over $5,500 per year at grocery stores last year.

The Top 10 Supermarkets (The Biggest Arenas: annual sales and geographic spread)
Wal-Mart: $312,427 billion, 4,304 stores in all states but ND (but more than just food)
Kroger: $60,553 billion, 3,700 stores in Mid-Atlantic, Midwest, Southeast
Safeway: $38,416 billion, 1,775 stores in western, Midwestern and Mid-Atlantic regions, as well as western Canada.
American Stores: $19 billion
SuperValu Stores: $16 billion
Winn-Dixie Stores: $13 billion, 690 in Southeast
Tosco: $13 billion
A&P Stores: $8 billion (German owned)
Food Lion: $9 billion, 1,225 stores in the South
Stop & Shop: $11 billion, 249 in Northeast
(Dutch owned)
Others (smaller):
Publix: 521 stores in South
Wegmans: 54: in East
Albertsons: $35.6 billion, 2,287 stores in the North
King Soopers: 88 in CO, NM, UT, WY
Giant Food: 161 in DC, DE, MD, NJ, VA
Vons: 173 in CA, NV
Piggly Wiggly: 110 Stores in South Carolina and the South

Let's examine just one arena in depth.
Kroger Stores–A Profile
Founded in 1883, Kroger is one of the oldest grocery chains in the U.S. The man behind the chain is Bernard Henry Kroger (1860-1938) of Cincinnati, Ohio. He grew up over his parent's dry goods store and had to go to work early. His first job in the business was as a door to door salesman for the Great Northern & Pacific Tea Company. That soon led the ambitious young man to start his own grocery, first as the Great Western Tea Company, then renamed as the Kroger Grocery and Baking Company in 1902. He did well, expanding each year. Today there are over 2,500 supermarkets with revenues estimated at over $66 billion annually.

Last year Kroger was named the top grocery retailer in the U.S. and the third largest general retailer (only behind Wal-Mart and Home Depot).

The stores are all organized in the same manner, and by (broad) categories:

- Beverages
- Health and Beauty
- Produce, Meat, Deli
- Household Products
- Dairy

- Cereals
- Canned Goods
- Frozen Foods
- Picnic Supplies
- Cosmetics

Kroger Floor Plan

There are twelve aisles, specifically organized as follows:

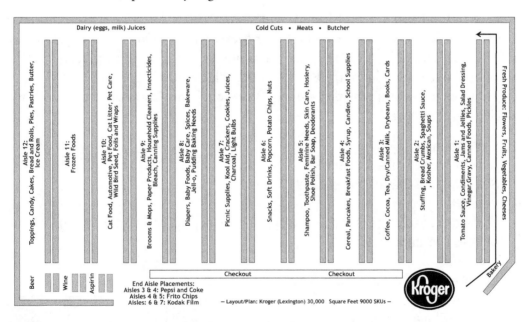

Aisle 1: ketchup, condiments, jams & jellies, salad dressings, vinegar, pickles

Aisle 2: spaghetti, kosher, Mexican, soups

Aisle 3: coffee, cocoa, tea, books and cards

Aisle 4: cereal, pancakes, syrup, candy, school supplies

Aisle 5: shampoo, toothpaste, skin care, feminine needs, soap

Aisle 6: snacks, soft drinks, potato chips, nuts

Aisle 7: picnic supplies, crackers, cookies, juices

Aisle 8: baby care needs, diapers, baking goods

Aisle 9: household cleaners, mops, brooms, etc.

Aisle 10: pet supplies, food, cat litter, automobile materials (limited).

Aisle 11: frozen foods, meals, etc.

Aisle 12: dairy products, milk, eggs, cheese, butter, ice cream, etc.

And on the perimeter walls, bakery, produce (fresh lettuce etc.) meats, orange juices, butter and margarine, ice cream, beer and wine, customer service and cigarette section, and the pharmacy. There are ranks of display shelves on each side of each aisle and super marketers call them "gondolas."

Dominance in the store is determined by two factors:

> **Brand leadership:** where they can demand the most space and best position
>
> **Packaging innovations:** which can attract attention with unusual shapes, colors and space savers.

Dominance in food and beverage brands: Coca-Cola, Pepsi-Cola, Tropicana, Budweiser Beer, Campbell's Soup, Lay's potato chips, Oscar Meyer wieners, Dole's products, Doritos chips, Breyer's ice cream, Nestle, Kraft Foods, Dannon yogurt, ConAgra products, Cadbury, Schweppes and of course, a lot of the Procter & Gamble brands.

Top contributors to U.S. supermarket growth: PepsiCo, Nestle, Coca-Cola, General Mills, Campbell Soup, ConAgra

Profit Margins

Top categories for the supermarket:

Soft drinks: 0% (particularly Pepsi and Coke)

Beer: 5%

Health and beauty aids (shampoos, etc.): 10-20% (depending on which brand)

Cookies and crackers: 20%

Wine: 30%

Over the counter drugs (OTC): 38-40%

Produce and bakery: 50%+

Note: profit margins are kept confidential, from store chain to store chain. These came from the manager at our local store and are probably similar to all stores. The question to consider is why would soft drinks be carried in the store with a profit margin of 0%? Because they are "loss-leaders," they are in such demand that the store manager knows he needs their "draw-power."

The dairy section of the Kroger Store.

Where it all goes

Display arrangement and brand positioning is very carefully controlled and, in the Kroger case, dictated from Cincinnati each month. They issue display/arrangement notebooks, called "Planograms," which dictate product placement. Kroger will display merchandise on each side of the twelve aisles, along the back wall and side walls. They all lead inexorably to the checkout counters along the front of the store.

Stock Keeping Units

SKUs are unique identifiers for products or product groups found in a store, particularly a supermarket. Their purpose is to enable the merchant to track inventory, in and out (along with the UPC system). If an item (say a can of Pepsi) is assigned a tracking number (SKU), this can represent either a single unit or a group of products (brands). It's up to store (or warehouse) management. The Kroger store in our town estimates approximately 9,000 SKUs, which may represent as many as 40,000 brands. In Europe they are referred to as EANs (European Article Numbers).

The psychology of the arrangement/store layout

Most customers enter and turn right. This is a natural phenomenon since most customers are both right-handed and right-headed and is based on research.

So for that reason they almost immediately pass the bakery, where the smells of fresh baked bread, cookies, etc. are evident in the air and the average healthy customer begins to get hungry.

He or she will next pass the produce section, where fresh lettuce, tomatoes, potatoes, broccoli, etc. are displayed and available. This is one of the areas with the highest profit margin. Here a simulated rainstorm is "arranged" with misting of the lettuces, etc. from spray heads, accompanied by the sound of thunder.

As he/she turns the corner and starts left, they will begin to notice the displays on the ends of each aisle. These are called "endcaps" and are highly desirable. This is where one will find Pepsi and Coke products, price off items, etc. All the major brands want to dominate the endcaps.

The supermarket concept involves five basic principles:

1. Self-service and self-selection displays
2. Centralization of customer services at the checkout counter
3. Large scale, low cost physical facilities
4. Emphasis on low prices
5. A wide assortment of merchandise, stimulating multi-item purchases (2 for 1 offers)

And another product line that has become a feature in most supermarkets–HMRs. **HMRs** are **H**ome **M**eal **R**eplacements, or prepared, ready to eat foods. A bachelor or temporarily single dad while his wife is away can keep himself going with frozen dinners from the freezer section of the supermarket from Lean Cuisine or Weight-Watchers, etc. He can also pick up precooked meals near the deli section. This is a direct reflection of the fast pace many modern families live, sometimes when both spouses work and there is little time to prepare food in the afternoon (mentioned at the beginning of this chapter).

The two basic drivers of all supermarket purchases
All of the facings (brands) in any grocery store or supermarket will appeal to shopper's intellect in one of two ways:

> **Rational: "I need that" (as Aspirin)**

> **Emotional: "I desire that" (as cookies)**

Most customers think neatness is a virtue, so savvy store managers will display all Frito Lay products for instance, at a neat, even right angle. Managers, again anticipating human traits, will sometimes put up a sign that says "Limited to four to a customer." He hopes this will communicate that the sale item is a really great deal and he is trying to be fair.
Another psychological trick is when store managers utilize the opposite effect of neatness by having dump-bins at end-aisles with casual chaos of sale items and with hand-lettered signs. This communicates the need to reduce inventory quickly.

Copy Cats
Another interesting phenomenon is the "Copy Cat" concept. Most stores, like Kroger, will have their own brands, bearing their own private label. These are called "Store-Brands" or in the UK, "Own-Brands." Sometimes they have a surrogate name, like "American Brands" or "President's Choice," but often they just use their store name. And they often produce look-alike packaging of the brand leaders, and shamelessly display them side by side at a price discount. Why don't they get sued?
They avoid lawsuits for plagiarism because the brand leader wants to maintain a good relationship with the retailer and a lawsuit wouldn't help the cause.

Let's examine the process of Buying and Selling (or retailing)

Shopping (buying) inevitably combines a small, interrelated group of human notions: discovery, examination, and ultimately, judgment. It is personal and subjective, but it is vulnerable to outside influence. There are many big chains, but there still exist small mom-and-pop businesses. Almost nine out of ten retail companies employ fewer than twenty employees. According to the National Retail Federation, 95 percent of all retailers operate just one store.

One of the most copied is Warner-Lambert's Listerine package

Contrast that with the nation's (world's) biggest retailer, Wal-Mart.

According to the most recent Wal-Mart Annual Report, the store enjoyed $312,427 billion in net sales.

They divide their retail spaces into three categories:

Discount stores: offering general merchandise and limited food products with an average of 98,000 square feet in size.

Supercenters: which average approx. 187,000 square feet in size and offer a wide variety of general merchandise and full size supermarket.

Neighborhood markets: 43,000 square feet in size–full line supermarket, limited general merchandise.

And then they have Sam's Club-a membership warehouse Club that sells items in bulk sizes at discount prices. These stores average approx. 127,000 square feet in size.

It is estimated that Wal-Mart's annual U.S. sales alone account for about 5 percent of all U.S. retail sales.

Not surprisingly, the U.S. economy is heavily dependent on retailing. Retailers ring up over $3.18 trillion in sales, annually–almost a third of the nation's gross domestic product (GDP). And Wal-Mart is only one of the retail behemoths. Some of the others are: Kmart (now merged with Sears), J.C. Penny, Albertson's, Target, Home Depot, and Costco. All enjoy revenues of well over $30 billion each year.

Meet the Gladiators

And who are the biggest, toughest gladiators (of packaged products) in the retail arena?

Altria (formerly known as Philip Morris Companies): annual net revenues of $97,854 billion
Their champions are: Marlboro cigarettes, Benson and Hedges, KoolAid, Maxwell House
coffee, Cool Whip, Bran Flakes, Grape-Nuts, Oreo cookies, Nabisco, Kraft, Altoids, Cheez
Whiz, Grey Poupon, Velveeta and Oscar Mayer.
Tobacco products: ($46 Billion), food products: ($30 billion), beer: ($2.5 billion).
Nestle (headquartered in Switzerland): $69,207 billion
Brand leaders (It's not just chocolate): Nestea, Taster's Choice, Dreyers, Edys and Haagen
Daz ice creams, Libby's juices and fruit, Carnation milk, Alpo dog food, Stouffer's, Perrier
and Poland spring water, as well as chocolate.
Procter & Gamble: annual net sales of $68,222 billion

Twenty-two brands bring in a billion dollars in sales, each. Among the champions are: Pampers, Tide, Luvs, Tampax, Charmin, Folgers, Pringles, Ariel, and Pantene. Here are some of the P&G product categories: Paper products
($12 billion), fabric and home care ($11 b.), health care and beauty ($7 b.), food and beverage ($4 b.).
And now they own Gillette, which allows them to dominate the toiletries category.

Twenty-two P&G brands have billion dollar annual sales

Heinz: annual net sales of $8,643 billion
Some of their leading brands: Heinz ketchup, HP Sauce, Lea & Perrins, Smart Ones (snacks), Poppers, and infant foods.
General Mills: annual sales of $11,640 billion. Brands include Cheerios, Total, Wheaties, Betty Crocker and Pillsbury.
Colgate: annual net sales of $11, 398 billion
Leading brands: Colgate toothpaste, Palmolive, Ajax, Lady Speed Stick, Softsoap
Pepsi-Cola: annual sales: $32,562 billion
Leading brands: Pepsi-Cola, Mountain Dew, Sierra Mist, Tropicana, Lay's, Tostitios, Fritos, Cheetos, Quaker Oats, Aunt Jemima, Gatorade.
Coca-Cola: annual sales: $23,104 billion
Leading brands: Coca-Cola Classic, Diet Coke, Sprite, Dasani, Minute Maid, Powerade, KMX

Johnson & Johnson: annual sales: $47,348 billion. Brands include: Band Aid, Tylenol, Aveeno.
Unilever: annual sales: $54,423 billion
Leading brands: Knorr, Slim-Fast, Lipton, Hellman's, Wishbone, Axe, Lux, Dove, Ponds, Omo, Comfort and Surf.

All of these, whether sold in the juice aisle, the beverages aisle, the health and beauty aisle or the household cleaners aisle, are all competing for your attention, affection and loyalty.

An In-Store Dilemma

Sometimes the product and the retailer find themselves at odds. This happened in England in the mid 1990s when Ocean Spray cranberries found itself competing directly with two of the three largest supermarket chains in the U.K.: Tesco and Sainsbury's. The dilemma Ocean Spray had was twofold: regain market share, and maintain good relations with the two grocery chains.

The Ocean Spray Story

The brand was in decline in the U.K., steadily losing market share to the two house brands of the two largest grocery chains, Sainsbury's and Tesco. Both were offering cranberry sauce in the same size container, but they discounted it by as much as 10 percent. In short, Ocean Spray didn't have control of the retail arena and they didn't dare alienate their retail partners. We got the assignment in mid 1994.

The Ocean Spray marketing director decided on a bold strategy: to bring out a totally new product, one with an added ingredient, in a new package, and sell it 40 percent above the standard price. The added product was to be Cranberry Sauce with Mulled/Spiced wine. In addition, he planned to keep the old product in the market to cannibalize from the competition and increase Ocean Spray's brand share for the whole category.

The target audience was mature (30-60 age spread) housewives from all socio-economic levels who had a love of tradition and the appearance of quality.

The marketing (and packaging) objectives were to: recover brand leadership, increase usage occasions, communicate appetite appeal and the new added value. Finally, our firm had to provide a

Britain's Ocean Spray Cranberry Sauce

133

package that had shelf impact and a sense of quality. The design followed this strategy by creating a strong central target shape, one that wrapped around the bottle and utilized a still-life scene of berries, grapes, cinnamon sticks and nutmeg. To give it the look of even more tradition and quality we had a professional fine artist paint the scene in oil on canvas. The final touch was the hand-lettered secondary logo, "Gourmet" which we printed in gold.

The strategy worked, even though it took two years. Today, Ocean Spray regular and Ocean Spray Gourmet is again the brand leader and still selling in Sainsbury's and Tesco.

They solved the problem through new packaging and a bold marketing strategy.

Positioning

A retail establishment can be categorized according to its level of service, product assortment and price. Specifically retailers use the three variables (service, assortment and price) to position themselves in the marketplace.

Positioning is critical to retail success.

The development of any marketing mix depends on this process-which influences customers' overall perception of a brand, product line or the parent company.

Position is more than physical space in a store. It's mental–often psychological.

Position is the place a product, brand or group of brands occupies in a consumer's mind. It is an aesthetic condition–hopefully a favorable one for the company whose product is going to compete in the arena.

P&G's Eleven Different Soaps

Tide: Tough, powerful cleaning – 31% market share
Cheer: Good cleaning but with color protection – 8.7%
Dash: Value Brand (a good buy) – 1.8%
Dreft: Good cleaning on baby clothes, safe for tender skin – 1.0%
Ariel: Tough cleaner aimed at Hispanics (in the US-wider audience in Europe) – 0.7%
Ivory Snow: Fabric and skin safety on baby clothes – 0.7%

Positioning assumes consumers compare products on the basis of (1) features, and (2) price. From time to time the two big cola companies will attempt to capture a position with a new product. One such was Crystal Pepsi, and earlier, Pepsi Blue. They wanted to steal share from Coke's Tab. Consumers didn't flock to it, correctly perceiving that it was a marketing gimmick.

One that may work, however, is the rush to provide consumers with a new low carb drink-and to that end Coke has just brought out "C2," and Pepsi with "Edge." Both brag of having just one carbohydrate in their respective drinks. But it's an old story and the consumer gets jaded. These two companies compete like Siamese twins, when one moves, the other re-acts. To do it well, the company must assess the positions occupied by competing products, determine the important dimensions underlying these positions and choose a position in the market where the organization's marketing efforts will have the greatest impact. This can often be where the company's retail presence and strengths are best.

Another example of good positioning is Gatorade.
The marketing management of Quaker Oats (Gatorade) chose to position their energy drink in the juice section of the store, rather than the cola section.
This wise decision meant that they: (1) didn't have to go head-to-head with Pepsi and Coke for cola category dominance, and (2) they could enjoy a better profit margin in the juice section where juice drinks sell for perhaps 12 percent more than the same size in the cola section. This was undoubtedly another reason why Pepsi was willing to pay $13 billion for this brand six years ago.

Perception Mapping
A classic method of analyzing a product's position is a method known as Perceptual Mapping. Perceptual mapping is the process of graphing the location of a product, brand or group of brands in consumer's minds (i.e. how they "perceive" the brand) on a chart made up of two lines—one vertical, one horizontal.

A Perception Map
The top of the vertical is often designated high price, the bottom, low price.
The horizontal measures the brand's "personality." Is it fun-light hearted
(the left side) or is it "serious, no nonsense/effective,"(right side)? The marketing manager doing the analysis for his brand will place his brand or product in one of the four quadrants and the competition in their respective quadrants, and thus gain a visual map of where he is and where he needs to be.

Marketing managers use a variety of bases for drawing positioning maps.
Some examples they might use to establish a brand position are as follows.

Attribute: consider the product associated with an attribute, product feature or benefit. Example: The safety and security of a Volvo automobile.

Price and Quality: The product may stress high price as quality, or low price as value. Example: Target stores has positioned itself cleverly against Wal-Mart. Target is perceived as being a higher quality, yet still a low cost mass-merchandiser.

Target stores are doing just this by providing the perception of quality while still offering discounted price (like Wal-Mart).

Use/Application: sometimes a company can be differentiated from its competition by the way it does business. Avis and the "We Try Harder" campaign is a classic example. The L.L. Bean reputation for low returns because of high quality and their readiness to make returns easy or give full refunds supports this.

Product User: the customer may define the position for the store's or brand's position. Weight Watchers is an example, SnackWells from Nabisco is another.

Product Class: some products group together, in competing products. The margarines fit this definition, so do the artificial sweeteners (Aspartame, Nutrasweet, Sweet and Low, Splenda, etc.)

Competition: a company can define its product by its competition. For example, the over-the-counter drug companies/brands. Tylenol vs. Excedrin ("We are best for headache relief-Excedrin, vs. we are best for fever-Tylenol")

All of these are legitimate bases for establishing one's brand position and retail stance. And there are more; the comparisons can be endless. They all are used in perception mapping exercises.

Repositioning: Sometimes products, stores and brands need to be "repositioned."

This is the act of changing a consumer's impression of a brand, in relation to competing brands. It is almost always done as a defensive move against the reality of falling share. A classic example of successful repositioning happened with GAP stores.

The GAP

The Gap was founded as a retail clothier in 1969 and for many years had a strategy of selling Levi's jeans and identifying themselves with casual clothing. This worked for some time and the company made money until the early 1980s. Times changed, their look and position needed to change also. The Gap acquired a dated image and they elected to reposition themselves. They started with their logo by re-vamping the typeface from a lower-case look to a long, slender all cap typeface on a black square. By 1991 GAP had created an entirely new identity distinct from its prior identity, and dropped the Levi's line entirely. And they kept going. They decided

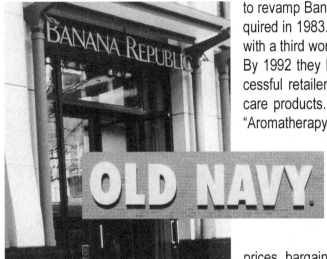

to revamp Banana Republic, which they had acquired in 1983. B.R. was a kind of novelty store, with a third world, jungle-theme image.

By 1992 they had transformed B.R. into a successful retailer of casual clothing and personal care products. Many stores resemble a sort of "Aromatherapy Spa." And still they kept going.

They started Old Navy in 1994. They created an identity made up of blocky letters. Store ambiance was warehouse-modern, with a rough, casual unfinished feel, to convey a message of low prices, bargains and good value. They focused on a target audience of a young family with kids and soon they were doing a brisk business with young mothers buying back-to-school clothes.

So, today GAP has a stratified segmentation of retail centers: each with its own identity, its own segment of an overall target market of young couples (married or non). At the high end: Banana Republic–fashion, smart stuff, low end: Old Navy; and in the middle, GAP stores.

The secret to GAP's repositioning effort is that: they (1) correctly identified their target market (TA), (2) found the graphic and image aesthetics to reach their respective TA, and (3) have stayed flexible. To keep their position they must stay timely with fashion, with ambiance. In 1995 GAP, Inc. opened 225 new stores. By March of 1996 it operated 1700 stores worldwide, including 444 Gap kids stores, 211 Banana Republic stores, and 139 Old Navy stores. Profits have averaged 28 percent per year for the last decade, although in the early twenty-first century (2004), their profits have fallen.

Store Types

All retailers fall into one of two types of retail formats: store-based and non-store based. Store-based formatted stores operate from a fixed location that requires consumers to travel to the store to view and select merchandise, services, etc. This means, in effect, that the prospect travels to the point of sale.

Essentially there are six basic types of store-based retailers.

Department Stores

This is the oldest form of retailing, going back to the 1800s, just after the Civil War. In the city centers they were represented by famous names like: Macy's, Filenes, Lord and Taylor, B.Altman's, Bloomingdale's, Marshall Field's, Saks Fifth Avenue, Hudson's, Wannamaker's or The May Company. Some were very grand and contained a broad product mix. A shopping trip to the city became an all-day social occasion, usually involving lunch. At Christmas time the State Street store of Marshall Field's (Chicago) featured a four-story tree which soared through the central atrium and families made an annual pilgrimage to shop and see the tree and the clever window displays. In New York it was the same Christmas experience at Saks or Lord & Taylor on

Fifth Avenue. These stores generally have 120,000 to 300,000 square feet of selling space. Department stores offered many services, including gift-wrapping, knowledgeable and helpful sales clerks, etc.

Sadly, the famous, popular old names (like Wannamaker's, Marshall Field's etc.) are being phased out. Recently Federated Stores (the biggest holding company) bought out The May Company (the other big holding company) and will now offer merchandise from stores that display just one of two brand names: Macy's or Bloomingdale's.

Discounters

Today the future of the department store is clouded by discounters at the low end of the price spectrum and specialty stores at the high end.

To counter this threat savvy retailers have refined the traditional method of selling and formed Discount Department Stores. This emerged as a defensive measure in the early 1950s. Like traditional department stores, Discounters feature low prices in a no-frills low service setting. They offer a variety of product lines inside a facsimile of the traditional department store format. Good examples are such stores as Wal-Mart and Target. They are invariably on one, maybe two floors, and located in the anchor position of a shopping mall and sell out of 40,000 to 100,000 square feet.

Specialty Stores

Specialty stores are relatively small-scale stores offering a great deal of depth in a narrow range of product lines.

One can find them typically in women's wear, men's wear, jewelry, footwear and electronics, sporting goods, automotive supplies and fabrics. Many specialty stores range in size from 3,000 to 7,500 square feet. Good examples are: AutoZone, Crate and Barrel, Ann Taylor, Radio Shack, Foot Locker, The Container Store, Best Buy, etc. They know their target market and position their stores décor and advertising directly at their TA. They reflect lifestyle and demographic factors big time.

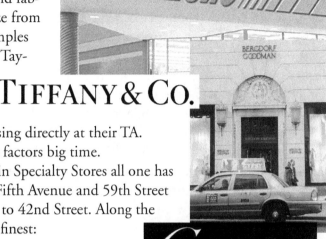

To experience the very top of the line in Specialty Stores all one has to do is walk from the Plaza Hotel at Fifth Avenue and 59th Street (in New York) south along the avenue to 42nd Street. Along the way you will pass some of the nation's finest: **Tiffany's, Cartier, Bergdorf Goodman, Fortunoff, Saks Fifth Avenue**, etc.

Non-Store Format

The other kind, the non-store based, attempts to catch the consumer at home, or at work, wherever he/she has a fixed location. In the last twenty years non-store format has grown massively. It began in the mid-70s with the proliferation of catalogs and with the beginning of specialty magazines.

Many of these catalogs have retail outlets as well, so a store like, L.L.Bean, J. Crew, Eddie Bauer or Orvis can offer fishing rods, boots and sports jackets, etc. from their catalog, or their retail store, or over the Internet. The growth of ordering online has more than doubled in the last ten years.

Saks Fifth Avenue Stores, a very traditional, old time, venerated department store in the old school mode, now operates out of many formats. Each format has its own marketing strategy, combining customized pricing and promotion mode.

Their online operation, called "Saks Off 5th" operates in thirty-nine states under the names of Parisian, Proffitt's, McRae's, Younker's, Herberger's, Carson Pirie Scott (another old line traditional department on State Street, Chicago) and Bergner's.

Supercenters

One of the newest competitive retail types within the store based format is the Supercenter. As the name indicates, these are huge, one stop facilities that combine supermarkets with discount department stores. The sizes of these stores range from 120,000 to 160,000 square feet-between 80,000 and 100,000 products.

Wal-Mart is, of course, the best example one can name.

Last year Wal-Mart's (combined) operating net sales were up 9.5 percent from the year before, at $312,427 billion. This is retailing on a grand scale.

Target

Target does many of the things that Wal-Mart does, but in a more upscale, uptown way.

And they do it well, with $48 billion in annual sales last year. They are bigger than Pepsi or Coke (in revenues) and nearly double Kmart and $5 billion greater than that of warehouse club Costco. They have only a little more than 820 stores nationwide and are headquartered out of Minneapolis. Even with the thin profit margins of the big discount store business, Target's $1.8 billion income for 2003 still sets a record. Dozens of retailers have tried to challenge Wal-Mart on price over the past few decades, and usually lost badly. Not so Target.

The company has built its reputation using a trendy assortment of distinct products and by crafting a unique approach to marketing. For example they offer their customers a popular, contemporary assortment of distinct products along with a unique approach to marketing itself and the store's image. Their ad campaigns are clever and witty. They utilize color (red and white) and their distinctive target logo with wit and punch. Target's secret, some say, is that while it remains in the same general business of discount retailing as Wal-Mart, it doesn't seem to act like it. They act as if they are a class act department store and people are accepting them as such.

Category Killers

This type of store retailing is really an outgrowth of the Specialty Store, but carried to an extreme. Their marketing strategy is simple and powerful. It is to carry a large amount of merchandise in a single category at compelling low prices, making it difficult for a potential buyer to walk away. He/she will say "All the competing brands are here, under one roof. Why not decide here and now." And they do.

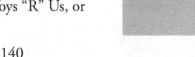

Good examples of these kinds of stores are Toys "R" Us, or Circuit City or Best Buy.

This category was probably named by an unfortunate competitor–the competition that got killed. Home Depot has prospered by this strategy. Last year Home Depot did $64 billion in sales, up 11 percent from the year before. In the past three years HD has grown sales by $19 billion, or 42 percent. They brag of 777 stores, and are still relatively young (twenty-four years old). Others in this category would be Lowe's, Blockbuster Video, Office Depot, Office Max, Bed, Bath & Beyond, Autozone, Barnes and Noble and Sports Authority.

Marketing Space
By Gerry Postlethwaite, retail marketing consultant
and Chairman Emeritus, RPA Ltd, London

The second half of the twentieth century (beginning in the 1960s) changed marketing in the retail space dramatically. This was due to three factors: the rapid technological advance in food preservation, packaging techniques and high-speed machinery. Packaging developments led to the self-service store, the supermarket and eventually the hypermarket or superstore, where the consumers have rapidly graduated from the corner shop and queuing to the vast space of the new concept stores. All this happened bewilderingly fast–in less than ten years. The superstores or hypermarkets (100,000-250,000 sq. ft) have evolved in the sophisticated Western market much more quickly over the last three decades and their customers have evolved with them and become familiar with increasing space and how to shop it.

The two global leaders in the field are Wal-Mart with their own unique development of the Superstore and the French chain Carrefour who have consistently set the pattern for the Hypermarket, with Britain's Tesco rapidly rising to No. 3.

The Carrefour concept of the hypermarket was a total failure in the USA. Outside the US Wal-Mart hasn't done much better, particularly in many of  the emerging markets. Both retail giants have had to learn costly lessons on the way, often for the simple reason of an unwillingness to adjust to a consumer with a totally different concept of shopping, different spending priorities and lack of credit facilities. In the emerging markets, feeding and clothing the family with necessities often took up 80-90 percent of available cash and almost everything else was a luxury. A hypermarket generates 60 percent of its sales volume in the food and general grocery section, but 60 percent of its profit margin is generated by all other merchandise.

Eastern Europe and South America

Since my own experience is largely in strategic planning and design development of large space stores in emerging markets, especially Eastern Europe, I started getting requests to help plan big stores for the Czech Republic and Poland as early as the late 1980s. I have worked with my clients to help them adjust to today's world. The biggest prize of all is now in sight–China. All the major retailers are announcing new partnerships in that market–not just Wal-Mart, Carrefour and Tesco but other giants such as France's Auchan and Germany's Metro Group with their real chain. One hopes that lessons learned in all the other emerging markets will be put to good use to meet this vast new retail challenge.

Convenience Stores

These are the smallest in traditional store format. They stock frequently purchased products such as gasoline, bread, tobacco, milk and snack items. Items purchased from a convenience store are usually consumed within an hour of purchase, and not by accident they are located along roads–at stop lights, truck stops, interstate junctions.

They are generally small: 2,000 to 4,000 square feet. C-Stores often charge higher prices but customers justify the price by the convenience being provided.

The biggest, and first convenience store is 7-Eleven. Unit growth is coming from major oil companies such as ChevronTexaco and Conoco.

It is interesting that when Gatorade initially decided to sell to the consuming public, they chose C-Stores as their venue, because of low competition from major brands and higher prices possible (higher margins attainable).

Non-Store Based Retailers

Other than catalog sales (covered earlier) the ability to order an item from the retailer over the Internet has revolutionized retail marketing. L.L.Bean was an earlier pioneer, but today the opportunities to buy most anything proliferate. There are, in fact, four types: Street Peddling, Direct Selling, Mail Order & Electronic Selling.

Street Peddling, of course goes back through the history of our country. In the eighteenth and nineteenth century peddlers sold merchandise from pushcarts or temporary stalls on Main Street. As a category, they have never totally died out.

Chain stores like Ann Taylor, Talbot's and J.Jill, etc. are in most major cities.

Direct Selling. This type of selling involves door-to-door, as typified by Mary Kay products, or Avon. Mary Kay and Avon have more than 12.2 million independent distributors, also known as representatives or consultants. They claim to generate sales of about $26 billion annually. In terms of worldwide sales from direct selling in forty-three countries, about $83 billion annually.

Mail order and electronic selling are self-evident. There is still another type of store that should be included—the store that sells and serves prepared food or beverages—in short, the restaurant. Some are small, quick stop places like a McDonald's, and some are larger and stylized to a theme. There is one (Starbucks) that fits between these two categories. It is small but highly stylized, it is franchised, it sells just one product and it is a wonderful success story.

Ambiance matters

Specialty stores have long understood and valued the presence of "ambiance." Pottery Barn uses music with an attractive, busy décor; Restoration Hardware with its spacious grey and tan atmosphere plays another tune. There is one store that while physically small and sells just one product (coffee), is an ambiance masterpiece—Starbucks.

The feeling one gets in a Starbucks café is largely based on a compelling aesthetic style, one that is tasteful, comfortable and clever. CEO Howard Schultz hired interior designer Harry Roberts to create a clever mix of organic and manufactured components: light wood tones on counters, green and tan on signage, brown bags and a strong, slightly mysterious logo. The logo was in fact adapted from a stylized Nordic mermaid with two tails. Most stores are about 600-1200 square feet. The full result is upscale, a touch European, a touch contemporary, a touch "old shoe comfy."

IKEA

This store is unique in several respects. First the name. It is an acronym made up of the first letters of the founder's name (Ingvar Kamprad) plus the founder's farm name (Elmtarrd) and his home village (Agunard) in Sweden. Second, it was (founded back in 1943) the first to offer furniture, designed by the founder that was sold "knocked down," that is the customer has to assemble it himself at home. This turned out to be an advantage, for shipping, for carrying home and for small apartments and homes. IKEA is focused on providing utilitarian, well-designed modern furniture that is economically priced. The target audience was and is young working women and men or newlyweds starting their first home together.

The stores themselves are also unique. They are generally large, mostly windowless big boxes

143

(invariably blue). Instead of the typical open plan of a Wal-Mart or Target, theirs are "enclosed" requiring the customer to follow a "one-way" path that akes them past everything along the route (interior maps are provided for the lost or confused). Finally they seem to be following a marketing strategy of "less is more." To date they have only built 273 stores worldwide (in 36 countries), usually on the edge of large cities where they think their target customers live.

The result is flexible, adaptable home furnishings echoed in their motto "Affordable Solutions for Better Living." They had $26.5 billion in revenues last year.

Part II
Early Retailing

Just what was the retailing scene like two hundred and fifty years ago? What were the stores like, the merchants? Were there any? A late twentieth century marketing phenomenon called "scrambled merchandise" is actually a throw-back to the colonial and early nineteenth century. It is the role that the general gtore played. Scrambled merchandise means that the store (now the supermarket) offers its customers diversity in unrelated lines of merchandise. Today it might be (besides food items): lawn chairs, socks, magazines, tools, light bulbs, flowers.

Colonial Williamsburg
The best place to study early retailing (as well as early logos–Chapter 2) is again, Colonial Williamsburg in southeastern Virginia. For seventy-seven years (from 1699 to 1776) this village was the political center of Virginia and one of England's largest, wealthiest and most populous colonies. It was a center for government and trade with more than twenty stores all doing brisk business. The people of Williamsburg, and those who visited from the surrounding areas, were growing wealthy and began to demand more items such as: clothes, fabrics, furniture, books, perfume, fine china and silver. By the mid eighteenth century, Williamsburg had taken on a more

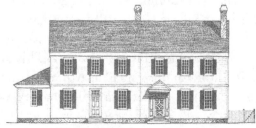

John Greenhow Store and House

modern look, with retail stores that had display windows filled with merchandise from anywhere and for almost anyone's taste.

A typical day was lively.

Market Square was the hub–from here, before dawn each market day (weekly, then as much as six times per week by 1790), farmers arrived in creaking wagons loaded with produce. Cattle and sheep were driven to the square, vendors unloaded meat, eggs, milk, butter, fish, crabs, oysters, fruit, vegetables which were laid out and displayed on makeshift counters made of pine boards supported by trestles. And the customers arrived: housewives, cooks, kitchen slaves–all fulfilling a daily chore in an age before refrigeration. Along with the merchandise, often there were puppet shows, horseraces, cockfights, dancing and fiddling. There were auctions of slaves, goods and land.

John Greenhow was one of five General Merchandise Stores in Williamsburg

The Prentis Store

One of the first stores was The Prentis Store. From 1733 until the Revolution, the firm of Prentis & Company operated a highly successful general store in a handsome building on the west end of the Duke of Gloucester Street. Its architectural style is typical of the period–a two-story brick building with the gable end facing the main street, display rooms in the front, the counting room in the rear. Two dormer windows faced east and gave light to the storage area that comprised the entire second floor. This store was highly successful-even celebrated. In the 1730s Lieutenant Governor Alexander Spotswood declared that the Prentis Store is "one of the most considerable trading stores of this country."

The value of the stock was appraised and valued at seven thousand pounds sterling in 1733–the time of the modern and final partnership. This was a considerable treasure for a store in those times. And evidently William Prentis, manager and part owner in the business, was a very good retailer. In the first thirty years of its existence the stock increased in value to 17,391 pounds sterling-more than 50%.

Prentis was at first paid on a percentage of sales basis, plus expenses. This was altered to an annual salary of 200 pounds, and finally 300 by 1759.

What is most surprising is that the store carried a very wide, sophisticated range of merchandise. And it was mostly imported.

In 1774, for example, The Prentis store imported and sold more imports to domestic products by a ratio of approximately 50 to 1.

This was a growing trend and shows how dependent the store, and by extension the village, was on its European connections. It also reflects the growing acquisitiveness of the Virginia colonists because this merchandise wouldn't have been imported if it wasn't likely to sell. The streets of Williamsburg must have been very fashionable indeed!

And it all came to a crashing halt two years later with the Declaration of Independence and the Revolution that followed.

How He Got Supplied
Prentis' cargoes were sent from Southampton, England, across the Atlantic (in 5/6 weeks), into Chesapeake Bay, up the York River, arriving by way of Queen's Creek to Capitol Landing-about three quarters of a mile from Williamsburg.

Until the outbreak of the American Revolution, the merchandise came from such countries as: Turkey, Italy, Spain, Portugal, France, Belgium, Germany, Norway, Denmark, Sweden, Russia, Holland, Ireland, Jamaica, Africa, Canary Islands, East India and China.
Some of the hottest items were: raw silk from Istanbul, wine and oil from Genoa, Spanish wool from Valencia, lemons and other fruits from Lisbon, fine lace, velvet, and perfume from Paris, furs from Moscow, linen from Dublin, ginger and cocoa from Jamaica, and, sad to say, up to thirty thousand African Americans each year, as slaves to work the plantations.
What was the store like inside?
The sales area was open, unobstructed to the perimeter walls, and was bordered by open shelves built against blank white walls. A counter ran along the west side of this room, and items such as leather tankards, shoes and wicker baskets hung from cords which bisected the room overhead.

Prentis got his goods from ships like these which took 5-6 weeks to cross the Atlantic.

The inside of the Prentis Store.

Retailing in the Nineteenth Century

Fast forward 100 years to examine retailing in the middle of the nineteenth century. The Civil War, of course, affected the number and type of stores that were found throughout the south. What was the typical nineteenth century country store like?

The country store in the south, and in New England (with variations) was the center of life in most communities of less than 1,000, even 500 people. The storekeeper was all things to his community besides a purveyor of merchandise.

He served as banker and credit source, as the recreational center, as school trustee, railway agent if the town was near a rail line, social adviser, postmaster and as a public forum for debating the issues of the day. His store was the hub of the local universe.

These small country centers were known and vital to the well-being of the cities. Wholesalers in the cities, like Atlanta, personally knew the crossroads merchants, and treated them very well when they came on their annual buying journeys. Because so many of these stores could be reached only after long, arduous road journeys, the store and the merchant was the true center of trade, and millions of dollar's worth of goods were collectively sold each year, emanating from the big city wholesaler.

To do business in 1870 required capital of from five to fifteen thousand dollars, because a stock sufficient to supply the trade for six months was bought at one time in either Philadelphia or Richmond or Baltimore. The retailer, at least in western Virginia, had to make a long trip by wagon to the marketplace and buy for his customers, plus a bit more for the general trade. He would often carry with him memorandums of what his customers wanted and he had to carry the cash to pay for these purchases as there were no banks. There must have been highway robbers so the retailer making one of these trips would have to have been armed. He went to Philadelphia, for example, made the purchases, paid for them and saw them packed and shipped before departing the city. Smaller items, like saddles or tackle, or rakes and shovels he might bring in the back of his wagon.

This demonstrates that a large portion of the sales were on credit, and very large.

The General Store

Here are Some Typical Sales

Most general stores sold whisky in the early days, at 12.5 cents per quart, or 37.5 cents per gallon. One of the bookstores in Lexington, Virginia, sold whisky and books, side by side. One such bookseller, John Blair Lyle, conducted an "automatic bookstore," meaning that if you found a book you wanted you left a note on the counter and paid later. Another item Lyle sold was stationery, pens, papers, sealing wax, ink, etc. He also advertised: "Newspapers, magazines and wall paper, books for sale, hire or exchange, circulating library, will be glad to supply all you want without buying."

Lyle was a much loved man who treated his business as a social practice and never let making a sale get in the way of enjoying the company of his customers and friends. When he died, he was buried in the family plot of one Colonel Preston and the whole town mourned.

The Drummer Makes the Scene

The only other way that country stores could be supplied was by a traveling salesman, sometimes called "Drummers." Shortly after the end of the Civil War, traveling salesmen began to venture out on the rough, often muddy roads in a two-horse buggy stuffed with merchandise. When they hit the road it was often for weeks at a time and they had to find lodging with farmers or with the storekeeper, in the local church–wherever they could bed down. A story appeared in the *Boston Advertiser* in 1866 when they sent a reporter south to see how the former Confederate states were coping. He reported, "I found the countryside full of drummers from Louisville and Cincinnati... representing all branches of trade, and they were getting many orders."

Drummers habitually wore derby hats

The origin of this nickname for a traveling salesman isn't known except that some salesmen carried a drum on their wagons and hired a local boy to beat it as they came into town. Doubtless this is the origin of the term, "To drum up business."

While there were different kinds of drummers, they all, for some reason, wore derby hats. There were dry goods salesmen who were agents of the expanding wholesale businesses in the north (and soon in the south) whose trunks bulged with bolts of cloth from the knitting mills of Rhode Island or Massachusetts.

There were hardware drummers who didn't need to bring trunks filled with samples. They were selling familiar/known products: harrows, grass rakes, plows, harness. The hardware drummer had to pay close attention to the consistency of the lands through which he traveled, the look of the fields, the nature of the weather, as an indicator of future clientele.

There were Medicine Drummers. These were often slick-talking, flashily dressed dandies representing makers of Patent Medicines, such as Dr. Josiah Bull of Louisville, Kentucky; Dr. Shoop of Racine, Wisconsin, Lydia Pinkham of Lynn, Massachusetts. Thus while drummers served their (wholesale) houses as salesmen and information sources, they also performed duties as advertising agents.

Riding behind a slow team, they had much spare time, so it was a simple matter to take boxes of samples, folders, memorandum books and tin pie plates and pitch them out at crossroads, on church and school grounds, at farm gates and around mailboxes. This was an excellent way to advertise medicines, needles, thread, soda and baking powder, flour and farm machinery. Sometimes they even nailed signs to doors and walls (and tore down those of their competition).

The drummer also had to be a good judge of the situation, and the person to whom he was selling.

Octagon soap by Colgate was popular with nineteenth century customers.

Different Strokes

To offer a devout tea-totaling deacon and community pillar a drink was to ruin prospects for business for a long time to come, yet to fail to offer another merchant a drink might also do serious harm. Some merchants had to be "liquored and yarned" but others would not permit liquor or racy stories in their stores.

Musical instruments were sold in the general store. One store in Tennessee advertised, "For sale, a good shaped fiddle, red shaded, put up in a paste board box, for as little as 68 cents." They had a more upscale model, called the "Stradivarius," which sold for as much as $2.80. It also was put up in a pasteboard box. Banjos cost more–$3.00, and, of course, guitars. The top of the line guitar came with a series of pearl position dots on its neck and strings that "gave forth soft tones which blended perfectly with the sounds of the night, and made an overpowering don of its owner." That beauty sold for all of $5.00.

Watches from R. H. Ingersoll and Brother's famous stem-wound Yankee model retailed for a dollar. When a merchant sold a watch he created a market for both a chain and a charm, and charms were available, such as the popular horse head, or dice, skulls and crossbones or girls' legs.

Most appealing at the time was Tappan's Sweet Bye and Bye powder, which was highly recommended because it "cannot injure the enamel of the teeth and gives breath a delightful fragrance and hardens the gums and comes in beautiful oval bottles with polished nickel screw caps."

The Power of Packaging–Even Back Then

Perhaps the most colorful drummer tale involved one Colonel W. H. Bradley of Kentucky, who brought to his pitch the as yet unknown "Mexican Jumping Bean." The newspaper, *New South* (Elberton, Georgia) wrote up his visit as "a terror to all who witnessed the magic 'Electric Bean that jumped on its own." Large crowds gathered and sat in wonderment. Thanks to his Electric Bean, Col. Bradley sold lots of dry goods–of inferior quality. He wisely never called on the same customer twice.

For at least twenty years after the Civil War ended, rural southern women made all the clothing for their family–and they always chose black, dark blue or grey. Drabness was the style, despite the growing trend for color and fashion in the cities. The long list of textiles, which passed annually over the counters of the general stores, tell a vivid story of southern clothing. Life brightened up near the end of the century (1890) when the most popular fabrics were calicoes, plaids, red and gray flannel, hickory stripes, and, most shocking for the country sensibilities–the slit skirt. They came into style with the bicycle and when ladies began riding horses like men, instead of side-saddle. By the 1920s modern magazine advertising made southern women style –conscious and cheap ready-made dresses were placed in stock. With that the dry goods shelves began to go bare.

Many general stores in the old, post war south, were near crossroads, and often had large open fields adjacent. Since they were the community centers, hitching grounds around the stores were scenes of most of the baseball games. Baseball caught on almost immediately, a craze which took hold after the Civil War. Merchants stocked balls, bats, gloves and masks and supplied the local teams with equipment. In Georgia nearly every store had its baseball team and brass band. Some of the team names were: the Fork Flyaways, the Pop-and-Gos, and the Paioli Blues.
Home base was usually about twenty yards from the front porch and the porch contained the brass band. The merchants made money, thanks to this sport, and not only from the soda pop they sold during the game. Twenty-four members of each team paid $12.65 as dues, balls cost $1.60, bats, $.50, water carriers were paid $0.25.
The only ones who weren't too wild about this new sport were the farmers whose fields joined the baseball diamond. One farmer, in a letter to the *Shelby Guide* (1875 in Alabama), accused roughnecks from Columbia, Alabama, of ruining his village. "They were galloping up and down the road catching fly balls, running all over the hill encircling the bases, scaring horses and raising sand in general." It does not, he went on, "elevate the moral level of its players, and recommend true gentlemen to play the game." Baseball flourished, as we all know.

The Many Faces (and places) of Retail

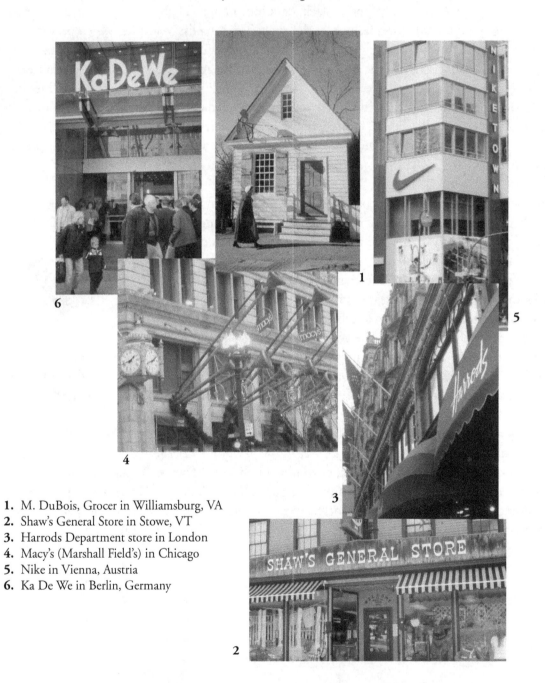

1. M. DuBois, Grocer in Williamsburg, VA
2. Shaw's General Store in Stowe, VT
3. Harrods Department store in London
4. Macy's (Marshall Field's) in Chicago
5. Nike in Vienna, Austria
6. Ka De We in Berlin, Germany

SECTION III

PROMOTION BY DESIGN

Ganter Bridge, Switzerland, built: 1980

7

SALES PROMOTION

Advertising's (not so) Little Sister

Many of us think of sales promotion in terms of a store's display.
FAO Schwarz is a good subject.

Their Fifth Avenue store is a perfect example of a store that pays close attention to display, to its retail environment. They should, they have a prominent location-just across from the Plaza Hotel at 59th and Fifth Avenue. As you enter the store music greets you as well as clown-costumed employees and on display are big stuffed animals, huge rotating dolls and a new toy everywhere you look.

An even larger example is the new Toys "R" Us at Times Square, with its big, working, four floors high indoor Ferris Wheel. These two represent display promotion on a grand scale.

A more modest variation occurs in a local store in my town. Peebles frequently offers a "Red Dot Sale," explained and hyped on window displays and newspaper ads. The Red Dot event is simple—any item in the store that carries a red dot on its sales tag can be purchased at 20-30 percent off the normal retail price.

Both of these stores, FAO Schwarz and Peebles illustrate one facet of sales promotion, but in this chapter we will explore the subject wider and deeper.

Retailers spend a lot of time enhancing their space, or as they would term it, "their retail environment." This is proper and smart and has proven effective over many years. Environmental aesthetics can drive business positively.

On Main Street

Promotions in stores lengthen the time that consumers stay in the store and the longer they stay in the store, the more likely they are to purchase. Sales promotion coupled with an appealing environment is most effective of all.

The advantages of a good display are hard to overestimate.

When a display is positioned well in a retail space, at the end aisle of a supermarket for example, or in the street window of a special shop on Fifth Avenue, it can help lower selling costs, increase sales and produce a higher profit per square foot of floor or counter space. There are studies that indicate that about 51 percent of the merchandise in a supermarket is bought on impulse–and usually off a display.

But display is only one of the more obvious forms of promotion.

Promotional activity can pull people into the store without a display, to look and to buy. When the general public wasn't so hardened to free give-aways, stores would offer simple items for the youngsters like kites, balloons, paper caps, etc. imprinted with the name of the store, or the product which the merchant would in turn offer to his customers for coming in the store. They were simple traffic builders and from the end of the nineteenth century to the middle of the twentiethth, they worked!

Some early examples were: in 1880, Adolphus Bush initiated a sampling promotion in beer gardens and pubs when he gave away pocket knives for trying his new beer; Procter & Gamble ran a give-away program with Ivory soap wrappers in 1890; and in 1914 Ford ran a rebate program–$50 off for each Model T sold.

Other promotions used by merchants (not manufacturers) in the past to build store traffic were:

—A store in Fort Wayne, Indiana in the 1940s, celebrated its anniversary with a big birthday cake in the window and customers were invited to come in, get a slice of cake and look around.

—A store in Winnetka, Illinois in the 1950s had a prize window and customers were invited to look over a windowful of products and find items whose first letters spelled out the name of the store, then come in and fill out a form making them eligible for a prize, the winner's name to be drawn from all of the filled out forms.

—In New York City Greek Airlines once filled a huge fifty gallon container with jelly beans and passers-by were invited to guess the number in the container. An accurate guess (within 10 percent) could win a round trip for two to Athens.

—A store in New Canaan, Connecticut, sent a congratulations card to every young couple who had had their first baby. Included inside was a coupon for diapers, or a fuzzy toy redeemable in the store at a future date.

A store in Sisters, Oregon, staged a wood-chopping exhibition. The maker of Fayette R. Plumb woodcutting tools toured the state setting up woodcutter demonstrations. A well-known master woodcutter came to Sisters and competed against local woodcutters.

The store and venue was the local hardware store, and the manufacturer and hardware store split the cost of prizes for the best choppers, at different age levels. Those who could chop through logs of differer diameter, faster, more cleanly, etc. won the prizes—all of which were Plumb Axes, of course. There was

The woodchopper's promotion was popular and effectively promoted Plumb Axes in Sisters, Oregon.

also a safety instructor to teach youngsters respect for a fine axe. Simple and charming as these promotions were, they had a narrow range. In addition, they are all examples of early promotions and a time when customers could be lured to a store more easily.

Sometimes they were packed into packages. The prize you got as a child in the bottom of a Cracker Jacks Box (Borden Foods) is a good, simple promotion.

The premise: buy Cracker Jack, win the prize.

That's an old concept and product–same for baseball cards and bubble gum.

And fifty years ago kids sent in five Wheaties box tops for the famous Captain Midnight decoder ring–as I did.

Sales promotion has changed, has grown up.

Early Days in Promotion

Today, there are sizable corporations that specialize in custom promotions and get fat fees for creating and executing them. In the 1970s when service and supplier companies began to grow, and opportunities opened up for people who knew how to combine consumer marketing expertise with knowledge of such things as product sampling, retail merchandising, display, premiums offers and fulfillment, a new form of sales promotion began.

One promotion pioneer was Ralph A. Glendinning, who left advertising agency life to found his own sales promotion marketing firm called Glendinning Associates. He located his building atop a lovely trout stream in Westport, Connecticut. A few years later three sizeable firms started up in Chicago: Bud Frankel founded Frankel and Company in 1962, and William A. Robinson started Robinson and Maites, and Lee Flaherty started Flair Communications in 1964. These three firms became known as the "Chicago School" of promotion. In the mid 1970s a man named Dan Pratt left Glendinning Associates to start Marketing Corporation of America (MCA), and it grew and soon occupied a number of buildings along the Westport River. MCA now does a major portion of the nations' sales promotions every year.

And once there was an interesting specialty promotions firm, founded by a charming guy named Courtney Randall, which was aimed at college students. It was called National Student Marketing. They sold premiums to students who were encouraged to build a business with representatives on campus, a sort of pyramid scheme, for which the student representatives on campus were paid a fee. NSA went public and was a Wall Street darling for a few years, until false earning reports sank it–and CEO Cort Randall did a little time for his role in this scheme.

All of these are examples of clever entrepreneurs working in a business that was and is fast moving and lucrative.

Today, sales promotion is offered under the umbrella of the big advertising agencies as part of their effort to provide a basket of creative services to clients. Young & Rubicam has Wunderman & Associates ($378 million in revenues), McCann Erickson has a youth advertising/promotions group called TAG, and D'Arcy Masius Benton & Bowles (Publicis Groupe) has the former Connecticut Consulting Group/Ted Colangelo Associates-now called Clarion ($28 million). And there are more.

Sales Promotion has become big time.

Sales Promotion vs. Advertising

What exactly is Sales Promotion and how is it related to (and different from) advertising? Both are marketing methods, with the common goal of increasing sales of given products. Both merchants (retailers) and manufacturers use sales promotion to offer customers incentives to buy their product. The focus isn't on the product's benefits, it is on the benefits to the customer–invariably involving price savings. When done well, they can get results fast. Merchants and manufacturers know it works and as a result an entire industry exists for conceiving and launching promotions–valued at between 150 and 200 billion dollars annually (No one knows for sure).

Sales Promotion is a marketing activity–another marketing activity that when planned carefully and executed with skill and timing, will move the corporation's product.

Furthermore, it is a marketing activity that is growing.

The Basics

Promotion isn't only personal selling, advertising and public relations, although these three activities will stimulate consumer purchasing and help the trade. It is and can include: sampling programs, premium offers, product demonstrations, coupons, displays, trade shows, contests, lotteries and sweepstakes. And more.

Sales Promotion is many-headed, as this chapter will show. It is also extremely diverse, more so than any other marketing communications tool in the marketer's arsenal of tools. When it is conceived and executed from a single objective and strategy, the same one that a corporation has designated for its other marketing activities, it can work exceedingly well.

Designing Promotions

The essential characteristics of a promotion are:
1. The creative concept or the offer
2. The vehicle or system for delivering it
3. The fulfillment of the reward promised in the concept or offer

Creative Concept

The creative concept in a promotion is the idea or proposition that gets the consumer to act. The concept of promotion is a behavioral rather than a communications medium, as in "your action will be rewarded."

This is a good case of where the medium is the message, as in a promotion concept where the proposition for participants to acquire the product by behaving in a certain way–i.e. buying the product being promoted.

The best promotions aim at one or two specific brand objectives:
> –the generation of new product trial and repurchase
> –the protection of market share in the face of a competitive threat
> –brand purchase continuity over a period of time
> –"pantry loading"or saturating the market with players to the detriment of the
>   competition.
> –generate trade support and good relations.

Promotion Planning

The best promotions are planned, carefully and in considerable detail.

The promotion plan is a logical extension of the marketer's plan–designed to fulfill the objectives set out in the marketing plan. The process can be described in five basic steps.

A. Promotion Strategy—Establish the promotion strategy based on fulfillment of marketing goals–identifying market priorities regarding target audience, packaging and key distribution channels, and timing.

B. Promotion Tactics—Based on promotion strategies, determine the most appropriate promotional tactic that will accomplish these goals. Promotional tactics mean the different executional devices available, couponing, premium collections, lotteries, etc.

C. Promotion Design—The key goal is to take the appropriate promotion tactics and creatively design them so that they stand out from competitive activity in the marketplace.

Consideration should be given not only to promotion excitement and consumer appeal, but also to brand imagery.

D. Promotion Execution—Creative and strategically sound promotion events often fail due to poor execution. The key objective of this step is to identify up front the executional steps needed to assure a successful promotion event.

E. Promotion Evaluation—As part of the executional timetable, a post analysis should be completed follow-

Singer Saleathon: sometimes a simple price off sales event does the trick.

ing the event, to assure that the success or failure of the event is determined on facts and not on isolated opinions. A regular post-mortem will help avoid repeating mistakes.

Examples abound.

Restaurants, especially fast-food restaurants, will offer price offs with meal purchase: a Coke, Big Mac and fries for $3.50. They may offer premiums with a meal pur-chase: "Win the Hamburglar figurine with the purchase of a Big Mac meal," for instance.

Movies promote shamelessly–especially kid's movies. Disney's *Monsters, Inc.* and *Shrek 2* are both offered with tie-ins at various fast-food restaurants, offering action figures or puzzles and games tied to purchase of a meal.

When manufacturers provide promotions that drive customers to specific places, like fast food outlets, they are called "Trade Promotions."

Trade Promotions. This is a very active, growing area of promotional marketing. Special in-centives are provided by the manufacturer through the distribution channel to facilitate price discounting at the retail level. They may offer buy-back allowances, price discount incentives and co-op advertising programs, sometimes all three.

Why does the retailer do it?

He does it because the manufacturer's promotion will bring increased business to his store–incremental business. The retailer will find these kinds of promotions useful for building retail inventories as well as increasing sales volume.

Trade allowances are another incentive that the manufacturer can resort to. Trade deals, are many and various:

Off-invoice Allowances in which the retailer is able to deduct a fixed amount from the full price of the product at the time the order is placed.

Forward Buying is another term for off-invoice allowances, because the retailer is shifting business from the future to the present.

Diverting is still another refinement of off-invoice allowances. In this practice, the retailer and wholesaler buy large quantities at the deal price (off-invoice allowance) and then trans-ship the goods to other geographic areas not covered by the manufacturer's offer. It is not unlike the arbitrage in financial circles where men simultaneously buy and sell securities in different markets, to profit from unequal prices.

Direct Marketing is an offshoot of sales promotion. Its techniques are the same as tradition-al sales promotion. It differs in that it is a direct to the customer or the business solicitation. Direct marketing depends on the U.S. Postal Service for delivery.

It is a valuable technique for generating leads (from the business), or generating traffic (from the customer). It uses direct mail to achieve this.

Some years ago my firm designed collateral materials for a direct marketing program for Canadian Mist whisky. It utilized both in-store solicitation (flyers placed on bar tops in restaurants or liquor stores), or direct mail (the same flyers mailed to a list of adult potential customers). It was called the **"Canadian Mist Trading Post."**

The offer was simple: purchase any of the items in the Canadian Mist Catalog by mail, use the receipt from the purchase of a bottle of Canadian Mist whisky to achieve a 5 percent dis-

count across the board. All of the items we offered originated at the prestigious outfitter store in Maine, L.L.Bean. Bean changed the labels on the garments so that they displayed a Canadian Mist logo. We photographed all the items in Central Park in New York City, and made it look like the north woods! The Canadian Mist promotion is a good, simple example of a price discount wrapped in a colorful mantle.

The Hook. At its basic level, all promotions involve the use of a price-off or value-added offer as an incentive for purchasing a specific product (over its competitor).

Promotions work best when they are coordinated with an advertising campaign. One has as its goal setting up an image or a perception about a product in the mind of the consumer (advertising) versus stimulating the consumer to make the purchase, either in the store or by mail (promotion).

Sales promotion is often described as "below the line" advertising–as opposed to media ad-vertising, or theme advertising–which is a budgeted, above the line item.

It's All About Price.

Promotions techniques, no matter how presented, amount to price reductions, even though they often go under different names:

—Coupons

—Rebates

—2 for 1 Sales

There are essentially three different categories of sales promotion.

—Consumer Promotions: $33 billion spent in 2000

—Business to Business Promotions: $36 billion in 2000

—Direct Mail Promotions: $41 billion in 2000

This totals $110 billion expended in 2000. Big business indeed! When you realize that the total spent on advertising in the same period was around $150 billion, it qualifies for the big leagues.

Consumer-Oriented Sales Promotion

There are several promotion techniques that seem to be the most popular and that appear year after year.

1. Coupons and Refunds

Discounts offered on the purchase price of goods or services is a classic coupon technique, and it is estimated that approximately 90 percent of all marketers use it.

ProKeds Promotion

In this case the nation's least popular shoe wanted to get back into the game.

Consumers initially find the coupon in the local paper, clip it out and take it to various retail outlets to execute. They usually involve a percentage off the purchase price of a stated item. The retail outlets then redeem the coupons from the customer for which they receive a handling charge from the manufacturer. This industry is estimated at over $5 billion alone. There is slippage, there always is, and many marketers dial this into their marketing budget. The marketer must look to the best, most cost-effective method for distribution of coupons.

Some tools at his disposal are: direct mail, magazines, newspapers, package insertions, and lately, the Internet. Free-standing inserts usually appear in Sunday newspapers.

Advantages of Couponing
—Couponing to consumers helps ensure that savings are passed directly to the consumers.
—While the consumer receives the benefit of a cost savings, it is perceived as a temporary special offer, rather than as a permanent price reduction.
—Coupons can create traffic for retailers, which pleases them and helps the relationship with the manufacturer to the retailer.

Various promotional techniques for attracting consumers and retailers.
Couponing

Here are some of the variations used in couponing.
—Cents off. The product is purchased at a dollar amount off the regular price.
—Free
—Buy one, get one free.
—Multiple purchase. The coupons work when more than one unit of the product is used.
—Personalized. The coupon names the consumer in the sales literature. This is very effective with large ticket items.
—Sweepstakes. The redeemed coupon becomes an entry into a sweepstakes promotion.
Unfortunately, couponing is so popular that it isn't considered "fresh" with consumers. Some people have the opinion that couponing is used as a life support mechanism for weak brands, others say couponing is used primarily by existing loyal users whose business you already have.

1. SAMPLING Strategic application: Trial	• Strongest trial device • High subsequent purchase generator • Good trade participation	• Very expensive • Inefficient for established brands • Can be administratively complex
2. COUPONING Strategic application: Trial and Loading	• Strong trial generator • Can be selectively targeted • Can enable tie-in with specific trade sectors	• Can be very expensive • Wastage. Low redemptions mean that high percentage of set-up costs are wasted
3. CONSUMER PRICE-OFFS Strategic application: Loading	• Easy and reliable volume generator • No other special activity needed to support offer • Acceptable to trade	• Lack of uniqueness • Heavy subsidizing of existing user • Danger of "price-wars"
4. BONUS PACKS (Extra product for the same price) Strategic application: Loading	• Method of costing allows greater consumer "value" but at low brand cost • No other special activity needed • Can encourage "trading-up" • Usually acceptable to trade	• Considerable extra factory problems • Need to offer significant extra product to be effective

Trial means getting the consumer to buy the product.
Loading means getting the retailer to carry the product.

Sampling

Sampling refers to the free distribution of a product in an attempt to obtain future sales. Samples can be distributed door to door, by mail, via demonstrations in stores or at events. Sometimes they are packed into existing products.

Sampling is a very effective way to get customers to test a new product, without risking big bucks. In fact, research shows that most of the consumers who receive samples, try them. There are some variations on the techniques of sampling.

—The Bonus Pack. This is when the manufacturer gives the consumer a larger quantity of the product without raising the price. Shaving cream that contains 10 percent more product is found frequently.

—Premiums. These are the items that are given free or at a reduced cost with purchases of other products. To be effective, the premium should have some relationship with the product being promoted–travel mugs for a new coffee blend, for example.

Contests and Sweeps

There is a subtle but important difference between a contest and a sweepstakes and a good marketer must know when to use each. A number of states have laws against sweepstakes, but not against contests, so the latter is usually resorted to when this situation exists.

Contests require entrants to solve problems or write essays, and may involve showing proof of purchase to qualify. The questions are usually easy–the goal being not to stump the participant but to move product (remember the proof of purchase requirement).

The entrant mails the entry to a post office box or deposits it in an on-premise container. Marketers often choose contests over sweepstakes simply because proof-of-purchase can be required.

Sweepstakes choose their winners by chance, so no product purchase is necessary. They are more popular with consumers than contests because they do not take as much effort to enter. Marketers like them, despite the non-purchase requirement because they are inexpensive to run and the number of winners is predetermined. They also like them because they usually attract a much larger pool of participants than contests. "Publisher's Sweepstakes" is perhaps the best known of this type.

The Holiday Inn Story

In 1977 my firm created a promotion for the Holiday Inn Corporation that combined two techniques, for two separate but connected target audiences.

There were two marketing objectives.

—Lure traveling salesman to Holiday Inns for the night, over rival Howard Johnson's or Hilton, by offering an incentive.

—Improve the performance level of the inn-keeping staff.

There were two marketing tactics.

When the customer arrived at the front desk to register the innkeeper would give him/her a folder which contained various items redeemable in the lobby restaurant or bar. These included: a coupon for a free cocktail, a coupon for a price reduced meal, a coupon for a free newspaper, and a coupon for a free (long distance) telephone call home.

When the customer arrived at the front desk, the desk clerk would receive bonus points for treating his new arrival courteously. He would be rated by the supervisor, as well as the customer (who had a rating sheet in his folder). If the employee did well in this social situation he was given an entry in a sweepstakes. The prizes ranged from premium items, cash, S&H Green Stamps to a grand prize–a week stay at a Holiday Inn in Florida, Canada or Puerto Rico.

The Promotion Execution

A group of four graphically related brochures were given to the Holiday Inn Manager. One said: "You're the key to the Inner Circle;" the second one said, "The free Newspaper Benefit;" the third one said, "The fine points;" the fourth one said, "Here are some tools to help."

The Holiday Inn inner circle promotion was aimed at customers and the innkeeping staff.

The overall brochure said, "The Inner Circle is big and getting bigger."

It was all linked by circles, half and quarter circles and colors.

The promotion worked. And in it we combined two interrelated promotional techniques-couponing and sweepstakes to two audiences: the consumer and the trade.

Specialty Advertising

If you have ever seen a person wearing a tee shirt with a slogan or brand on it (and haven't we all), you have just seen an example of specialty advertising. This is big business, estimated at $8 billion each year. T-shirts are big, but cups, baseball caps and jackets are all hot specialty items. Also calendars, glassware and pens and pencils are heavily used. The purpose is simple, to reinforce the advertising message of a nationally advertised product. Consumers like these giveaways and they do get the ad or logo or slogan around.

Continuity Promotions

In a promotion like this the consumer is rewarded for re-peat purchase or use of a product or service. The whole objective here is to encourage purchase loyalty and frequency. These promotions are best typified by the now popular Frequent Flyer programs offered by virtually all the airlines. Versions of the Frequent Flyer programs of the airlines have turned up in special credit cards tied to earning miles, for purchase ($1 equals one mile on American Airlines, etc.).

Hot air balloons with promotional messages on them are another form of specialty advertising.

All of these promotional techniques are "continuity" programs aimed at building returns and brand loyalty. Finally, there are Scratchcards.

Scratchcards

Scratchcards are a technique for offering customers an incentive to purchase a product. They are traditionally structured on an instant win basis, or sometimes delayed-win requiring multiple purchase, or collection.

Scratchcards are relatively simple, yet very effective promotional tools. Because they are easy for consumers to undertand, they usually have immediate acceptance.

The hardest part of a scratchcard promotion is the preparation of the card. There are only two or three printing firms in the U.S. who have the equipment to prepare the cards. The easiest part is that the entire promotion is contained in the single card. To activate your card, customers merely scratch off a specified area of the card to determine winning cards.

Pepsi License Plate Lottery

The classic card design involves two sections, top and bottom. The top section is often a "match and win" game, while the lower portion is a set completion. A good example of this might be the spelling of a word, like P E P S I. Cards are printed up with a number of covered boxes (or circles). nside each covered box is a number, or a letter, or even a picture. The box is covered with a material (graphite) that can be rubbed off with one's thumbnail, or a key or penny.

The customer buys a product from a newsstand. Along with the product (e.g. a pack of cigarettes) he/she finds a scratch card lightly adhered to the package. The customer will scratch off all his boxes to see if he can complete a known, and displayed word, like "bike," which is the grand prize of the promotion. If he rubs off "b i k e," he wins the grand prize. He might also rub off "c a p," and he wins a cap with the cigarette company logo on it. The instant win on the top of the card encourages the customer. The completion of a word at the bottom of the card stimulates repeat purchase (and loyalty).

The best feature is that the execution is easy. Retailers collect the cards from winners and send them to the promotion firm handling the promotion for the manufacturer. And the customer can easily perceive how it works and knows instantly if he/she is a winner.

Above is the scratch card for Pepsi's license lottery promotion.

Regulations for Pepsi's License Lottery

1. Print no less than ten times the number of cards for the number of customers you expect in your market area.
2. The ratio of winners should be on the basis of 1 per 100 cards sold (for lower level prizes), 1 per 1,000 for second level prizes, and 1 per 10,000 cards for top level prizes, or 10 percent winners (lowest level), .01 percent winners (middle level) and .001 percent for top level prizes.
3. Winners in the top level must scratch off the license plate letter/numbers that match the license plate on the display poster in the store where the cards are sold. If he matches, he wins (odds being 1 to 10,000) the car.
4. Winners in the lower level must scratch off five letters, completing the word, PEPSI, to win a second level prize, such as stereo equipment, an iPod or small television.
5. In the lowest section of the card the customers may uncover a symbol of the Pepsi logo. This is redeemable for a free Pepsi at the participating store.

Licensing

Licensing, when it is an integral, coordinated part of the marketing strategy, can be a powerful sales tool.

The main players of any licensing agreement are:

—The licensor (the property owner)

—The licensee (the purchaser of the rights to the property).

The types of properties are broad and various:

—**Sports:** athletes in almost all the competitive games: from golf to football.

—**Cartoon characters:** Super-Heroes (Spiderman), Hanna Barbera characters (Yogi Bear) Disney (Mickey Mouse), Sponge Bob Square Pants.

—**Music and Musicians:** Michael Jackson, Britney Spears, Madonna, Tina Turner.

—**Toys:** Barbie, G.I. Joe, Hot Wheels, Transformers, etc.

—**Fashion:** use of names on product/promotions, like Ralph Lauren, Donna Karan, etc.

Tina Turner has been a licensed promotional celebrity for Pepsi for years.

Usually when the licensed property is to be the central incentive in a sales promotion program, they buy the rights for a flat fee for a specified length of time. One of the advantages to the licensor is that it will generate awarenss of their properties, thus advertising the event or the person itself. These work well for new motion pictures that launch with a lot of publicity. Licensing programs work best when they are tied to some aspect of the product itself–**James Bond and 007** with toy cars that emulate the Bond BMW or Aston Martin, for instance.

Pepsi sponsored a number of Michael Jackson's concerts and tours, and had the use of his name and image for their ads.

Event Promotion Marketing

Events offer what no other medium can, entertainment tied to a product. They are complicated to put together, but when they work, the effect is powerful. Advantages: an exciting environment, total association with the sponsor, a captive and receptive audience, a chance to satisfy all the key players: trade, media, consumer and brand enhancement.

167

How it Works

Fundamentally, a sponsor is picked who associates with the event/property. It might be a rock star, a band, an athlete, the Super Bowl, or the Olympics. The sponsor, who usually pays handsomely, will be able to "trade-off" on the popularity of the event.

The first step is to identify the sponsor's objectives.
All event marketing is multidimensional and must be identified up front.

The second step is to plan and identify the strategy by which the objectives would be achieved.

Finally, **the last step**, is the execution.
Execution is the most important element in event marketing. It is important to work with professionals who have the experience to run a concert.

You will have to deal with such issues as:
—renting the concert hall
—setting up the ticket sales and advanced bookings
—hiring the talent who will play at the concert
—having security on site during the concert
—controlling the sale of beverages at the concert
—sales of premiums (albums, t-shirts, etc.) before and after the concert
—arranging for the press (TV, radio and newspaper) to cover the event

It is so complicated and dependent on experience and contacts, that you might want to hire a reliable manager to handle all of these details.

The Pepsi Resource book was created to help promotion managers around the world, plan, execute and evaluate their programs.

168

Choosing the Right Promotion Technique

A number of techniques have been listed and explained on the previous pages. They are all tried and true-tested by promotion marketers in all parts of the world. The difficult part is picking the right promotion technique for your product.

Promotion planning should be as carefully undertaken as any in the marketing mix.

Step One: Establish clear and concise objectives

Step Two: Develop a strategy to meet these objectives.

Step Three: Select the promotion techniques which best fit your strategy.

Incentive Techniques

All promotions, by their very nature, will offer an incentive to act, participate. Incentives are either instant, or delayed.

Instant means money back on the spot (or something of value: product, a t-shirt, etc.)

Delayed is self-evident.

Delayed Incentives	STRENGTHS	WEAKNESSES
1. CONTESTS/SWEEPS	• Can be set up quickly • All costs are known • Gives impression of activity, but at relatively low cost • Can stimulate displays • Stronger than self-liquidating premium offer • Sweeps attract attention	• Low consumer appeal • Usually no effect on sales • Sweeps illegal in many countries
2. IN-STORE LOTTERY	• Consumer excitement • Relatively low cost • Generates trade acceptance and displays	• Can be legal risk • Requires special handling
3. CASH REFUNDS (on mail-in basis)	• Can generate high levels of response • Can gain good trade support	• Needs to be high value to attract attention • Danger of higher redemption than anticipated • Pre-testing essential • Uncreative
4. FREE MAIL-IN PREMIUMS	• Can be strong volume builder • Can offer consumer genuine value • Very flexible technique adaptable to many needs • Can be distinctive	• Pre-testing essential • Danger of redemption miscalculation
5. SELF-LIQUIDATING PREMIUMS	• Very low cost • Can help gain displays • Creates impression of activity but at low budget level	• Usually, very low consumer and trade interest • Involve greater set-up effort than results justify • Severely over-used technique in developed markets
6. COLLECTION	• Inexpensive • Repeat purchase encouraged • Creative opportunities	• Heavily used technique

Guerrilla Marketing

This subject is discussed in Chapter 12. It is a bit hard to categorize, being new, but probably it should be considered a promotion technique.

Examples abound.

In the 1980s my firm developed a program in which Pepsi put brand logos and images on Volkswagen Beetles to promote their family of soft drinks. The cars were "borrowed" from college students and young working people, painted white and then decorated with giant Pepsi decals. These same (now decorated) cars were leased back to their driver/owners to use on their daily trips around their cities and campuses. The cars became "moving billboards" and were a highly successful guerrilla marketing campaign.

Here are more examples.

A company in Paris places ads under the glass of the small tables used by the cafés and bars that border their lovely boulevards. A company in Berlin places ads on paper towels that you can read as they are pulled from their dispensers in public restrooms. Taxi cabs in New York City now carry advertising messages on the back of the driver's seat and on the roof. All are examples of guerrilla marketing in action.

You can find guerrilla techniques everywhere, including: hot air balloons, sidewalk painting, coffee cup holders, computer mousepads, ATM screens, waste bin covers, t-shirts, NASCAR racing cars and driver's uniforms, matchbook covers, beer coasters, sun shades and signs on the sides of buses.

Ethics

Promotion is the element in the marketing mix that raises the most ethical issues.

Promotion gets a bad rap.

Hollywood has personified a promotions man as a "huckster," one who sells anything for a buck, with false promises and hustle. There is some truth to this illustration, at least the way Hollywood practices it.

In New York taxi cabs often carry advertising messages on car tops.

Publicity campaigns to promote a new movie, on air plugs, TV and radio programs, are all examples of the bottom rung of sales promotion. You could say the same for the auto industry, with its banners, hype and special holiday sales, which always seem to expire sometime in the following week. It is associated with what is called "Whistles and Balloons" premiums of questionable value given out just for entering the dealership. Wall Street hasn't helped the image. Promoters who hype a stock using inflated or unreasonable numbers are as guilty as used car salesmen. The practice of sales promotion is far more disciplined, sequential and close to advertising in its planning and execution than one might imagine.

The practice of sales promotion is also mandated and controlled by law, by the Robinson-Patman Act.

Robinson-Patman Act

This Act was created by congress in 1936 to put a curb on unethical practices, resulting in unfair trade practices that victimized the customer. Their initial goal was to prevent discriminatory practices when using promotional allowances in the sales of commodities in interstate commerce. In practice, it is intended to prevent discriminatory pricing and price fixing and to maintain open and free trade.

Basically the Act is intended to prevent a manufacturer from giving more help in any form to one retailer over another.

The Robinson-Patman Act is one of three which are considered America's "antitrust laws."

Guidelines to Planning a Fast Food Promotion

The same degree of careful planning and consideration that must go into selecting a new store location, is required in planning a promotion for a food service establishment. This is a step by step process and very necessary to achieve an effective promotion marketing method. Success depends on thoroughness. Don't attempt to hurry or short cut the process.

Process	Do	Don't
Step 1 **Establish the promotion *objectives***	1. Be specific *Example: Build breakfast sales on Mondays* 2. Identify one major objective 3. Have an objective that is measurable. *Example: You must be able to read the results of your promotion objective to build breakfast sales on Mondays.*	• Don't be vague, too broad or general. *Example: To build sales* • Don't try to achieve more than one objective at a time. • Don't try to tackle an objective that cannot be achieved with reasonable effort and time. • Don't expect inspiration to hit you like a bolt from the blue.
Step 2 ***Evaluate* the promotion objective**	1. Ask yourself: a) Will accomplishing the objective do something worthwhile to the business. b) Is the objective "do-able." c) Will the costs be properly related to the reward.	
Step 3 **Develop the promotion *strategy***	1. Identify certain guidelines to help you achieve the promotion objectives. *Example: Is advertising support needed? What is the target market profile? Select the time of year for the promotion.*	
Step 4 ***Create* the idea**	1. Get in the "promotion frame of mind." Raise your level of consciousness. 2. Look at what is going on in magazines, newspapers etc. 3. Talk to people 4. Look for help from suppliers and vendors.	

The other two are: the Sherman Act of 1890 and the Clayton Act of 1914. Together the three acts make doing business in America one of the fairest in the world.

The Robinson-Patman Act was created, initially, to curb demonstrations. In 1969 the U.S. Supreme Court ordered the Federal Trade Commission (FTC) to write and enforce guidelines for the use of advertising and promotional allowances. These guidelines are known as the "Meyer Guides."

Coop Advertising

Cooperative advertising is closely watched by the FTC, the enforcing body of the Robinson-Patman Act. In principle cooperative advertising is simple–the sharing of advertising costs between the retailer and supplier. It can be effective, is legal, and varies from year to year in popularity.

When a manufacturer establishes a relationship with a retailer, he will probably also establish a co-op ad program. The manufacturer will pay all or a portion of the retailer ad costs, if he, the retailer, uses the materials the manufacturer supplies, and advertises up to a mutually agreed frequency. The retailer usually retains the control of media used, timing and content. The goal is to attract customers to the retailer's stores. The goal for the manufacturer is to attract customers to buy his product from the stores involved in the program. The ads are the tools. Ethics is a larger issue than simply providing a level playing field for business. It raises the issue of influencing customers who may not be old enough or strong enough to regulate their behavior as a result. Cigarette advertising has been outlawed on television because it encourages kids to smoke. Camels has been restrained in the use of its Joe Camel campaign, which proved too effective in getting new customers from some ethnic market groups.

Pepsi/Grease promotional tie-in with Paramount Pictures gave consumers the chance to get movie tickets by collecting Pepsi bottle caps.

Liquor advertising on television is another controversial area. Beer marketers advertise heavily on TV and spend far more on advertising in print and outdoor media than any other group. Finally, there is the issue of exaggeration. All ads and promotions exaggerate to some extent, it's the nature of the beast. Consumers can usually tell, and they accept it. Sometimes however, the exaggeration goes too far, when claims of benefits or efficacy of a drug, for instance, promise too much.

As a result there is another controlling act–the Uniform Commercial Code–which standardizes sales and business practices throughout the U.S. Essentially, it obliges the company to stand behind its claim.

Two Basic Marketing Methods

Not many years ago only advertising was king. Manufacturers of consumer products concentrated on advertising to focus the retailer to handle the products and to pull the customer into the stores where their products were sold. This is classic "pull marketing."

"Push marketing" is what sales promotion is all about and now consumes as much as 40 percent of the annual marketing budget. The promotion budget for a company like Procter & Gamble could be as much as one third of its advertising budget.

A Different Approach

Sometimes promotion programs and their materials take a different approach – usually dictated by the nature of the product or service or the prospective audience being solicited. If the concept is not price related, or calendar related (i.e. "Buy One, Get One Free, or This Offer Ends Next Week!"), the message and the method is different, more nuanced.

The promotion pitch for subjects such as: an expensive townhouse on Fifth Avenue in New York, or a fancy condo on the beach in Hilton Head would fit this category. There would be no reference to a time frame and maybe to the price at all, but the location and the ambiance would be emphasized.

The examples on the next page are still other, more indirect, less aggressive promotions.

A Different Promotional Approach

1) **The Ludwig Institute for Cancer Research:** promotes the good research work of the institute in seeking the answer to the disease, and the appeal is for funding.

2) **Carnegie Hall:** is an appeal to corporations to sponsor (buy) a performance at the famous concert hall, thus burnishing their image with their customers.

3) **CBS:** the promotion of a TV documentary tells the story of the making of the film but also the CBS commitment to the arts, literature and quality programming. The inference is to purchase advertising time on the show.

4) **Dupont/Lycra:** fiber companies have a special marketing problem. They must promote to the mills that weave the cloth (which is ultimately bought by the design/retail houses, and then the customers). This brochure featured the glories of Lycra (the firm's elastic fiber). To further emphasize comfort benefits, a sports shirt and slacks were included in the promotion package, selected to the general size requirements of each individual buyer.

5) **Pepsi-Cola:** the goal is to educate marketing managers and directors outside the United States in new, tested promotional techniques. It was a quarterly magazine written, printed and distributed for over eleven years.

All were brochures and all were designed by my firm.

8

THE COLA WARS

They Never End

Coke arrived first, in a south that was still recovering from the effects of the Civil War. A former Confederate cavalry officer named John Styth Pemberton created Coke in May of 1886. Both before and after the war Pemberton worked as a druggist, living and working in Atlanta, Georgia. For some six months following the war he had been searching for a patent medicine that didn't rely on alcohol to relieve headache, nausea or indigestion. Pemberton felt if he could invent one without alcohol, and it worked, he'd have a hot product. Other southern inventors had been pursuing the same goal, such as Dr. Tucker's Specific and Dr. Mitchell's Coca-bola, or Nyal's Compound Extract of Damiana, all of which made liberal use of cocaine and opium. Cocaine, by the way, was not illegal in those days–quite the opposite. Doctors in the late nineteenth century prescribed it regularly for nervous conditions, or chronic pain.

Pemberton wanted to form a company, and he needed backers. He solicited his friends and contacts, and perhaps because he was a recognized Confederate war hero, he succeeded. With $160,000, The Pemberton Chemical Company was formed. His early experiments centered around removing the alcohol from a popular French product called "Vin Martiani," a Bordeaux wine laced with whole-leaf cocoa.

Secret Formula

Pemberton labored long, brewing his concoctions in a large brass kettle over a fire behind his laboratory. He was constantly adding or subtracting extracts–trying to improve the taste. Finally in May he hit on a combination of oils and flavors of the extracts that he liked. This combination became the base formula of Coca-Cola.

What he hit on, what resulted, stems from some interesting base ingredients.

Coco leaves were regularly imported from Bolivia to the United States in the 1870s, and the basic plant, the Coco Plant, is the same from which cocaine is derived. To do so, one must refine and process it in a certain manner to create actual cocaine.

The other main ingredient was the Cola Nut, which came from West Africa, first introduced by the slaves that chewed the leaf to increase their work effort. So, two natural agricultural products, popular with nineteenth century Bolivian indians and West African natives, became the base ingredients of Coca-Cola.

Other ingredients were: sugar, caffeine, which came from the Cola extract derived from cola nuts, and oil of cinnamon, oil of coriander, citrus oils, vanilla, water and lime juice.

How do the ingredients of today compare to the ingredients in 2004?

From the label of a 2006, 8-fluid ounce bottle of Coke Classic, we find:

Carbonated water	Natural flavors
High fructose corn syrup	Sugar (27 grams)
Sucrose caramel	Acid
Caffeine	Sodium (1%)
Carbohydrates (9%)	

Pemberton's next step was to market it.

In June of 1886, he and his colleagues sold it into several Atlanta drugstores and it was billed as a "Temperance Drink." It was a thick, dark syrup, and needed to be mixed with water to drink. They packaged their brew in pint-sized beer bottles.

It worked, it relieved headaches, but is still was flat.

One day a customer came into Jacob's Drug Store and wanting instant relief for a headache, asked the counter man to mix him a glassful on the spot. The counter man accidentally used the soda water that was on tap, and effervescent Coca-Cola resulted and it was good! Soon it was copied all around town.

Coca-Cola helped alleviate more than just headaches, it became a symbol.

From the beginning it was very well marketed, and today it can be found in almost any store, luncheonette, fast-food restaurant (not linked to Pepsi) or sports arena in the world. Because of its marketing effort, Coke has found a place for itself that is on a higher plane than all other soft drinks. In the next 100 years Coke became synonymous with America and what America stands for: baseball, jazz, apple pie, the good life, optimism, the flag, and much more. The beverage entered many worlds not normally associated with a soft drink–like, the movies, paintings, sculpture, books and songs. It became a portable, refreshing, convenient symbol of America around the world.

It became its own creation, **"The Pause that Refreshes."**

Asa Candler Takes Over

The next owner of the secret formula was Asa Candler, in 1888. Candler was a very ambitious, vigorous man and he began marketing the product big time. His goal was to sell Coke to every soda fountain he could. Soda fountains, like Jacobs in Atlanta, or the Penn Drug Company, in Sidney, Iowa, were very fancy places with marble counters, gilt-edged mirrors, decorative iron chairs, checked tablecloths at round tables and the customers often dressed up for the occasion. They were truly social centers and most elaborate. Mahogany walls, large baskets of fruit overflowed on tables, sometimes dozens of silver spigots blossomed out of the marble counters. The drinks were served from glasses set in silver-plated holders by a pharmacist who wore a white jacket and a black bow tie. They were egalitarian, a place where men, women and children could gather around the marble and polished onyx counters, enjoy ice cream and visit. It was the south's version of a European spa, like Baden-Baden, without the music by Strauss.

There were many syrup-based beverages on the market at this time, but few had the drive of an Asa Candler behind them. He traveled throughout the south, pushing Coca-Cola as a "Brain Tonic that would cure headaches, exhaustion and jangled nerves."
By 1889 Candler had made Coke into a megabrand, 2,171 gallons of syrup sold to soda fountains. By 1894 sales topped 64,000 gallons.

Yet, as popular as these soda fountains were, it wasn't until Coke was bottled that the product really became a nationwide beverage.

Bottles Make the Scene

A new partner of Asa Candler, Joseph Biedenharn (from Vicksburg, Tennessee) began experimenting with putting Coke in bottles. He needed a bottle that was airtight and portable and found it in something called a "Hutchinson bottle."
These ingenious bottles had a rubber stopper attached to a wire that could be yanked up into the bottle's neck after it was filled, and which would seal the contents.
When a person wanted to open a Hutchinson bottle he would smack the stopper down into the bottle with his palm and a "Pop" sound would occur, caused by the escaping carbonated gas. That sound is how "Soda Pop" got its name–synonymous with a sweet, fizzy drink that came from a bottle.

The Hourglass Bottle

While Coke was now a national drink, it still had no standard bottle. Asa held a contest for the best designed bottle. A number of designers responded to the opportunity and Candler had many to choose from.

He selected the design submitted by Earl Dean, a man who worked for the Root Glass Company of Terre Haute, Indiana. It was shaped like an hourglass, made of thick green glass, and patented in 1915 and approved by Coke management in 1916.

Three years later every Coke bottler was using the new bottle. Designer Dean felt he was emulating the look of a coco bean when he put ribs down the sides and top, leading to a heavy, fat base.

By the 1920s Coca-Cola had become bottle-oriented. Five years later (1925) more coke was sold in bottles than at soda fountains. Candler knew it was the future.

Pepsi Comes On Stage

The year was 1893. It was also the old south.

Caleb B. Brabham started a pharmacy in New Bern, North Carolina. The main money maker for Brabham was his popular soda fountain, a true social center for the small town on the Trent River.

Like Coke's Pemberton seven years earlier, Brabham loved to tinker with new concoctions to sell in his soda fountain. One of his elixirs became an early favorite. It was a combination of sugar, vanilla, oils, spices and the African Cola nut. It was advertised as a remedy for dyspepsia and peptic ulcers.

He knew he needed a catchy name and that same year he created one: "Pepsi-Cola."

Nine years passed before he incorporated the Pepsi-Cola Company, with the corporate address as the back room of his drugstore. He had early success and in the first year after incorporation sold 7,696 gallons of syrup–$1,888.78 worth.

He also advertised from the start.

Brabham, like Asa Candler, was able to capitalize on the temperance movement that was gripping the south. He had early success as a substitute for alcoholic drinks. Also like Candler, he grew by expansion–selling franchises across the nation. By 1909 he had assembled a bottler network of 250 companies in twenty-four states.

The rosy future of Pepsi-Cola was undercut by World War I. The war affected manufacturing–causing the cost of labor and materials to soar. Sugar was the worst–jumping from 5 1/2 cents a pound, to 22 1/2 cents a pound during the war, which caught Pepsi and its bottlers in a deadly squeeze. Caleb Brabham couldn't keep up and in 1922 he went bankrupt.

The next to try his hand at Pepsi-Cola was Roy C. Magargel, a Wall Street financier. He bought the trademark and assets from the ruins and started a new Pepsi-Cola company in Richmond, Virginia. He couldn't revive the company and meet the staggering expenses and in 1932 Pepsi went bankrupt again.

The third, and this time successful savior, was Charles Guth, owner and CEO of Loft, Inc., a bustling candy company located in Long Island City, NY.

Guth had the financial base from his candy company to fund the third start-up of Pepsi–this time in New York.

Even though Pepsi was a puny competitor to Coke, the Atlanta company decided to harass the new owner with a lawsuit. Coke sent spies to the Loft stores in New York to confirm that customers were being served Pepsi when they wanted Coke. Guth countered by sending his own spies to Atlanta to claim that Coke had made up these charges just to harass and malign Pepsi-Cola. The struggle went to court, where it wasn't decided until 1942.

This was probably the opening salvo in the Cola Wars.

The weapons used in the Cola Wars were matched on each side, but not always equally. They were: Advertising, Packaging, Promotion, Salesmanship, Political maneuvering and Legal Activity.

Twelve Full Ounces, That's A Lot

Charles Guth was an impatient, ego-driven despot and he soon tired of his new company-and wanted out. It appeared that Pepsi was about to fold for the third time when a bottle dealer suggested to Guth that Pepsi be packaged in used beer bottles. The problem was that all beer bottles at this time were 12-ounces, while Coke's were only 6-ounces–the standard size for soft drinks. The bottler argued that this was an actual advertising advantage–that Pepsi could fill the extra 6 ounces of soda for little extra expenses, and offer it to the public under the advertising headline, "twice as much, and a nickel too." The concept of twice as much for the same money was compelling, they tried it and sales of Pepsi soared.

Guth learned some early lessons: first, that sales were a direct result of promotion, packaging and price, and second, that expansion would drive volume. He put both principles into practice, sought new bottlers and by 1934 he even had one in Montreal, Canada.

Despite his success and much needed aggressiveness, the Pepsi-Cola Board wanted a new style of leadership. They went looking for a new chief executive.

They found what they were looking for in Walter Staunton Mack, Jr., one of the partners of The Phoenix Securities Company. He proved to be a good chief executive and reigned for the next ten years.

Mack was good for Pepsi. He was a big, imposing man, given to wearing bowlers or wide-brimmed straw hats. He was outgoing, friendly and very much the showman. He brought the beleaguered brand a much-needed sense of style and identity.

The Cola Wars broke out a second time in 1938 when Coke sued Pepsi for trademark violation. Coke claimed that Pepsi couldn't use the word "cola," which belonged to them.

Pepsi countered that the word "cola" was generic, that neither company could protect, or claim it as proprietary. Mack and Coke CEO, Robert Woodruff settled the matter over breakfast at the Waldorf. Coke agreed and signed off on an agreement to never attack the Pepsi-Cola trademark in the United States.

Peaceful coexistence didn't last long, however. Coke tried again, this time suing for trademark infringement in Canada–and it went all the way to the British Privy Council. Mack traveled to London to argue his side of the case and his lawyer was the celebrated politician, Wendell Wilkie The Privy Council decided in favor of Pepsi and required that both companies coexist in peace.

The Two Cola Giants in WWII

In 1941 America went to war and Robert Woodruff executed a brilliant strategy. He declared

Illustrated ad from the 1940s shows Air Force pilots from America and China enjoying a Coke after a mission.

that the Coca-Cola Company would make Coke available to American servicemen for a nickel a bottle–anywhere in the world. This grand gesture impressed Secretary of State George Marshall, who informed area commanders that they could order entire bottling plants directly to the front lines along with food and ammunition. It was felt that the presence of Coca-Cola on the front lines was a morale booster. Coca-Cola became synonymous with a "slice of America," a symbol for which the soldiers fought. Such a gesture left a mark on the hearts of the American public and became the core of the enduring relationship between the brand and the nation. During the course of the war Coke established sixty-four bottling plants just behind allied lines. Beginning in North Africa and moving up into Italy, the bottling plants followed the battlefronts, picking up and relocating as the fighting advanced through Europe. Plants were established in France, Germany, India and the Philippines. General Dwight Eisenhower was a big fan and demanded abundant supplies of Coke wherever the armies went.

Coke's German market was well established and popular, even before hostilities broke out. Bottling plants had begun to appear throughout Germany, France and Belgium, and Max Keith, a German bottler, managed to continue to bring Coke syrup in with the help of Air Marshal Hermann Goring. As the war got hotter, the flow of syrup finally got cut, but Herr Keith managed to create a similar tasting formula from available ingredients, which he named "Fanta." The name survives and is still sold to this day (2008). When the bombings grew intense, Keith moved his bottling operations to the countryside and the beverage continued.

Near the end of the war Max Keith was liberated by the U.S. Marines.

Coke's wartime status was the best public relations campaign that a company could imagine-establishing the beverage as the symbol of America. Coke had become the deity of consumer products. Woodruff's decision to supply the war effort was a marketing stroke of genius.

Pepsi Fights Back

Meanwhile, up in New York, Pepsi CEO Walter Mack was making plans to beat Coke at its own game. He was energetic, combative and imaginative–qualities he would need to accomplish his task.

In the late 1930s Pepsi still had a lackluster image, which Mack determined to fix. He hired an advertising agency named Newell-Emmett and then promptly wrote his own jingle. Against the agency's objections he put it on air at independent stations in New York and New Jersey. The jingle was genius and quickly became famous. A survey conducted in 1942 revealed that the Pepsi jingle (Mack's jingle) was the best known tune in America. In one stroke Mack had changed the tone of radio advertising, and had given Pepsi a big shot in the arm.

The jingle was called **"Twice as Much for a Nickel"**

The words were:

"Pepsi-Cola Hits the Spot
Twelve full ounces, that's a lot
Twice as much, for a nickel, too,
Pepsi-Cola is the drink for you."

(the tune was from the British ballad, John Peel)

The jingle was played an estimated six million times on over 450 radio stations nationwide. Next he moved the headquarters office from Long Island City to fashionable space on 57th Street in Manhattan.

181

Mack loved promotions, like art shows, square dances, scholarships and community activities. He even tried sky-writing, hiring pilots to write Pepsi-Cola in smoke in the skies above America's major cities. He got celebrity cartoonists like Peter Arno to come up with funny and racy drawings for magazines like *The New Yorker*. And during the war Pepsi sponsored the "Portraits of America," in which servicemen could have their portraits drawn or painted by name illustrators like Norman Rockwell and James Montgomery Flagg and sent home. By 1947 Mack approved an advertising budget of $4,500,000, up from $600,000 in 1939 but still peanuts against Coke's $15 million a year.

His energy, imagination, and marketing efforts were working, however, and by the end of World War II Pepsi was the second most popular soft drink in the nation, having passed Dr. Pepper, Royal Crown Cola and Seven Up.

Despite these successes, Pepsi was still a long way from catching Coke.

Pepsi's sales had leveled off at $45 million, and earnings were modest. Coke outsold Pepsi by a five to one margin at home and approximately four to one outside the U.S.

Pepsi Changes Leaders

Walter Mack was running out of ideas, and maybe energy. He had run Pepsi for more than ten years, and his spirit, imagination and tenacity had been the major reason it was now the second most popular soft drink in America.

In 1949 the Pepsi Board of Directors decided to change leaders.

In a few more months they were able to elevate Mack to Chairman of the Board and make a successful offer to a Coca-Cola Director, Al Steele, to take over the CEO job. They gave him a free hand to do and try anything to give Pepsi a competitive edge.

Steele was good for Pepsi also, but he had a rocky start. For years, thanks to the Nickel campaign, it was perceived as the "bargain" drink, not necessarily the quality drink of choice. Clearly Pepsi had to revamp its image, or raise its price.

Steele began by redesigning the 12-ounce bottle. He made it sleeker, more modern looking. This fit with his new strategy, to go for dominance in take-home sales.

By 1950 sales had increased significantly and they had 120 company-owned bottling plants in fifty countries.

Steele played the political game as well, currying favor with Republicans. Coke favored the Democrats. When a Republican was in the White House, deals could be struck for bottling plants in foreign countries, and vice versa.

In 1955 Steele married film star Joan Crawford and she proved a genuine asset. She was brilliant at bottler conventions; she wooed the shareholders and flirted with the bottlers. "She played the part magnificently," said Pepsi's public relations officer Robert Windt. She relished her new role of being Pepsi's "first lady" and freely used Windt as her advance man. The two worked well together from 1959 to 1965. She made whirlwind tours to bottling plants and openings, drawing bottlers from an entire region for a Pepsi event. She brought glamour to the product and the business. The press loved her.

Al Steele died in 1959, after a strenuous traveling public relations tour.

Steele, like Mack, had been good for Pepsi. Under his leadership nearly 30 percent of all soft drinks sold nationally were Pepsi's. He had closed the cola gap and was outsold by Coke by only a narrow margin.

The Moscow Trade Fair

Steele's biggest public relations event, which he never lived to see, was the trade fair in Moscow.

It was called the American International Exposition, sponsored by the State Department and the U.S. Information Agency. The show was to be a display of the consumer might of the United States before the Russian people. Steele talked the State Department into including a portable soft-drink plant, where on one side they would make Coke, the other, Pepsi. Coke declined because they didn't want to appear side by side with Pepsi. Donald

The 1959 Moscow Trade Fair
(L to R) Don Kendall, Nikita Khruschev, Richard
Nixon and a party official sampling a Pepsi-Cola.

Kendall, a Steele protégée and head of Pepsi's overseas operations, spearheaded it and in October of 1959 Pepsi and 200 other U.S. companies put on their show.

Kendall had only one goal, to get a Pepsi-Cola into the hands of Khruschev and have it photographed. He arranged for Vice President Richard Nixon to steer Russian Premier Nikita Khruschev to the Pepsi booth. He did, and the cameras caught it.

Khruschev liked Pepsi, quaffing seven in total. It was a public relations bonanza!

This move, and its worldwide publicity with Khruschev holding and drinking the beverage of the "decadent" capitalistic center of the world, also assured Don Kendall of his ultimate position as CEO of Pepsi. Kendall was a salesman's salesman. He made liberal use of his powerful contacts from the start.

One of these was, of course, Richard Nixon, who was out of office but now serving as Kendall's attorney. As Nixon pursued his interests, and ultimately the White House, Kendall benefited, particularly from Nixon's international contacts. Another area in which Kendall was well connected was to big business. In September of 1964 Kendall bought the company that made Mountain Dew.

In 1965 Kendall merged the Pepsi-Cola Company with the Frito-Lay Company of Dallas, a move which protected Pepsi from a takeover move by CBS (rumored at the time) and gave the firm much needed diversification. "Potato chips make you thirsty, Pepsi satisfies thirst," so said Don Kendall. One of his strategies was to strengthen the company through diversification and mergers.

Keeping Burger King
By John Gillin, Senior Vice President with Coca-Cola

I held a number of marketing jobs at the company (Coca-Cola) and was Marketing VP for the Fountain Division in 1980 when Don Keough, Coke's legendary President and COO, told me we were about to lose our second largest customer, Burger King, to Pepsi. Don sent me to talk to the President of Burger King to try to save the business. As I left, Don said: "You have the worldwide resources of this company behind you... keep that business." I did. I promised Burger King a better marketing plan than they currently had and we delivered on it and kept the business.

That set my career in a whole new direction. The company now regarded me as someone who had a unique ability to retain major customers.

The War Heats Up

By the beginning of the 1980s, the struggle between Coke and Pepsi was more than standard business to business competition, it had become personal. Pepsi was determined to catch "King Coke," and Coke wasn't about to relinquish first place.

Pepsi's sales force jargon took on military tones, such as speaking of fighting Coke for share as "invading" Coke's markets, or referring to their sales force as "Shock Troops, or Panzer Units." Coke was also diversifying and merging. They acquired Minute Maid Company, in an exchange for stock, and set up a separate division for the company in Houston, Texas, called Coke Foods. At this time Coke's share of market was 30.4 percent, while Pepsi's was only 14.3.

Coke/Pepsi Marketing Strategies

The two soft drink giants have always maintained opposite views in their marketing strategies-as expressed by their advertising and promotions. It can be seen most clearly in their positioning. In its advertising, Coca-Cola attempts to become the manifestation of a metaphor between the refreshment of its soft drink, and the good life of the (American) people who enjoy it. In other words, the good life is Coke.

Pepsi-Cola in its association with Michael Jackson (or Britney Spears or rock music) is attempting to link the enjoyment of its beverage with a kind of edgy, iconoclastic, thrilling world that is slightly dangerous. Pepsi is definitely (intentionally) not your parent's choice of a soda and thus, becomes highly appealing, a badge brand of teenage rebellion. In other words, living dangerously is Pepsi.

Both Pepsi's and Coke's points of view are broadly divergent, yet both work, in their own way, are brilliant conceptions.

Pepsi and Coke ads present divergent versions of life itself, coached in choice. These can be: happiness vs. sadness, we vs. them, cool vs. un-cool, in-style vs. out-of-style, turned on vs. turned off. And the commercials or print ads or promotions then suggest the same solution: consume our product. At the time their marketing position(s) were represented in their ad slogans. The difference is evident:

Glorify the Product (Coke) vs. Exemplify the User (Pepsi)

Advertising Tag Lines:

Coke's:

1907: Good to the last Drop
1920s: The Pause That Refreshes and Thirst Knows No Season
1940s: Everything Your Thirst Could Ask For
1950s: The Best is Always the Better Buy
1960s: Things Go Better With Coke
1970s: It's The Real Thing and Coke is It
1980s: Coke Is It
and today: Coca-Cola Now

Pepsi's:

1939: Twice As Much for a Nickel Too and Pepsi-Cola Hits the Spot
1940s: Why Take Less when Pepsi is Best
1950s: Be Sociable, Have a Pepsi Day
1960s: 70s: You've Got a Lot to Live, Pepsi's Got a Lot to Give
1970s-80s: Come Alive, You're in the Pepsi Generation
1980s: The Choice of a New Generation
and Today: Generation Next

You've got a lot to live
Pepsi's got a lot to give

185

Pepsi and Coke Go Global

By the middle of the 1980s both companies were well ensconced in foreign markets. Coke dominated Europe for the most part, while Pepsi dominated the Middle East and the Russian republics. Asia was more in balance, although Pepsi only had about a 6 percent share. Latin America was dominated by Pepsi, although individual markets were often in play. In the mid 1990s, for example, Coke managed to steal Venezuela out from under Pepsi's nose.

A Venetian Gondolier delivers Pepsi to a market outside the Gritti Palace.

Keeping Up with Coca Cola
By Pedro Vergara, Chairman Emeritus- Promos S.A., Santiago, Chile

In 1982 I moved from Porto Alegre, Brazil, to Purchase, New York, to take over the job of Promotions Marketing Manager of Pepsi-Cola International.

The situation I inherited at Pepsi was of great concern to me. Sales Promotions were being launched and executed with little pre-planning, with no evident discipline as to expenses, and there existed no process in place to measure the effectiveness of the promotion after the event. If Bolivia had what appeared to be a popular UTC (Under the Crown Promotion), then Colombia, or Costa Rica would simply copy it. It was a free-for-all. And Pepsi lost money through needless expenses, poor planning and worst of all, gained little or no market share. In any case we couldn't tell because there were no post-promotion programs in place to measure them. It was frankly, a mess.

We were a headquarters department responsible for all of Pepsi's promotion planning and execution for 57 countries. Every week I would get requests from as many as 70 regional market managers, looking for new ideas.

My staff consisted of one experienced secretary, one consultant, and soon a young assistant.

I doubt if we were any match for Coke's promotional efforts anywhere in the world.

I began by instituting an overall two-part plan: focused on (1) better communications between country marketing directors and headquarters, and (2) a clearly defined Promotion Planning process.

Better Communications: involved reviving a small but well-targeted promotion magazine so that ideas could be shared from one office or country to another. For example, when Spain ran a TV show with Disney-like cartoon characters from the legend of Don Quixote, I made these films and promotion opportunities available to Spanish speaking countries in Latin America.

Better Promotion Planning: involved setting up guidelines for planning and executing a sales promotion campaign. I directed the creation of a Promotional Resource Book which would direct future planning of promotions along an organized, measurable process. When the field offices called in for ideas I was able to control the planning, execution and post-promotion analysis.

It took about three years, but I got the department on an organized, functioning basis.

By the mid-80s the Cola Wars had been raging for fifty years and showed no sign of letting up.

THE COLA WARS

The story of the global corporate battle between the Coca-Cola Company and PepsiCo Inc.

J.C. Louis and Harvey Yazijian

Taste Tests

It started modestly in Dallas and was to have far reaching effects for both companies. In April of 1975 Pepsi unveiled an unusual promotion, largely out of frustration at their the low 6 percent share of the Texas market. It was called "The Pepsi Challenge." Pepsi invited customers (in shopping malls) to participate in the test by drinking and choosing between two unidentified cola drinks marked "Q" and "M" while a hidden camera rolled. The surprising result was that Pepsi won this "blind taste test" each time by a decent margin. The hidden camera became the core of a series of commercials, which they then aired on local Dallas TV. "More Coke drinkers like Pepsi than Coke," was the tag line of each commercial. It might have blown over had Coke not over-reacted.

Coke responded vigorously and from 1979 to 1980 publicly challenged everything Pepsi said and did. Coke churned out a blizzard of statements to refute the challenge–such comments as "It takes more than one sip to appreciate a Coke, or that most people have a psychological preference for the letter M over the letter Q." No one believed the excuses proffered. They ran ads with Bill Cosby, selling Coke as "The Real Thing." They redesigned their vending machines, increased promotional activity in supermarkets, and came out with yet another new slogan, "Coke Is It!"

BBDO, Pepsi's agency sensed a weakness and responded with a new set of taste tests using the letter L and S, and the result (of the taste test) was still favorable for Pepsi.

Coke responded with a satirical spot spoofing the test. Now Pepsi knew it had found a genuine weakness. They took the Challenge to eleven cities in the next year, boosting Pepsi's sales and badly frightening Coke's bottlers. Newspapers picked it up and this was the first time the term "Cola Wars" came into general usage.

Pepsi was about to take its Challenge Campaign outside the United States and my firm was intimately involved.

Patrick Duffy (Bobby Ewing) was Pepsi's spokesperson in Spain in 1982

Dallas Captures Spain

In the early summer of 1982 the marketing manager of Spain decided to launch the first taste test challenge in his country and he wanted to wrap it in the proven popularity of the hit TV show, *Dallas*. I was asked to fly to Dallas and sign their romantic lead, Patrick Duffy (who played the lovable Bobby Ewing). On a blistering 100-degree day in July, I turned up on the TV set at the ranch. We had a memorable meeting in his trailer just off the set - which turned very negative when I told him I only had $5,000 to offer him (as his fee) for spending a week promoting the Spain Challenge. I was immediately ushered out of his air-conditioned trailer and into the Texas heat. With permission, I hung around and at the end of the day Mr. Duffy beckoned me over. I followed him into the ranch house and he produced two cold beers (a good sign I thought) and we sat down. He said he'd been thinking it over, that he did want to do something with Pepsi and wondered what else might be possible. I indicated that outside of more money, anything was possible. o, after a little haggling and for a few extra perks (like taking his wife and agent and friends to Spain for a slightly extended stay) he did sign the contract and the campaign went forward. It was to be called "Accepta El Reto Pepsi," which means "Take the Pepsi Challenge."

Happily the promotion was a big success and Patrick did a splendid job, reacting warmly to the crowds who followed him through the streets of Toledo, or applauding when he did an impromptu Flamenco Dance at a nightclub in Madrid. He was in the newspapers every day and the extra cost of the perquisites I had granted to sweeten the deal were forgiven by Pepsi management.

Pepsi liked the results and tried it again with a taste test in Germany in 1983, called "Mach den Pepsi Test!"

It was bitterly contested by Coke, which interpreted German law as forbidding comparative advertising or promotions between two rival brands. Pepsi fought them in court and introduced a third brand into the contest–the popular but smaller brand of soft drink, Sinalco. It went all the way to the German Superior Court, which finally ruled in favor of Pepsi. This promotion ran the same way as Spain's except that we staged it in city centers in Bavaria rather than outside grocery stores, and the results were again much in favor of Pepsi over Coke. The Pepsi Challenge was doing damage to Coke's image and more practically–sales and share.

The reality was that the actual difference between Pepsi and Coke was not in the products, per se, it was in the images put forth in their advertising.
But, of course, Pepsi didn't stop and Challenge ran in many more countries in the next years.

Project Kansas
Coke Chairman Robert Goizueta felt he had to do something about the Pepsi Challenge. His bottlers and top marketing officers were demanding it. Too many market surveys showed Pepsi creeping up on Coke. In January of 1985 Pepsi sales figures for 1984 revealed that its market share had increased in the U.S. by 0.7 percent, while Coke's share had been cut by 3.1 percent.

The Pepsi Taste Test was equally successful in Germany in 1983.

They ran taste tests at Coke headquarters, and determined that Pepsi wasn't lying. In blind taste tests in Atlanta, consumers also responded in favor of Pepsi. It was definitely sweeter. Apparently people liked it.

Goizueta commissioned a top secret plan to be led by Sergio Zyman, Coke's marketing chief, and a small group of trusted top executives. It was code named "Project Kansas."

Zyman, a former Pepsi manager, had joined Coke in the late 1970s and distinguished himself straightaway by directing the marketing behind the successful launch of Diet Coke. Zyman was well suited to the task. He had a fresh outlook, he was smart and assertive. His thinking was original, not immersed in the traditions ingrained in most Coke officers.

He conducted research. The goal was to come up with a new formula and introduce a "new" coke. First he had to find a new taste. Not an easy task.

Formula change

Evidently the breakthrough in Project Kansas came from the R&D people that created Diet Coke. The company's chemists tried reversing the traditional method of making a soft drink. They substituted sugar for high-fructose corn syrup, which gave it a smoother taste. They also reduced what they called, "Merchandise No. 4," phosphoric acid, and added citric acid, which had a less biting taste. They also adjusted the caramel, caffeine and vanilla and eliminated Merchandise No. 5: the Coca and Cola traces. They also altered Merchandise No. 7X— the super-secret blend of flavoring oils. The result was New Coke: less tart, sweeter, slightly lemony and smooth.

Zyman and his team decided to conduct taste tests-on a grand scale. They conducted 190,000 taste tests-made up of participants from all age groups, all geographic areas. The results were encouraging, the new Coke beat Pepsi by six to eight points, whereas before they usually lost to Pepsi by ten to fifteen points.

By the end of 1984, research showed that Pepsi was closing the gap in the cola market, and now trailing by fewer than three points. This was the catalyst that made Goizueta pull the trigger and launch his new cola.

Zyman briefed his agency (McCann Erickson) and set a target date of mid-April 1985. The agency was charged with creating ads for New Coke in just four months.

Secrecy, which had been maintained, became strained and by early April word was getting out. Goizueta decided on a major press conference at a popular theatre in New York, for April 23.

On April 23rd Coke announced that it had created a new and better drink.

Sensing what was to come, Pepsi CEO Roger Enrico decided on a preemptive strike and on the day of the Goizueta press conference, placed full page ads in all the major newspapers in the United States, proclaiming that they had "Won the Cola War!"

At eleven o'clock on the 23rd Goizueta began his announcement by saying, "The best, has been made even better."

The reaction was big and not what they'd hoped for.

A groundswell of protest was unleashed by consumers with some 1500 daily telephone calls and letters to Coke's Atlanta headquarters. And it didn't let up; it went on through May and

June, even increasing in intensity.

The surge of emotion was a total surprise to Coke management. Curiously, the outrage wasn't just from Coke drinkers, it was from citizens who felt that their old way of life was being abandoned. It demonstrated how deeply ingrained Coke had become as a symbol of America. It was totally unexpected.

Of course Pepsi had a field day. I remember that day well at Pepsi's offices in Purchase, NY. The Pepsi PR department created many press releases, some sarcastic, some just emotional. One featured a distraught teenage Coca-Cola drinker looking at a can of new Coke and saying, "Can somebody out there tell me why they did it? They said they were the real thing, they said they were it. And then they changed."

After picking up a can of Pepsi and drinking she says, "Now I know why."

Pepsi-Cola USA reported that its May sales figures rose 14 percent vs. the prior year, producing the highest volume in its eighty-seven year history. New data revealed that 46 percent of the New Coke samplers said they'd drink less Coke or switch to another brand. Another group said they'd switch to Pepsi by a margin of 75 percent!

Coke management could recognize a crisis when it saw one. And this was certainly one.

Coke Caves

They decided to reverse course, and on July 11, 1985 made another announcement-that the old Coke would return under the name "Coke Classic." They also said that New Coke would remain as the company's flagship brand, and be marketed alongside Coke Classic.

What was the final assessment?

The Challenge campaign and resulting formula change reveal that even data and research cannot measure the deep emotional attachment of the original Coke–how ingrained it had become in the American psyche.

This was never anticipated or realized in Atlanta.

Coke's Don Keough, (in a July press conference) went on to say, "Some critics will say Coca-Cola made a marketing mistake. Some cynics will say that we planned the whole thing. The truth is we are not that dumb and not that smart."

The telephones lit up again, this time in praise of the move.

Pepsi continued its ridicule when President Roger Enrico held a press conference to ask if his rival planned to start a "Cola of the Month Club." The late night comedians had a field day, crying "Coke Are It."

But there was a happy result, albeit undeserved.

From the start Coca-Cola Classic proved to be very popular and immediately began outselling New Coke and ultimately it overtook Pepsi again in early 1986. Within a year New Coke had shrunk to a 3 percent market share and may now be obsolete.

There is still more irony in this tale.

In the mid eighties the Coca-Cola company began using an artificial sweetener (aspartame) in its Diet Cola formula, and accidentally created a sweeter, smoother soft drink. Diet Cola took off and became the third best-selling soft drink in the country. Diet Cola now tasted a lot like New Coke—so in a way, Diet Coke became New Coke.

The Right Question
By Sergio Zyman- Former Marketing Chief at Coca-Cola

The big stumbling block that kept coming up in research was taste. At Coke, we ran taste tests too and found that Pepsi wasn't lying. In blind tests, consumers also told us that they preferred the taste of Pepsi to Coke, basically because Pepsi is much sweeter. At first try, people would get a smoother taste on a sip-by-sip basis.

We never asked the right questions.

Now, because we ourselves had fallen for Pepsi's point-that taste was the only thing that mattered-we decided that if we wanted to sell more Coke we should think about reformulating it (something never done in more than ninety years).

Sergio Zyman

We conducted research ourselves, and asked such questions as, "What they thought of Coke?" They would say, "Coke is part of my life. It's the one that understands my feelings. It's the one that's been around for a long time..."

We also asked them, "What would you do if we gave you a product that tasted better than Pepsi, but still was a Coke?"

They told us, "I would buy it."

"Would you like it?" we asked.

"Sure I would like it," they said.

The problem was that even though we were asking the right type of pre-search questions, we didn't ask The (Big) Question. In truth, the only question we really needed to ask was, "If we took away Coca-Cola and gave you a New Coke, would you accept it?"

And that led Coke to decide to change its formula—with disastrous results.

(Excerpted with permission, from his book, T*he End of Marketing As We Know It.*)

The Combat Continues

Despite the formula embarrassment, the Cola Wars were still showing no signs of cooling off. In the early 1990s, Coke began bringing out what they call "flanker brands" with names like Caffeine-free Coke, Caffeine-free Diet Coke, Diet Cherry Coke, Diet Sprite, Lymon, Mello Yello, Mr. Pibb, Fresca, Fruitopia, etc.

Pepsi responded with flanker brands of its own, including Aquafina, Slice, Sierra Mist, etc. Soon the supermarket shelves were overcrowded, and the lesser brands were being crowded out.

Coke brands now had 41 percent of the overall market, outselling Pepsi's brands by eight points. This lasted into the mid nineties.

In 1989 Pepsi commissioned a massive pubic relations campaign in the form of a book called "A Pepsi Day." This book was designed and executed by my firm (Congdon, Macdonald & Shear) to show the proliferation of Pepsi product in any country in the world where Pepsi is sold.

It was presented as follows.

"A day in the life of Pepsi-Cola is indeed a day of opportunities seized. And on September 14, 1989, for 24 consecutive hours, in 49 countries, 65 of the world's leading photographers will set out to capture it on film. It is a typical day in which 200,000 Pepsi employees will help push the Pepsi enterprise forward, two hundred fifty million bottles of Pepsi-Cola will be filled, tens of thousands of Pepsi trucks will carry them to market around the world." Our intention was to capture the day through the lens of many places and countries.

The book which resulted presented Pepsi in a unique way: on a single day, through moments frozen in time, from San Diego, California, to Sydney, Australia, Pepsi was seen being consumed by taxi drivers in New York, Arab Sheiks in Dubai, football players in Indiana, in gondolas in Venice, on oil rigs in Texas, street vendors in Mexico City. We even learned that the bottler

The cover of a giant picture book for Pepsi International created in 1989.

delivery trucks were crossing the lines in Beirut, Lebanon (It was a divided city separating Muslims from Christians), so we sent photographers there as well.

The design was simple but effective. The harder part was coordination with the marketing managers and photography teams in the forty-nine countries.

The book was dedicated to Don Kendall. A half million copies were printed and distributed to every marketing firm, bottler and major press representative in the world.

The results were what we hoped for–compelling evidence of the popularity of the drink around the world.

A New Logo is Born

In 1992 Pepsi decided to change its logo, replacing the "book-ends" logo of nineteen years (1973).

We were part of a team effort (with New York design firm Petersen Blyth) to apply the new logo to various real-life situations. Pepsi management hoped to achieve a modern, more cutting ege look with this new logo–compatible with its new style of TV commercial, and association with the emerging and popular rock stars of the day (Jackson, Madonna, Tina Turner and ultimately, Britney Spears).

After the initial design was presented and accepted (it was nicknamed the "Action logo" because it leaned forward), the real work began. We had to adapt the new logo to every conceivable application we could think of. These included: outdoor and indoor signage, packages, cans and bottles, umbrellas, vehicles (from small vans to 18-wheelers), cups, glasses, vending machines, print ads, caps and tee shirts. We also had to show how the logo would look in foreign languages as diverse as Cyrillic (Russian) to Kanji (Japanese), to Farsi (Arabic).

Gatorade

The two soft drink giants were constantly looking to diversify and the appeal of energy drinks had caught their marketing department's attention. Gatorade became the next field of battle. Coke decided to buy the parent organization, Quaker Oats, and made a bid of $14 billion to do the deal.

Pepsi also wanted Gatorade, admiring the growth and potential of the energy drink created thirty-nine years before at the University of Southern Florida.

If it could buy Gatorade it could move ahead in the sports-drink category. The push was coming for non-carbs in soft drinks.

Coke made their offer on November 18, 2000, and they assured Quaker executives that the Coke board had been informed of the proposed acquisition. Quaker agreed and the price was settled and the terms agreed upon.

The Coke board was not in agreement, however, and voted unanimously not to make the offer–already made!

This was an embarrassment to the new CEO, and it was rumored later that big investor and board member Warren Buffett was (again) pulling the CEO's strings.

More damaging still, Pepsi had also made a move to buy Quaker, and after negotiating with the Federal Trade Commission, did buy the company for $13 billion (one billion less than Coke had agreed to). They also had to agree to certain terms regarding advertising and marketing but ultimately did the deal.

Gatorade has flourished for Pepsi, and in PepsiCo's recent annual report, Gatorade amounted to 13 percent of the beverages of the North American product mix, roughly equal to that of Diet Pepsi, and revealed a market share of U.S. sports drink brands of 82 percent, against Coke's Powerade at 15 percent.

Today (in the twenty-first century) Gatorade's annual sales are over five billion, they have expanded the flavor variety and size offerings and largely

The Pepsi Mobile Media promotion was launched in 1980 and was an international success.

dominate the juice aisle of most supermarkets. The Quaker/Gatorade acquisition broadened Pepsi-Cola's product range, now reflected in its annual revenues.

It Never Ends

In the cola wars, Pepsi has wisely kept the focus on just one issue, taste. The Pepsi Challenge is an extension of that focus, negating all of Coke's normal advantages which are: history, emotion, constancy and stability.

Coke learned an even larger lesson (albeit by accident), the realization that Coca Cola, the drink, was more than a beverage, it was a symbolic core value of the American way of life. They never realized that they possessed this treasure until they tried to kill it. Two years ago Pepsi-Cola Incorporated had revenues from all sales of $32,562 billion while Coca-Cola's were only $23,104 billion. However, Coke still dominates in terms of market share, 41 percent vs. 33 percent.

Pepsi thinks the potential pool of customers is more than sixty million persons. Both beverages are made with high-fructose corn syrup as a sweetener, low sugar and carbohydrates. Both companies are betting that Americans are paying more attention to their diets–wanting a more healthy life style.

The real reason may be more economic. The editor of *Beverage Digest* reported in the spring that growth in soft drinks has been losing market share, slipping 74.1 percent in 2002, 72.6 percent in 2003. Only diet drinks have been gaining.

Sergio Zyman, former Chief Marketing Officer for Coke, described it thus, "While Coke stands for continuity and stability, Pepsi on the other hand, does stand for choice and change." This is how each chose to position itself, and market itself. It began a long time ago when Pepsi's Charles Mack dreamed up his jingle and slogan, "Twice as much for a nickel too." From this jingle to the 1990s, Pepsi defined each brand's position (in their view) thus: one drink is for the older folks, one for the young. When they brought out the Pepsi Challenge they repositioned Coke yet again by declaring that all that matters is taste. It is an example of what Zyman extols, "Positive comparative advertising."

The Cola wars are far from over, indeed may never end. Some have observed that the two big beverage companies are "joined at the hip", that they each need each other, that they are defined by each other. Top executives in both companies would vehemently disagree, I expect.

However, as with any hundred years' war, the fortunes of the two soft drink giants will surge back and forth. They are, perhaps, as American as apple pie–the spirit of competition that resides at the core of capitalism.

The Coca-Cola image of goodness and American values has given them an advantage that they didn't realize they had until they tried to change the formula. Even Santa Claus has been a Coke ally in the ongoing Cola Wars.

Can't Beat The Real Thing.

9

ADVERTISING

The Image Makers

Advertising used to be called, just, Madison Avenue.

Movies were made about advertising, starring such actors as: Clark Gable, Jack Lemon, Tony Randall, Rock Hudson and most recently, Mel Gibson.

Jokes were created about advertising such as "Let's run it (i.e.- a new ad concept) up the flagpole and see if anyone salutes," or "Let's throw it against the wall and see if it sticks."

An industry that is defined not by its product (let alone its location) but by its color and, frankly its excesses, reveals what an integral part of America it has become. It is unprecedented.

From the beginning "Madison Avenue" implied a lifestyle, a look, a reputation. It was (and is) a business that lacked tangible assets, only people with their skills and contacts.

It was (and is) always about persuasion.

It was (and is) never ignored.

Advertising is big, pervasive, growing and impossible to overlook.

> "Maggie, in the world of advertising there's no such thing as a lie, there's only the ***expedient exaggeration.***"
> - So said Cary Grant playing Roger Thornhill- advertising executive, in the classic 1959 movie, ***North by Northwest.***

Back in 1962, *Time* magazine estimated that the average American was exposed to 10,000 TV commercials a year. What's changed? What's diminished? Certainly not the ad volume. Today, there are approximately 500,000 commercials aired every year, adding up to about

1,600 messages every day. Furthermore, just last year nineteen minutes of every hour of TV programming was given over to commercials.

That's bombardment.

The question is, is it effective? How did it get this way? We'll see in this chapter.

Research reveals that the average person notices fewer than 150 commercials in a year, and remembers only about twenty. That's only a 13 percent (of .0003 percent) chance of success.

There are an estimated 14,000 advertising agencies (all sizes of course) and the big ones have all merged. How did an industry which generates so much revenue each year (estimated at over $240 billion in billings and fees in the U.S. alone) and is so vital to the American economy begin?

History of Advertising

The business of advertising items for sale began a long time ago, fueled as it was by the growth of media. Like packaging, a series of "inventions" had to occur. Here are a few highlights.

First came signage, as in "My cow is for sale."

Then the newspaper, in **1784,** in Philadelphia. Packaged goods began to appear (**1884**-Quaker Oats in a box) and with it branding. Then radio (**1920**–the first radio station starts, in Pittsburgh. Then RCA starts the first radio network in **1926**). CBS radio is organized and opens in **1927**, glossy magazines (**1936**–*Life* publishes its first edition), television makes the scene in **1941**–the first TV spots go on air for Bulova Watch.

This growth of media opportunities led to advertising opportunities as American businesses sought to sell their products. This growth was clearly fueled by consumers. As Americans became more affluent, so did their appetite for things (some needed, some desired). It was in many ways a mirror reflecting both the growth of advertising and ourselves.

1882 – Procter & Gamble places early ads for Ivory soap

1899 – Campbell's Soup spends $10,000 to buy streetcar posters in New York, Philadelphia

1906 – Kellogg's places its first ads for Corn Flakes in six midwestern newspapers.

1928 – Lucky Strike sponsors a dance music show on radio, called "Your Hit Parade"

1948 – V-8 juice features Ronald Reagan in an ad

1954 – CBS (Columbia Broadcasting System) becomes the largest advertising medium

1956 – The Marlboro Man debuts on TV and print

And what followed, like bees to flowers to honey, were the advertising agencies

1868 – N.W. Ayer opens in Philadelphia

1878 – J. Walter Thompson starts in New York
1923 – Young & Rubicam in New York
1928 – Batten Barton Durstine and Osborne (BBDO)
1936 – Leo Burnett in Chicago
1943 – Foot Cone & Belding in Chicago
1948 – Ogilvy and Mather in New York
1949 – Doyle Dane Bernbach (DDB) in New York

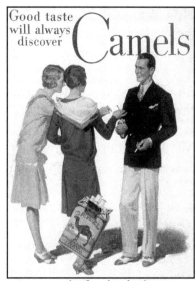

1980 to 2000

The years to the end of the century saw a number of changes and growth in advertising. The deregulation of AT&T led to the "Baby Bells," MCI and Sprint, all of whom now competed for customers and used lots of advertising to get to them. By **1994** the telecommunications sector of advertising was over $3 billion. Nike became one of the leading sports marketers with its brilliant ad campaign: "Just Do It." Apple computer made its classic commercial "**1984**" and infomercials began. The ad agencies,

In 1915 the first big budget cigarette campaign was launched. The agency was N.W. Ayer.

responding to client pressure, spun off their media departments into separate and independent media divisions. In **1999,** *Advertising Age* editors picked the five greatest marketers of the century. They honored: Nike for edgy creative work, Anheuser-Busch for understanding its target audience, Coca-Cola for creating the first global brand, McDonald's for consistent quality advertising, and Procter & Gamble for setting the standard in product marketing and research.

Madison Avenue, USA

In the beginning, almost all the major advertising agencies were in New York City and were located on (or very near) Madison Avenue, roughly between 34th Street and 59th Street. Within those twenty-five blocks you could find all the big names–famous names that defined an era. At 40th and Madison was Young and Rubicam, where it still is to this day. At 43rd

Madison and 42nd Street

and Lexington, J. Walter Thompson was located and around 48th and Madison was Ogilvy & Mather. Other notable agencies in this Madison Avenue urban canyon were McCann-Erickson; Batten, Barton; Durstine and Osborne, Grey Advertising; Doyle, Dane Bernbach, Cunningham & Walsh; Benton & Bowles; D'Arcy Advertising; and Campbell-Ewald. Only

N.W. Ayer in Philadelphia, Leo Burnett and Foote Cone & Belding in Chicago were big and located outside the city. They, and others less well known (or smaller), competed fiercely for a piece of the advertising pie. "Madison Avenue" is more the symbol of the industry than the reality.

All will agree, no matter what their address, that advertising is very big business. Almost 300,000 persons are employed in the business (overall). Of that, about 50,000 are creative people (16 percent of the total) and 100,000 are women (or approximately 33 percent).

Consolidation

"Merger Mania" was the narcotic of the late twentieth century, a phenomenon not exclusive to the advertising business. Philip Morris bought Kraft; Kodak bought Sterling Drug; Ford bought Jaguar; KKR bought Nabisco, etc. Whether it is good or bad for the nation's economy, in the last decade many corporations have merged: ExxonMobil; PriceWaterhouseCoopers; JPMorganChase; and others have been on an acquisition kick, Pepsi and Quaker Oats; Sears and Kmart; Procter & Gamble and Gillette; Federated Department Stores and The May Company. Which means they are getting larger, and fewer.

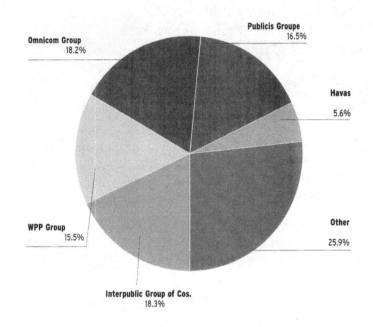

Ad agencies were doing the very same thing–merging and going public. Some were happy about it, some hostile (as with Ogilvy and Mather), some were reluctant (as with Y&R). It began in 1960 when McCann Erickson restructured as Interpublic. Then in 1986 Needham Harper, BBDO and DDB merged to create Omnicom Group–the largest ad agency in the world, at the time. It is sometimes referred to as "the Big Bang," the year when a number of other ad agencies merged and the big agency holding companies became commonplace. Today there are six big agency groups (holding companies).

Omnicom Group - $11.46 billion in annual revenues
Interpublic Group - $6.2 billion

WPP Group (London) - $10.8 billion
Publicis Group (Paris) - $5.9 billion
Dentsu (Tokyo) - $3 billion
Havas (Paris) - $1.87 billion
As you can see, they are global, as advertising (and the client's marketing) is today. Taken altogether these six agency groups represent approximately $30 billion in worldwide revenues (from fees). A few individual agencies had the following revenues: J. Walter Thompson Co.($1,178.5 billion), Ogilvy & Mather Worldwide ($706.3 million), Y&R Advertising ($215.7 million). Taken with foreign and U.S. media spending, it approximates $400 billion.

> **Note:** All of these numbers, holding companies and lists of ad agencies, have been generalized and not all of each entity's properties are included. All have extensive company-owned properties that specialize in public relations, or graphic design, or buy and place media. The sources are the 3rd Annual guide to Advertising & Marketing—as printed in *Advertising Age* magazine-Crain Communications, Inc., 2005.

These new **super-agencies** are able to offer their clients a plethora of creative services, like: logo and packaging design, sales promotion planning, public relations and retail display, as well as traditional media-based advertising.

So, with the consolidation (through merger or acquisition) of agencies into giant holding companies, and clients into multi-brand diversified corporations, naturally "one-stop shopping" is now offered, and I think, preferred.

One Effect of the Consolidation (mergers) of Advertising Agencies
By Ralph Rydholm, Chairman Emeritus, TLK/Euro RSCG, Chicago

The agencies have been given conflicting tasks.
1. They must work with all the companies in their company mix, and when they can, even try to promote them.
2. They also must make more and more profit every year on their own.
3. How do you do it, if you lose control with your client? That is the biggest problem I had to deal with, the whole integrated marketing movement.
Ironically, you need the holding company–they are the only one entity with common interest. In the end, however, the only person who can really control it are the client and the brand people.

Young & Rubicam Inc.

The Whole Egg at Work

It goes by many names, but Y&R started it all with their Whole Egg concept in the 1970s. Let's examine this agency as representative of a typical multi-services market communications firm in the twenty-first century.

Young and Rubicam has a network of 339 agencies, (including worldwide affiliates) which are located in seventy-three countries and that span every communications discipline. The breakup of their communications "team" as they put it – follows. It has ten parts.

1. **Y&R advertising:** full service consumer advertising, creative, research, marketing and media buying and planning.

2. **Wunderman:** also a full service, global consulting and communications firm that provides strategic, customer-centered solutions for business (i.e. direct response marketing, promotion and business to business advertising)

3. **Brand Dialogue:** strategic development database design and management

4. **Media Edge:** Media specialist/purchasing

5. **Burson Marsteller:** Public Relations - "perception management" as they say

6. **Cohn & Wolfe:** Public Relations

7. **Landor Associates:** Brand and graphic design services

8. **Sudler & Hennessey:** health care communications, medical services and product advertising

9. **The Bravo Group:** communications to the Hispanic community

10. **Dentsu Y&R:** (a joint venture to offer advertising services in the Asia-Pacific markets). That's how Y&R breaks down. Examine any (or many) of the other large agencies and you'll find a similar structure. All the main ad agencies are set up to offer integrated marketing concepts, from many diverse sources, most of the time owned by the agency of record. This structure is widely practiced now in most of the big agencies and is the very essence of the "Whole Egg" concept.

A modern advertising agency is agreat deal more than it used be – it has become a "one stop shop." Because of the changing habits of consumers and new media delivery systems, a marketing mix is required. Media opportunities abound and may now include (after traditional advertising in print or broadcast), the Internet, gaming devices, music players, cell phones and video on demand. The TV and the PC are becoming fully integrated. A typical and effective mix might include: sales promotion, direct mail, publicity, packaging, the Internet and Guerrilla marketing.

Going Global

With the merger mania in place, and one-stop shopping the norm, all that remains is a big enough stage to make use of all this talent in one package. So naturally, advertising has gone global. Agencies have branches in most of the major cities of the world to serve the needs of the big U.S. and European corporations (product companies) around the world. And companies sell their brands globally–no one more so than Procter & Gamble. Brands are global, campaigns are global. Consumers are global. Well, sometimes, with some brands.
It sounds great, most promising. In practice it is less smooth.

One problem that is endemic with today's big global, many faceted agency, is the problem of coordinating the work from the various sources within the agency's basket of goodies. The 3M company recently moved from using thirty-four agencies in twenty-three countries, to one agency, Grey Worldwide. This will doubtless lessen the possibility of misinformation and a fractured presentation. It may also lessen the creative output, however. Other large agencies that offer such services are: BBDO, DDB, Leo Burnett, Ogilvy & Mather and Young and Rubicam. It often sounds better than it is in practice. It almost seems like a creation made to persuade, rather than to explain. The large agencies may have a tendency to emphasize their creative advertising work, despite talk about integration, or true IMC. Ironically, the smaller, mid-sized agencies often present integrated services with more equanimity, agencies such as Cramer-Krasselt, Fallon Worldwide or Crispin, Porter+Bogusky.

How Does an Advertising Agency Work?

Let's start with a definition. Advertising is: to make something known, in an impersonal way, by arousing public attention and by emphasizing (its) desirable qualities.
There is, of course, a lot more to it than that. The trick is how you make something known. Some of the most memorable advertisements these days do it with humor, some with sex. David Ogilvy (founder of Ogilvy and Mather) might have disagreed when he said, "I do not regard advertising as entertainment or an art form, but as a medium of information." Ogilvy might have agreed, however, that the true mission of an advertisement is to plant an

image in the mind of an existing and/or future consumer. This is in many ways the toughest job of all. Image building is highly subjective, varies widely from consumer to consumer, from geographic region to region, from male to female, etc.

To successfully plant an image is what spells success or, leading to initial sales, repeat sales and ultimately brand loyalty. If the mission of the advertisement or logo is to provide a short-hand reference to a brand (i.e. "I like the Dell Inspiron because the recent ad campaign amused and informed me"). That's the image part.

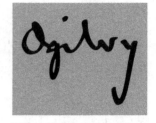

It works differently for a packaged product, like Pepperidge Farm's Milano Cookies. There the moment happens in a large busy supermarket. The customer sees the package, notices the logo, remembers the taste, picks up the package and reads the back panel copy, and hopefully drops it in his or her cart. At its best, it is a carefully crafted, seamless marketing effort, all designed to persuade the consumer.

An advertising agency is nothing less than a tool of marketing whose goal is to increase sales and, ultimately, profits for the (client) corporation.

To do this with accuracy and economic efficiency, every ad must be planned to achieve a specific goal and that goal must be related to the marketing mix.

The Basics
A typical advertising agency has five basic functions:

Write the Strategy

Create the Ads

Plan the Communications

Placement of the Ads

Maintain Client Relations

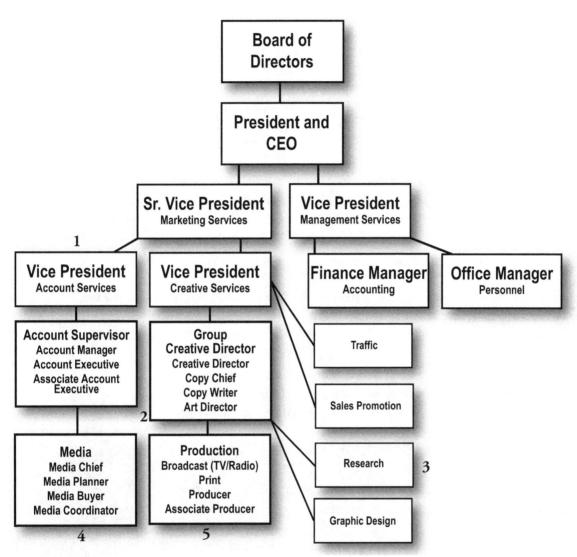

Here is a typical agency structure—

Strategy, Creative, Communications Planning, Placement, Client Relations

These five functions are fulfilled out of five essential departments: the Account Services Department, the Creative Department, the Research Department, the Media Department and the Production Department.

1. The Account Services Department

There can be no advertising without clients–the life blood of the agency. To put it simply, the account services department has one primary, overall mission, to keep the client happy. And this doesn't mean, or imply, that the client must be wined and dined. Clients these days are disciplined marketers and what keeps them happy is to know that they are getting good work, well targeted at their consumer group and fairly billed from an organized advertising agency. There are four positions in this department: Account Supervisor, Account Manager, Account Executive/Director, Account Coordinator–in a descending order of importance and remuneration, influence, etc. The size of each of these positions will vary by agency, but they usually follow the same pattern. The role of the Accounts team follows.

Account Planners:
Account Planning is a process, newly expanded and made respectable by British ad agencies about twenty years ago. It started at BMP (Boase Massimi Pollitt) Ltd., the London agency that claims (through the person of Stanley Pollitt) to have invented The Account Planning position and methodology–although others dispute this.

Here's how Christopher Cowpe, Managing Partner of BMP, described the process. "To be truly effective, advertising must be both distinctive and relevant, and planning helps on both counts. The role of the planner is vital to the creative effort in that he/she must interrogate the data and consumer-preferences until it reveals the shape of an insight that, then, allows the creative people to move forward." That's a fancy job description. A simpler one is to know what our targeted consumers are all about–intellectually and intuitively. They are like detectives.

To do this they must meet with the target audience (the consumer) and find out where and how he lives, what he likes and doesn't. He will initiate and oversee research either of the qualitative (focus groups) or quantitative kind (mall intercepts).

The essential difference between an Account Planner and a traditional Account Services person is that one (the former) must study and grasp the trends, fads, socio-economic patterns of the world as a single picture and how they will impact on the sales for all packaged goods (for example); while the typical account director is more tightly focused on the financial health and welfare of his client or brand, as it compares to its competition. The Account Director's role is just as important as that of the Account Planner, although it is somewhat more "micro."

Account Executive on his way to a meeting.

206

Relationships
By David Ogilvy, Confessions of an Advertising Man,
Athenaeum publishing, 1957

In some agencies the account executives are allowed to boss the creative people. This makes a good impression on some clients; they believe that their advertising is safer in the hands of 'business' men. But it (also) creates an atmosphere which inhibits copywriters, and the client winds up with second-rate advertising... the account executives are little more than waiters who carry confections from the campaign-builders, to the clients.

The Account Director

As said, they are equals in the agency, each with a vital role in keeping up the health of the agency and its clientele. The account director brings more of a business perspective as opposed to the planner's consumer orientation. Ideally they should work together on strategic positioning and spend as much time as necessary with the creative teams to be certain that they are designing ads that are on target.

In the end, the Account Director runs the account. It is he who maintains and watches the budget, the operations and the timeliness of the result. He is like the president of a small division, the division within the agency that does the Procter & Gamble business (for instance). This is an ideal arrangement when it is in balance and working smoothly. The account planner must have some removal from the account's daily needs in order to think on a broad scale and the account director must maintain the relationship with the client on a day to day basis if necessary.

Duality

The Account Team (Director, Supervisor or Manager) has a tough role essentially "schizophrenic." The typical account director must answer to two masters, both of whom can affect his welfare.

For the agency (where his paycheck comes from) he must provide proactive, intuitive top level account management.

For the client, he must also do exactly the same.

In effect, he must appear to have each respective party's best interests at heart-telling it like it is to the agency, telling it like it is to the client—making each think he really has their best interests at heart. It requires a certain "duality," and probably is the root of the reputation that account people are shallow, insincere, **"empty suits."** It isn't true and is basically unfair.

The Creative Brief

The next step is to create the advertising. It all starts (or should) with the Creative Brief. At some agencies it is called a Work Plan but it amounts to the same thing–the moment when the account director meets with the creative team to brief them on what's needed.

The Young & Rubicam Creative Work Plan

1. Statement of the Key Fact(s)
    a. State the assignment as specifically as possible.
    b. State the specific deliverables (are they to print ads, TV ads, non-traditional?)
    c. State the deadline(s).
2. Definition of the Target Audience
    a. By gender, age, socio-economic level, geographic area, etc.
3. Definition of the Problem (or Opportunity)
    a. (i.e.)To arrest a sliding sales curve or recover market share to a specific brand, etc.
4. Statement of the Advertising Objective
    a. (i.e.)To build on the equity of the brand
    b. (i.e.)To counter a marketing move by the competition, etc.
5. Statement of the Creative Strategy
    a. Prospect Definition
    b. Principal Competition
    c. Promise/Consumer Benefit
        i. What will it do for the consumer?
        ii. How will it motivate the consumer to act?
    d. What will the competition do?
6. What is not written in ad terms?
    a. (i.e.) Consumers are "turning off" to traditional advertising methods and executions, due to clutter and overload.
    b. Does the client's product have a unique selling proposition (USP)?
    c. If the reader gets one idea out of the ad, what should it be?
    d. What action should the reader take after reading or watching the ad?

Now that the creative team has been briefed ,they must go away to create the ads. They usually work in teams of two. One is an Art Director (thinks visually), one is a Copywriter (thinks in words). They both must search for the compelling idea which will bring life to the opportunities and/or problems expressed in the Creative Brief.

2. The Creative Department

The creative department makes the ads. There are four positions here also: the Group Creative Director, the Creative Director, the Copy Writer and the Art Director. The Creative group produces the agency's product. The two person creative teams are usually referred to as "cells," and often they are paired to opposites, in background and temperament. When such a combination works, it is magic, each providing an ingredient to the creative work that the other may lack. The Creative Group is essential to the agency's life—because without good creative even the best managed, organized agency will fail. Even the most brilliant account executive can't sell thin air.

The Creative Group has only one goal, to generate ideas. Idea generation is an imprecise process and defies definition, but to be creative one must be: "intuitive, instinctive, scared and lucky... and also: rigorous, disciplined, logical and deductive."
(Source: Alex Kroll, Creative Director of Y&R in the 1980s)

The Y&R creative group for Sony (one of their biggest clients) has six teams of two persons each. In London, a big advertising hub, agencies even hire their creatives in pairs. They may interview together for jobs, they create ads together, they will share an office and they typically receive identical salaries. The agency has a difficult role to get the most out of their creatives. They must do two seemingly opposite things: provide a structure for the creative couples yet provide freedom for them to be innovative. They must provide discipline without being confining.

Phil Dusenberry joined BBDO as a writer in 1962 and developed into one of advertising's most imaginative creative forces. His work with Pepsi-Cola is legendary, spotlighting such pop superstars as Michael Jackson, Madonna, Lionel Richie and Ray Charles. Phil is a veteran of more than thirty years in the creative end of the advertising business on many accounts - like General Electric. He recently retired as Chairman and CEO of BBDO, worldwide.

Three Rules for Creating Effective Ads

1. One-Shot ads almost never work
The average American sees thousands of ads each year and only one out of nine, on average, is seen by the Target Audience. Average for mind retention is three times.
2. Quality Counts
Well designed ads are more effective than poorly designed ads.
3. Carefully identify your target audience.
Don't start the process by deciding what the ad will look like, start by deciding what you want your ad to do.

In many ways it is the way in which the brief is given that creates the most success. It should not be too specific or too dictatorial. Creative people are, by nature, instinctive and dislike regulations. It is important to respect this attitude.

Bottom line, the creative team must come away with:

1. An understanding of what their advertising needs to do
2. A realistic appraisal of what it might achieve
3. An accurate and "beneath the surface" analysis of the Target Audience
4. A clear direction on what or which message is most likely to "reach" the TA.

The Single Idea

In the movie *"City Slickers"* with Jack Palance (Curly) and Billy Crystal (the city slicker), the two men around the campfire talking about the meaning of life. Billy has just helped Palance deliver a calf and is full of the meaning of life, and says, "What does it all mean, Curly?"

Curly (Palance) thinks a bit, studies the fire, relights his cigar, holds up one gloved finger and says, "It all boils down to one thing, one single thing."

Billy (anxiously) "Yes, what is it?"

Curly, "I have no idea."

Another way to describe the Curly factor is as the "Unique Selling Position."

The USP

*This concept (and term) was coined by Rosser Reeves in his book **Reality in Advertising** and was advertising's child of the '50s. The premise was simple–find the unique benefit in your product and hammer it home, repeatedly until it grooves in.*

Rosser Reeves

Here's how he put it.

"Let's say you have one million dollars tied up in your little company and suddenly your advertising isn't working and sales are going down. Your future (and your family's) depends on it. Now what do you want from me–fine writing, or do you want to see the sales curve stop moving down and start moving up?" Some of his slogans were inspired: "M&Ms melt in your mouth not in your hands" or "Colgate cleans your breath as it cleans your teeth." He said, "You must make the product interesting, not just make the ad different."

In all creative briefs, good ones, there is also the final statement–what is the single factor that most sums up the product or mission? Some agencies call it "the proposition." It is hard to define because it is less what the ads, or campaigns must say, and more about what the consumer takes away from the ad.

It is, in many ways, the most important element in the brief. It should encapsulate everything else. Ideally it should be a single idea, expressed in one sentence (the Curly Factor again).

The "Got Milk?" campaign grew out of such a brief.

It was based on extensive research, conducted by the San Francisco Agency Weiden and Kennedy, to determine what and why people drink, or didn't drink, milk.

Milk appeared as a boring, necessary child-oriented product. Research did reveal, however, that milk was a companion product, one essential to the enjoyment of say, brownies, or cereal or a PB&J sandwich. But the agency realized that there was no humor in this, no hook, no curly factor. Milk could not create its own desire.

Then one researcher opined, "We know that people feel they need milk when eating a brownie, or in their coffee–that it is essential–so, what happens when we deprive them of their milk?

Hal Riney's *creative work is unique for its expression of American spirit, warmth and character. The campaign for Gallo (with front porch stars Bartles and Jaymes) is a perfect example of this, as well as his work with Saturn cars, Crocker Bank, Alamo Car Rentals and "Morning in America" for Ronald Reagan's re-election campaign in the 1980s.*

And from that was born the "deprivation" strategy, and from that the brilliant "got milk?" campaign.

The curly factor in this case was, **what happens when you take away the essential companion to foods we all love?**

Another way to look at the Curly Factor is to analyze it as the "Compelling Thought."

This should be an integral part of the brief. It isn't easy to isolate and identify, but worth the effort.

The Compelling Thought's credibility and persuasiveness allows the consumer to accept the competitive benefit in your strategy.

The Compelling Thought must be able to position and dramatize the communications strategy.

The Compelling Thought must boil the product's benefit down to a simple phrase, and have two qualities:

> –to endure over time through many repetitions
> –to separate the brand from the competition

Some examples of good Compelling Thoughts:

> –Kellogg's: "Frosted Flakes taste great" (as spoken by Tony the Tiger)
> –Black Flag's Roach Motel: "They check in but they don't check out"
> –Miller Lite's: "Everything you ever wanted in a beer, and less."
> –P&G: "Tide's in; dirt's out."
> –Gallo Wine's: "We will sell no wine before its time"(as spoken by Orson Wells)
> –Eastern Airline's: "The Wings of Man" (again, as spoken by Orson Wells)
> –Motel Six, "We'll leave the light on for you." (as spoken by Tom Bodette.)
> –Hallmark Cards: "When you care enough to send the very best."

The Creative Process

It has three basic stages, in this sequence:
1. Preparation – What do you know already?
2. Incubation – What is the most important fact, the least?
3. Illumination – The most appealing idea emerges (when you least expect it)

What is the Creative Person like?

He or she has to be able to think out of the box to look for and find untried ideas.
The creative person must look for and interpret the briefing strategy and translate it into terms that will build a relationship with the target audience. It should lead, ideally, to devel-

oping loyalty to the brand being advertised, the company behind it, and even the stores that sell it. The creative person must provide the visual, the copy line, and the layout that can add perceived value to the brand, one that is different from the competition.

Reflections on the Creative Person
By Mike Hughes, President /Creative Director of The Martin Agency, Richmond, VA

Creative people are a pretty diverse lot but I'd say the best of them have a lot of desire, a lot of curiosity, and a lot of heart. What is it that drives a writer to keep working on a headline until 4 or 5 in the morning? Why will an art director work all night on a project – and then throw everything out the next day and start over? You've got to have desire.

You've got to keep searching for what's new or what's best. I've seen moderately talented creative people with more desire succeed where their more gifted peers failed. I always hate to tell this to young people coming into the business, but I've never known a top-flight senior creative person who hasn't given some years of his life to the business.

I guess the good news that accompanies that fact is that the creative person in question usually enjoyed those years tremendously.

Mary Wells was the first woman to head a major advertising agency, Wells, Rich, Greene (in 1967). She started as a creative writer with Doyle, Dane & Bernbach and moved on to do outstanding advertising for Braniff Airlines and American Motors.

What qualities must he/she possess?

    –Intelligence to understand the potential consumer, the TA. Why do they buy, and in what way?

    –Curiosity, to delve into the personality, habits and mores of the TA.

    –Insight, to understand what the brand or product means to the TA

    –Boldness, to be able to question the established wisdom, either within his agency or from outside research. His doubts must be respected and catered to.

    –Confidence, to try unusual interpretations

What skills does he/she need to have?
- –Likes to write or draw
- –Originality
- –Go beyond the ordinary in execution
- –Create visuals that stand alone, tell the sales story
- –Copy lines that dramatize the product's promise.
- –Create confidence in the brand, presenting it in a way that inspires confidence in the TA.
- –To earn loyalty by avoiding the boring, pompous or didactic approach. To do all of these will build a brand, and a consumer relationship will result.

"The art director is the difference between advertising that stands still and advertising that stands out".
Leo Burnett, Copywriter (and agency president)

3. The Research Department

The Got Milk? campaign depended on excellent research, it would not have happened without it.

Most agencies have their own research departments, but often work (through their department) with larger outside research facilities. My old firm most often worked with a firm in New Jersey called Perception Research which had large conference rooms, separate entrances, viewing rooms where we could watch potential candidates for our ads or packages try and discuss their merits through one-way glass.

Research firms are often small, maybe two or three person departments, but are a vital part of the mix and often critical to the success of the agency. A research person is responsible for reviewing, recommending and deciding on the appropriateness of a new ad concept, the one that will best support the brand's positioning.

All ads, after being created and before they go before the client, are tested, either via Focus Groups (invited "customers" who speak their mind about an ad or a brand) or Mall Intercepts (researchers who go into the public forum to ask quick questions of potential visitors in the retail area). One (the former) is called "Qualitative Research," while the other is called "Quantitative Research."

Research's Mission
By Jon Steel, author of *Truth, Lies and Advertising*

"The goal of advertising research is to tap into the inner thoughts of the consumer, to reach a deeper level of understanding, to know how they think, feel and behave; and then use those observations and discoveries to kick-start the creative process..."

The research process leads from (1) gathering data about the target audience, where they live, what they buy, etc., to (2) digesting information and analyzing the product and its market, to (3) searching for insightful moments (what can you learn that may be subtle, or implied) to (4) a hopeful moment of inspiration when you discover something that wasn't there before (at least in your head).

Research should be available to all account planners and creative persons. You never know over whose head the light bulb will go off.

4. The Media Department

The Media Department has finally come into its own. In the traditional full-service agency, this department was a support facility for the creative department. What emerged when the ad agencies unbundled themselves of their media departments was the emergence of the independent media agency, which made media buying move from a cost center to a profit center and in so doing it became a growth industry. Today the six largest media agencies control approximately $40 billion in advertising spending, nationally and globally.

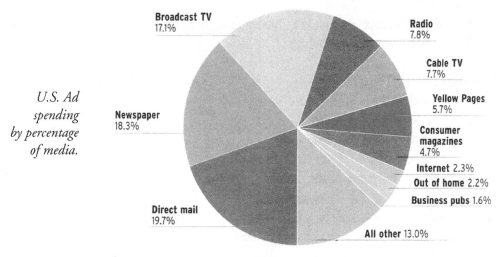

U.S. Ad spending by percentage of media.

Broadcast TV 17.1%
Radio 7.8%
Cable TV 7.7%
Yellow Pages 5.7%
Consumer magazines 4.7%
Internet 2.3%
Out of home 2.2%
Business pubs 1.6%
All other 13.0%
Direct mail 19.7%
Newspaper 18.3%

215

Advertising Totals by Media	
Medium	**US Ad Spending**
1. **Direct Mail**: 19.7%	($ 48.37 billion)
2. Newspaper: 18.3%	($44.84 billion)
3. **Broadcast TV**: 17.1%	($ 41.93 billion)
4. Radio: 7.8%	($ 19.10 billion)
5. Cable TV: 7.7%	($ 18.81 billion)
6. Yellow Pages: 5.7%	($ 13.90 billion)
7. Consumer Magazine: 4.7%	($ 11.44 billion)
8. Internet: 2.3%	($ 5.65 billion)
All Other: 16.7%	
Total (approximately)	**$236.11 billion**

Source: Advertising Age/Fact Pack - 2005

Another change in the advertising picture is the founding and rapid growth of Media Specialist Companies.

These organizations came about for two reasons:

a) Clients were complaining that their agencies were not buying media for their ads at the lowest, best rate.

b) Agencies realized that there was a great deal of money to be made from "independent" self-standing media placement companies, so they split their media department from the main body of the agency.

Starting in the early 1980s, six big media specialist companies were created. Their approximate (recent) U.S. billings are listed below.

1) **Mindshare** (WPP Group)	$9.40 billion
2) **OMD Worldwide** (Omnicom Group)	$8.33 billion
3) **Initiative Media** (Interpublic Group)	$7.51 billion
4) **Universal McCann** (Interpublic)	$7.40 billion
5) **Media Edge** (WPP)	$5 billion
6) **Optimedia** (Publicis Group)	$3.5 billion

Media is a message-delivery system, to a very big audience.

Because advertisers usually need to reach a mass audience as well as a specialized one, they need media buying services to do it for them. The advertisers could, but don't buy the media time or space they need, directly. It is too expensive, too dangerous and far too complicated. The media planning function is a major operation in advertising agencies and is perhaps the most important service the agency and its media planning entity can provide.

There are four positions in this department: The Media Chief, The Media Planner, The Media Buyer, the Media Coordinator.

The prime responsibility of the media department is to decide which basic advertising vehicle–television, radio, magazines, newspapers, etc. will be the most effective. Once this decision has been made, the specific publications, newspapers or broadcasts, must be selected on the basis of which will do the best job for the money allocated.

Media is separated into three overall classifications: traditional mass media, nontraditional media, specialized media.

Traditional Mass Media

Newspapers, magazines, radio and television are the basic categories in this classification. The advantages of this group are: they can deliver a large audience, they can deliver ads to special kinds of audiences, they have the ability to develop strong loyalties among audiences who have favorite shows, entertainment vehicles. Magazines are particularly good at delivering an ad to a specialized audience through the specialization of magazines themselves into interest groups: fashion, sport magazines, interior decorator magazines, gun magazines, etc.

Nontraditional Media

Sometimes it is called Guerrilla Marketing and can be as diverse as **matchbook covers**, **napkins, pens,** key fobs, tee shirts, television screens in airport waiting areas, posters, direct mail postcards, bus sides, commuter train cards and many more.

Guerrilla Marketing
By Jay Conrad Levinson

Guerrillas view creativity in marketing the same way that drivers view steering wheels in their cars. The creativity is supposed to guide the marketing toward its goal of producing profits just as the steering wheel is supposed to guide the car toward its goal of arriving safely at the destination. [Meaning: a guerrilla marketing concept must be creative in order to get you to your marketing goal]

Specialized Media

The publishing industry has spawned thousands of magazines for every special interest, and advertisers can buy space in skiing magazines to sell warm jackets, or gardening tools and books to homeowners who dote on their gardens, or bamboo fly rods to trout fishermen. The list is endless: money management, photography, antiques, wine or food. Sometimes this classification is referred to as niche media.

Sometimes the magazines themselves are provided free, paid for by the advertisers. Business-to-business advertisers are usually the most interested in these publications.

Handbills, direct mail and free-standing inserts (FSIs) in newspapers fall into this category as well.

It's a very complex industry.

The media planner will deal with certain specific questions for the client and his product:

> –How many prospects do I need to reach (to achieve the client's goal)?
> –How many times each day or month should prospects see each ad?
> –In which months (by season) should the ads appear?
> –How much money should be spent in each medium?
> –Where (by geographic area or market) should the ads appear?
> –In which medium (broadcast or print or special) should the ads be placed?

The Process

In today's world (from about 1998 on), Media purchasing is now divided between the agency's in house media planners, and the Media Specialty companies who make the actual purchases.

In this department, a complicated process must take place and work smoothly, efficiently and frugally.

The process evolves from a marketing strategy and consists of four interrelated activities:

> –Selecting target audiences
> –Specifying media objectives
> –Selecting media categories/vehicles
> –Buying the media (now done by the Specialist Companies).

Certain skills are required to be good at this.

Growing from the Media Tactics (which emerge as the methods to be employed to reach the Target Audience (like: "Which TV stations, Network or Spot buys, at what hour, what day of the week, what time in the year?")

It requires the use of:

> –Mathematical skills
> –Research tools
> –Common sense

These advertising organizations are all headquartered and located in North America, but have sizeable offices in Europe, Asia, and some in Latin America. All, or most ad agencies, also have three other divisions:

The Production Department

This department handles the production of an ad, making the artwork given them from the creative department, or the production of the TV commercial. These days, many agencies hire outside production departments, particularly for television commercials. Production, particularly for television commercials, can be very expensive. Production may involve the use of locations, actors, props, costumes, hotel accommodations, food, as well as camera crews, lighting engineers and sound. The biggest market for this work is Los Angeles, an off-shoot of the movie business. A typical LA shoot for one 30- or 60-second spot (or a recent big credit card company) ran as much as $300,000. As a result of this, many agencies (and their clients) have instructed their production companies to investigate filming in places like Vancouver, Canada, (cheaper actors who also speak English) or Wilmington, NC, (lower logistic expenses) or even Australia (but very far away).

The Traffic Department

This department has the simple, but important (vital even) task of following the course of an advertising assignment from initiation to production. Their mission is to see that what is intended actually happens. Many college graduates get their start in these departments.

Administration Department

This department is no different from that of any large corporation, consisting of: finance, accounting, office management and personnel (now often called "Human Resources").

Overview

All together the process of running an advertising agency is logical, integrated and functions smoothly. The work flows, or should, from the accounts department, to the creative (for a briefing), it is worked on and presented back to the account management, then taken to the client for approval (often with the creative director present), then if approved, it returns to the agency and the production department will see that it is produced (in print or broadcast form), the media department will find the right medium for the ad, present to the client and finally place the advertisement(s). Following along at the end of the line, the traffic department will make sure that it happens, when and where designated. Of course it doesn't always happen this smoothly; time pressure, unreasonable and last minute changes in creative work, attempting to buy media time in a crowded broadcast slot, can do severe damage to the process and the nerves of those trying to get it out.

Absolut – A Special Ad Campaign

 One of the most witty and stylistic ad campaigns at the end of the twentieth century were the Absolut ads (see also Chapter 4). The first of the Absolut Ads appeared in 1981 and variations ran continually for the next twenty-five years–more than 1500 ads in total. Always a print campaign (placed in upscale magazines), it moved the brand from an unknown vodka from Sweden to the third most popular in the spirits market (only behind Bacardi rum and Smirnoff). Today 40 percent of all imported vodka in the U.S. is Absolut, with over seventy-three million liters sold annually. It is the work of the agency, TBWA/Chiat Day.

The Mammoth Mirror

Writer Marshall Loeb, writing for *Time* magazine in 1962, called advertising a "Mammoth Mirror–a mirror on ourselves." It was a large mirror indeed, estimated at $12 billion spent on advertising by U.S. business. In 2004 (just forty-two years later) the total U.S. ad spending was $245.45 billion, with a projected 2005 estimate expected to exceed $250 billion. The broadcast portion of this expenditure (broadcast meaning radio and TV) was $76.58 billion, or 31.2% share of all advertising media expended. In this same year (2004), the cost of advertising on the Super Bowl was approximately $80,000 per second, or $2.4 million for one 30 second commercial. By 2008, Super Bowl commercials rose to $2.7 million or $90,000 per second!

The logical question is, who would spend such money? And for such a short moment?

The big advertisers on the Super Bowl last year were: Anheuser Bush, General Motors, Pepsi-Cola and Frito Lay–when they each spent an average of $2.7 million+ (each commercial) to run their 30 second spots. The reason they felt it was worth it? – about 110 million people watched the game last year–probably the only place where an advertiser can reach so many, at one time–all potential customers.

Putting aside the Super Bowl moment, just who were the big advertisers last year?

1. General Motors	$3.43 billion
2. Procter & Gamble	$3.32 billion
3. Time Warner	$3.10 billion
4. Pfizer	$2.84 billion
5. Daimler-Chrysler	$2.32 billion
6. Ford Motor	$2.23 billion
7. Walt Disney Co.	$2.13 billion
8. Johnson & Johnson	$2.00 billion
9. Sony Corp.	$1.81 billion
10. Toyota Motor Corp.	$1.68 billion

Procter & Gamble was number two in ranking, with annual expenditures of $3.32 billion, and they make the top five every year. Why? One reason P&G advertises is obvious–it works! At least twenty of their brands contribute $1 billion each to the annual sales. These are brands like: Tide, Pampers, Pringle's and Pantene.

A Powerful Commercial

One time a single commercial was aired (on the Super Bowl) that was so powerful that it had 72 percent audience recall and resulted in $4.5 million in new sales orders, the next day.

It was called "1984" and it had no spoken dialogue and just one line of copy.

The line of copy was, "On January 24th Apple Computer will introduce Macintosh. And you'll see why 1984 won't be like '1984' " – referring, of course, to George Orwell's classic book. It was the work of the ad agency Chiat/Day and the Apple in-house creative department. They never ran it again. They didn't need to.

They are all fighting for share of market and TV (and print and other means of marketing communications) help them achieve (and keep) their share goals. It is both aggressive and defensive. You will notice that four of the top ten advertisers in the previous chart, were automobile companies. All together these four spent almost $10 billion on advertising to increase market share–and lately Toyota (and Honda) are moving up.

Share of Market/ Auto Brands

Ford: 17.3% share (where each share point is equivalent to $34 million in sales)
Chevrolet: 15.8% share
Toyota: 9.6% share (newer figures put Toyota ahead of Ford for the first time)
Dodge: 7.3% share
Honda: 7.1% share

Share of Market/Beer Brands

Bud Light: 18.3% share (where each share point is equivalent to $5.6 million in sales)
Budweiser: 14.9 % share
Coors Light: 8.0% share
Miller Lite: 7.6% share

Measuring Market Share

Market share is the name of the game. The amount of advertising dollars spent just to increase market share by a fraction of a percent is staggering. "The competitive pressure on both advertisers and their agencies, is enormous," says Harry Jacobs, Chairman Emeritus of the Martin Agency of Richmond, VA.

Since the beginning of this century (and in the previous decade) we have been in the age of global branding and global marketing and the medium of choice has been anything wireless and handheld.

The things that affect and move us, the typical American consumer, are reflected (as always) in: music (jazz, rock, hip-hop), movies, television shows, sports, personalities and social changes such as growing fundamentalist religion, looser sex laws, the influence of politics, computer influence (email, broadband, Internet advertising), the economic situation, the consolidation of corporations (clients) and the imagination of advertising agencies. It's Mr. Loeb's "Mammoth Mirror" again, forty-four years later.

Five Memorable Ad Campaigns and Three Memorable Ad Men

The advertising campaigns which follow were shaped in large part by the styles and personalities of some advertising giants, men who, while different from each other, shared a love of the business and the craft of making ads. Here are profiles of three men and their signature ad campaigns.

David Ogilvy

He was the consummate English gentleman, and it was reflected in his ads. He assumed and played the role of the English aristocracy-with ease. He was handsome, he usually wore a tweed suit, smoked a pipe, and looked very much the British country gentleman. He was a real character in a business made up of characters. He wasn't born to English upper-class privilege, however.

He was born the fourth of five children in West Horsley, near London, in 1911 to an Irish mother and a Scottish father. Ogilvy won a scholarship to Oxford, but was expelled due to poor grades and study habits. He took off for the continent and got a job in the kitchens of the Hotel Majestic in Paris. Here he worked hard and considered this one of his happiest experiences as a young man. In later life and in his memoirs, he considered that his real life lessons were learned in the kitchens of the Hotel Majestic.

His first job in advertising was in London for Mather and Crowther. He flourished at that agency and after two years (and some pleading) got himself transferred to their New York office.

In Manhattan he became enamored of NBC and its radio advertising methods-and he met and idolized Rosser Reeves, an early advertising writer and creative director of Ted Bates & Co.

In 1948 he started his own agency. He was now thirty-seven and running America's first British agency. One of his backer/investors was his old firm, Mather & Crowther.

They played on their British roots; it gave them an image. It worked and they began to acquire clients: Hathaway shirts, and Guinness stout (in 1951).

The Man in the Hathaway Shirt

Hathaway was a Maine shirt manufacturing company, and Ogilvy approached the ads for this client in a unique way. He took what was a cheap, common shirt and presented it as a luxury item and set about creating a sense of sophistication for it. They found a distinguished looking model and used him in all the ads. He was respectable, middle aged, had a mustache, and they gave him a black patch over one eye for a touch of mystery.

The campaign, called "The Man in the Hathaway Shirt," appeared for the first time in *The New Yorker* magazine on September 22, 1951 and it was a runaway hit. Sales skyrocketed. David and his team went on to show him buying an expensive Purdy shotgun, painting a picture, conducting a symphony orchestra, always in an upscale situation. Many clients and successful campaigns followed: Schweppes and the bearded Commander Whitehead and his famous Rolls Royce advertisement in 1957.

Rolls Royce Campaign

For the initial ad, Ogilvy wrote one of the classic copy lines of all time. The ad featured a single RR Silver Cloud in front of a store and under the photo the immortal line, "At 60 miles an hour, the loudest noise in this new Rolls-Royce comes from the electric clock."

"At 60 miles an hour the loudest noise in this new Rolls-Royce comes from the electric clock"

Ogilvy had opinions, and he expressed them in print

–The headline is the most important element in almost all advertisements. It is the telegram which decides the reader whether or not to read the copy.
–The headline is the 'ticket on the meat'
–Every headline should appeal to the reader's self interest.
–Five times as many people read the headline as read the body copy. Include your selling promise in your headline.
And finally, - The pursuit of excellence is less profitable than the pursuit of bigness, but it can be more satisfying."
Confessions of an Advertising Man, by David Ogilvy, 1952

He retired early, at fifty years of age. He bought a chateau near Tours, in France.
In 1989 he fought and lost a hostile bid takeover of his agency, to the WPP Group. Under WPP ownership, Ogilvy & Mather grew to become the seventh largest in the world, with 377 offices in ninety-seven countries, 10,000 employees and 1,500 clients. David Ogilvy died on July 22, 1999.

Leo Burnett

As handsome and urbane as David Ogilvy was, Leo Burnett was not. He was half bald, had a sharply protruding forehead and a smooth face–remarkably free from wrinkles even in his sixties. He was short and pear-shaped and had a protruding lower lip. He was usually wringed in cigarette smoke and the lapels of his suit were almost always covered in cigarette ash. Some thought he looked funny; I thought he looked like a smaller version of the famous movie director Alfred Hitchcock.

No matter, he was a genius. He founded Leo Burnett Advertising in 1935 and in just twenty-four years he had built the fourth largest advertising agency in the world, with revenues of $120 million.

It was rare for a Chicago agency to grow to such size and prominence and most people think it had a lot to do with the particular personality of Burnett and his advertising.

Burnett was born in October of 1891, in St. Johns, Michigan. His father was a grocer, who did his advertising on a large sheet of wrapping paper with a fat, black pencil. Leo's first job was for a printer, later a teacher in a rural school. He saved his money for tuition to the University of Michigan and graduated in 1914. His first job after graduation was as a cub reporter at the *Peoria Journal* (in Illinois).

A friend lured him to Detroit with the promise of big bucks to be made in the automobile industry. Leo got a job with Cadillac, editing their in-house magazine.

It was while at Cadillac that he got his first introduction to advertising–but World War I interrupted his career. He served, and when he returned he went to work for an ad agency in Detroit. From that point on he embraced the profession with religious zeal.

In 1935 he opened is own agency in Chicago. He had just three clients and eight employees. From the beginning, the agency had two distinguishing features: a large bowlful of red apples, replaced fresh every day, and the company logo: a hand reaching for the stars. This logo derived from one of Leo's sayings, "If you reach for the stars, you may not get one, but you won't come up with a handful of mud either."

He loved Chicago and was fiercely proud of its personality. He was also very competitive and determined to show New York (Madison Avenue) what a good team in Chicago was capable of.

His credo was simple, honest and strong. It was a little like a Carl Sandburg poem.

Some Burnett Quotes:

"Our town is the Midwest, the heart, soul, brains and bowels of it."
"We are wide-eyed, unpretentious, creating ads that talk turkey to the majority Americans."
"Chicago advertising draws energy from the richness of American folklore, restoring it in a keen, lively way."
"There is an inherent drama in every product, our number one job is to dig for it, and capitalize on it."

Success didn't come quickly or easily, but it came and by 1939 the agency had six new clients and took over the fifteenth floor of its building at Michigan Avenue and the river. Their first big breakthrough was when they presented for (and won) the highly prestigious Santa Fe Railroad account.

Perhaps the watershed moment was yet to come, the birth of a legend account: the Marlboro Campaign.

The Marlboro Campaign

The year was 1954 and representatives from the Philip Morris Company were visiting all the agencies to see which one they would entrust with their Marlboro filter cigarette.

When they visited Burnett in his office the floor was littered with layouts for Marlboro. The Philip Morris men were impressed – and gave him the account.

The problem for Leo and his creative team was how to take a filter cigarette, with an effeminate aura, and make it a masculine brand.

Leo changed the package (using graphic designer, Frank Giannenoto), replacing the beige color with a deep red pack embellished with a V shape formed by white space, and changed the soft pack to a hard edged flip top box.

The most important decision had yet to be made, to determine the image of the type of man they would feature in the Marlboro ads.

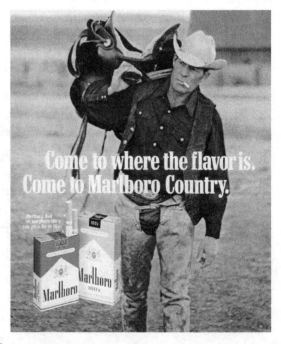

In a meeting at the agency, where they explored the icons of macho in American life one man posed the question, "What is the most virile American male you can think of?" In a moment everyone projected, "The American Cowboy!"

The first Marlboro advertisement with a cowboy appeared in January 1955.

Burnett and his agency went on to other distinguished campaigns, Nestle, United Airlines, the annual Pillsbury "Bake-Off" in New York's Waldorf Astoria hotel–but it was the Marlboro campaign that marked the agency. The trade press all talked of the Chicago school–a style of advertising that was gutsy, no-nonsense and strong. What they were really talking about was Leo Burnett. He was the Chicago school personified.

Leo Burnett died in 1971, at age seventy-nine. His work, his style and his agency lives on. The agency is now represented in 32 countries, employs over 4,000 people and is worth more than $900 million in worldwide annual revenues.

LEO BURNETT
COMPANY · INC.
ADVERTISING

William Bernbach

Of the three men profiled here, Bill Bernbach was the most unassuming in appearance and demeanor. He looked like he might be an accountant or professor. He was attractive but didn't stand out in a crowd. He wore glasses and dressed conservatively, if modestly.

But he was far from average in his creative skills. His creative work revolutionized the way advertising is approached today. It was innovative, intuitive and simple in style. He believed that "only a simple approach would make crystal clear and memorable the message of an advertisement."

In his long career, Bill Bernbach was able to create some of the most successful, beloved campaigns in the history of advertising–campaigns like Ohrbachs, Levy's bakery, Volkswagen and Hertz.

He was born in the Bronx in 1921 and after high school went to New York University and studied English, music and philosophy. His first actual job in an advertising agency was with the William H. Weintraub agency in 1940 where he started as a junior copywriter and soon became friends with Paul Rand, an art director and creative head there at the time. They merged talents on a number of accounts like the Dubonnet and Air-Wick accounts. He and Rand spent their spare time visiting art galleries and discussing images and good writing.

In 1949 he started his own advertising agency at 350 Madison Avenue. He had two partners, Ned Doyle, who was in charge of sales, and Maxwell Dane, who handled administration and finances. Bill was head of all creative work. They had thirteen employees.

DDB (Doyle Dane Bernbach) grew rapidly, but they kept their offices modest in appearance.

He felt it was necessary to follow intuition in creating ads and find the ideas that come from one's subconscious.

He had to make his reputation on smaller accounts and because he was able to do so, they, and he, were propelled into

CEO and Founder
Bill Bernbach

fame. His first triumph was Ohrbach's, the large but limited department store in Manhattan. He had to create ads to compete with those for bigger and better known Macy's or Gimbel's. The advertisements he created and ran in the *New York Times* were the first examples of the Bernbach style: it showed a man going into a store with a woman under his arm. The heading read, "Liberal Trade-In: bring in your wife and just a few dollars... we will give you a new woman."

The ads created a lot of stir and sales for Ohrbach's.

You don't have to be Jewish

to love Levy's
real Jewish Rye

His next breakthrough was the advertising he did for Levy's, an industrial bakery based in Brooklyn. Bernbach had a tiny budget, $40,000. He designed full page print ads for the *New York Times*. They were very clever and very New York. The campaign showed different ethnic types, an Irish policeman, a Chinese laundryman, an American Indian, each eating a rye bread sandwich. The headline read, "You don't have to be Jewish to love Levy's real Jewish rye." These ads, made into posters, are still being sold in stores in Greenwich Village.

The agency was gaining attention for its creativity and was beginning to attract top talent.

By 1957 the agency's revenues grew from $8 million to $20 million.

In 1958 they won five gold medals for creative work, awarded by the New York Art Directors Club.

The Creative Process of Bill Bernbach

The first step is to get thoroughly familiar with the product and the market. Then find a single purpose or theme to convey the product to the reader. This is more difficult. Bernbach and his creatives had the ability to intuitively find that single idea (the "Curly Factor") sometimes only one point of difference or importance that would strike a responsive note with the consumer. Once they found it, they pursued it tenaciously in the advertising campaign.

It is at this point, having determined the selling proposition, that Bernbach's genius was most impressive He would present that idea with such unique artistry and imagination that people would see it, remember and buy it.

Dick Coyne, from *CA* magazine in 1971.

The Volkswagen Account

Lemon.

In 1959 they picked up what was probably to become their most watershed account, Volkswagen.

It was a tough challenge, not one that everyone at the agency greeted with joy. It had the reputation (accurate) that it had been "Hitler's Car." Indeed Hitler had personally directed the Volkswagen project with the help of Austrian engineer, Ferdinand Porsche. The challenge, as one of his people put it, was to "sell a Nazi car in the biggest Jewish city in the world!" Further, it was lacking in charm, style, power and had no automatic transmission. There was much defection within DDB; many art directors or writers refused to work on it. So, Bernbach, and Helmut Krone (a first generation German-American) did it alone. The two men decided that all the defects should be made to appear as advantages.

The car's simple look reflected its price tag (low).

The car's underpowered engine meant it was more economical to run.

Art Director Helmut Krone designed a super simple, almost austere layout, which was one-third text, two thirds visual, all of which gave the ads a strikingly simple look.

229

The first Volkswagen ad to come out with this layout design bore the simple phrase, "Think Small." The follow-up copy below explained that the car was small in many good ways, small gas consumption, small engine, air-cooled and able to do 70 mph all day without strain, with a small price tag, etc.

They went on to create a series of clever, simple and highly effective print ads. They also utilized television with the same wit. One showed a VW driving up to a large garage, having no trouble in the deep snow. The headline read, "Have you ever wondered how the man who drives the snowplow drives *to the snowplow?*"

The ads, and the campaign, became a classic, even to this day. Furthermore, Volkswagen of America sold a lot of cars, and the world of advertising was mesmerized. The Bernbach style became the most sought after example of excellence in advertising.

In 1966 DDB was ranked one of the top ten agencies in the world with billings of $130 million. The agency was now established and preeminent. He had on his staff three of the best graphic designers of the time: Paul Rand, Bob Gage and Helmut Krone. Among his top writers were Mary Wells, (who went on to found Wells Rich Greene.), Julian Koenig and George Lois (an art director).

When the agency went public in 1964 (and today it is part of the Omnicom Group) it never functioned well as an ad agency with divisions and branches. It was, and remained, the creation of Bill Bernbach.

Bernbach on Inventiveness

"You must have inventiveness, but it must be disciplined. Everything you write, everything on a page, every word, every graphic symbol, every shadow should further the message you are trying to convey.

I warn you against believing that advertising is a science. It is [far more] intuition and artistry, not science, that develops effective advertising.

Find the simple story in the product and present in an articulate, intelligent and persuasive way.

Genuinely entertaining, involving, or dramatic advertising not only gets people's attention, it gets their affection."

Advertising, Wasteful or Useful?

Prominent men have attacked the business. Vance Packard in his book, *The Hidden Persuaders,* claimed that "Madison Avenue twists the truth and debases public taste." Harvard economist and teacher John Kenneth Galbraith argued in his book, *The Affluent Society,* that "Madison Avenue tempts people to squander their paychecks on un-needed possessions," and British historian Arnold Toynbee said that "the stimulation of personal consumption through advertising, is un-Christian."

Ad man Bill Bernbach rebutted Toynbee best when he said, "Mr. Toynbee's real hate is not advertising, it is the economy of abundance. Mr. Toynbee should really speak out against such a society and not merely against one of the tools that is available to any society."

Ad men defend their profession by pointing out that advertising is a vital cog in the wheel of commerce, allowing corporations to sell more units of a product through advertising than they ever could without. While advertising does induce the public to buy products that are not "needed," it also informs people of the availability of new or improved products, helps to create mass demand, which in turn makes possible mass production, with attendant employment, presence of retail centers, etc.

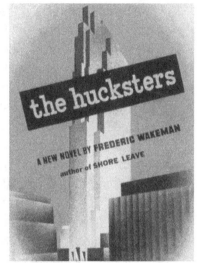

The Hucksters was a popular book and a classic movie.

Ad man David Ogilvy argues that while advertising may stimulate an urge for (say) whisky–harmful for an alcoholic, it also informs: stimulating the use of (say) toothpaste which improves oral hygiene, or travel ads which stimulate travel and knowledge.

Advertising is an aggressively creative, and effective force that makes cash registers ring by stimulating the public desire to acquire goods. It has become an indispensable force in making the U.S. economy move, a substitute for the personal salesman. It has become a magnet that draws customers into supermarkets and department stores, malls and specialty stores all across the country–a uniquely American contribution to global economic life.

Advertising is so effective because the best ads, and ad men, have learned to tap into the core of human psychology, with measurable results. The most heavily used themes of old evolved from three aspects of life: youth, sex and romance. Lately there have been three more added: financial security, health and humor.

In 1946, Frederic Wakeman wrote a book called *The Hucksters.* It was an exposé of the advertising business and its shallow goals. A movie was later made starring Clark Gable.

Time and Tide
By Kevin Roberts, CEO

SAATCHI & SAATCHI

The challenge was to get intimate with a whole new group of consumers (busy mothers). So, the first thing that P&G and Saatchi & Saatchi did was to take a long, hard look at the lives of what P&G affectionately calls "Moms."

Today's women live their daily lives on a punishing schedule. They deliver their children to and from school and their days are often packed with events and extracurricular activities. Then there is the planning and participating in family events on the weekends and running the household. Added to this marathon is the fact that the majority of mothers work full or part time. They live in their cars. They're constantly on the move. Clearly, Tide could no longer talk to these women in the way it once did–she didn't stand still long enough! The brand would have to catch her on the run–out in the world, not in the home, where its advertising messages had traditionally reached her. The message would have to be clear and quick. A message that showed how the brand empathized with her hectic and demanding lifestyle.

To talk with Tide's consumers, we developed the "Point of Dirt" campaign. This we figured, would represent all the classic situations where spillage and staining occur. In the car. On the bus. At the pizza parlor. A myriad of places. The strategy was to have Tide speak to mothers at the Point of Dirt–and to reassure her that in that instant, Tide would be right alongside her to clean up the mess. The advertisements that Saatchi & Saatchi created were light-hearted. Optimistic. Amusing. Ads that brought smiles to the faces of mothers and everyone else who identified their own personal sticky situations with the stories on the billboards (we created billboards that said "Takes Out, Take Out-Tide," or bus stop posters that said, "When your Popsicle suddenly becomes just a stick").

As one consumer told us, "Everybody's been there. It's so appropriate."

Another: "I think it's more personal when they speak to you at that moment. It's almost as if they knew what you were doing." The campaign was a rare and successful fusion of medium and message. An intriguing blend of information and intimacy.

The reward? Sales showed an immediate leap, and continued to grow year on year, in some markets up to twenty-five percent. Now that's a dramatic turnaround for

a brand that was running out of energy. By listening to the consumer, we created a very special moment of intimacy–a moment that reveals emotional understanding. A moment that proved to be the foundation of returning a brand, Tide, to its status as a true and enduring "Lovemark."

The lure of advertising is based on the merging of goods and values–illustrated through a series of images. It is also based on studying your target audience. The Saatchi/Tide campaign succeeded because they took the time to thoroughly understand their target audience–the busy, working mother and then create an ad message that reached them–what they called "The Point of Dirt."

When many ads for the same brand are grouped enmasse, as in a campaign, the cumulative impact is powerful.

What's it all mean? Just how powerful is advertising?

In 1999 two editors at *Advertising Age* put it this way: "Advertising played a key role in powering the miracle American economy of the past fifty years, and has had a profound impact – for good or ill – on our culture."

Marshall McLuhan (philosopher, scholar and communications theorist) put it another way. "Historians and archaeologists will one day discover that the ads of our time are the richest and most faithful daily reflections any society ever made of its whole range of activities."

Despite the many manifestations within the advertising industry, the pervasiveness of the business, the vast amounts of money spent every year and the many forms of stimuli bombarding the consumer, evaluating the effectiveness of advertising is still very difficult.

The "Milk Mustache" campaign began in 1994 to arrest the declining sales of milk by the American populous. It was the result of the creative team at Bozell Worldwide, under the leadership of CEO Chuck Peebler. It continues to this day with new celebrities and continuing success.

What? I know – you've never seen a cover girl with a mustache before. Well, get used to it. The milk, I mean. With nine essential nutrients including calcium galore, it's one of the best things around. Well, that and waterproof mascara, of course.

MILK
What a surprise!

10

SPIN

or the craft of public relations

Spin is the art of influencing opinion, a goal not unlike all integrated marketing communications.

Spin is widely practiced and very popular.

Spin works.

When done well, by a master like Karl Rove, it is highly effective.

It is, in many aspects, the "methode du jour" for marketers as well.

Its popularity grows from two current conditions: a general "turn-off "by the public for the more obvious methods of marketing (like copy-cat advertising, or hype with a too obvious, too repetitive message), and the apparent effectiveness of so-called "infomercials."

Politicians practice spin wildly, foolishly, some would say. David Ogilvy abhorred it, stating that "All politically directed advertising was fraudulent."

Trial lawyers use it most blatantly for high profile, celebrity clients (witness the Michael Jackson trial).

Army generals use it in reporting the success of a battle or progress of a war (remember the famous "Light at the end of the tunnel" projections of General Wm. Westmoreland during the Vietnam War).

Entertainers use it, often without moral scruples (witness the many efforts of Paris Hilton to stay in the public eye).

Even school children use it.

Spin, as practiced by a ten-year-old presenting an unfavorable report card, can be both inventive and highly imaginative and is, most often (to a wise parent), ineffective.

So, spin is ubiquitous. We all do it.

Spin is widely practiced, spin is calculated, directed and goal-driven.

Spin is another effective tool of marketers-especially when referred to by its more acceptable term, "Public Relations."

This chapter will explore the craft of public relations, how it all started, how it is practiced today and how its influence is likely to affect marketing communications for years to come.

Maytag and the Pillsbury Bake-Off

Maytag understands its image thoroughly and uses it adroitly in its marketing strategy. Its image is:

–Reliability (e.g. our machines are very well made–seldom break down)

–Old time values (e.g. we've been making great washing machines for years)

–We're always there for you. (The Maytag repairman is known and trusted.)

When Maytag recently launched Neptune, its new line of front-loading washers into a world made up of top loading washers, it crafted a clever public relations strategy to accomplish the launch.

They rented the ballroom of a New York hotel and threw a party, and the inviting host was "Ol Lonely" the well-known Maytag repairman. To emphasize the second quality of their image (old time values) they peppered the floor with seventies-era television moms, like Barbara Billingsley *(Leave it to Beaver)* and June Lockhart *(Lassie* and *Lost in Space)*, and of course, Florence Henderson *(The Brady Bunch).* Using those well-known, well regarded TV moms underscored the family values (by association) aspect of Maytag's PR program.

The second message that Maytag felt gave them a competitive advantage was that the Neptune was energy efficient. To demonstrate this they set up (in conjunction with the US Department of Energy) a live water-conservation test in Bern, Kansas. This town was ideal, image perfect. It is in middle America, it is attractive and best of all, it is small (population 204). This allowed Maytag to give half the town (102) Maytag Neptune machines for six weeks. The Department of Energy made it official by measuring the amount of water saved in each of those 102 homes (it was 38 percent). This successful demonstration was widely covered by the media, which provided the best kind of national publicity for the new washer line.

The Neptune promotion was public relations at its finest. It was (relatively) inexpensive, it was believable (with the Department of Energy overseeing the demo), and it was persuasive. Sales soared.

A good public relations program when it appears in the press, or is sponsored by a government organization, has the essence of apparent authenticity.

It can usually get around the normal skepticism of most consumers.

Who created this clever, integrated publicity program? Moreover, why did it work so well?

It was created by the public relations arm of Leo Burnett in Chicago. The public relations agency associated with Burnett through its holding company, is Manning, Selvidge and Lee.

More About MS&L

MS&L is, in many ways, typical of all of today's big public relations firms. This one is owned by the Publicis Groupe—one of the six major holding companies offering a plethora of marketing communications services. MS&L, as well as Burnett, is part of the Publicis Groupe, a Paris holding company and one of the five big holding companies who own and control nearly eighty-five percent of all marketing communications in the world. Publicis has billings of $13.91 billion, revenues over $4 billion, income of approximately $125 million (from recent records).

So, it is big business. And as such, they (the PR firm) have lofty (stated) ideals.

The MS&L mission, vision and values are:

–**Partnership** with their clients in creating exciting, effective PR programs

–**Collegiality** an open, even attitude about their work and its results

–**Knowledge** to constantly seek the truth, leading to creative insights

–**Initiative** to be bold, take risks, work outside the envelope.

Sounds a bit like motherhood or the Scouts, but it works and they believe in it and importantly, so do many of their clients; clients like General Motors, Procter & Gamble, Philips Electric, Pharmacia, etc.

The point here is that publicity is now big business, with serious goals and large scale operations. MS&L claims to have client relationships in 109 countries—although many are doubtless casual and based on the spread of offices of (Paris-based) Publicis Groupe, the fourth largest holding company.

The PR firms in the Ad Agency Holding Company Groups

Omnicom: Brodeur, CONE, Fleishman-Hillard, Karwoski 7, Courage, Ketchum, Porter Novelli

Interpublic: DeVries Public Relations

WPP Group: Burson-Marsteller, Cohn & Wolfe, Hill & Knowlton, Ogilvy Public Relations Worldwide
Publicis Groupe: Manning, Selvidge and Lee, Publicis Dialog
Dentsu: Renegade Marketing Group
Havas: Euro RSCG, Magnet Communications, Arnold Worldwide Integrated Solutions

The One Million Dollar Prize

Another public relations event that gained great popularity half a century ago and has enjoyed an enduring interest with the public, is the annual "Pillsbury Bake-Off."

Next year will be the forty-second such contest, although they have skipped a few years. The rules are simple.

Cooks wishing to enter simply submitted (via mail) their recipes to a central headquarters (in New York) where they were judged based on four criteria: taste, appearance, creativity and consumer appeal.

Entrants had to include two or more Pillsbury products listed on the entry form in their recipe and had to submit their recipe in one of six categories.

This year the top 100 finalist winners were invited to Miami, Florida, to actually bake their recipe and the grand prize winner won one million dollars and a GE Profile model oven.

The five runners-up contestants will also win prizes, like $10,000 and other GE products.

This year's winning recipe involved chicken with Pillsbury's waffle sticks-toasted. The winner was a housewife from Dallas and she won the one million dollars.

In my father's time (he was the Pillsbury Creative Director for the Burnett Agency) all 100 finalist contestants were transported (by train then) to New York City where they were set up in the Grand Ballroom of the Waldorf Astoria, with ovens and mixing tables. With television (and radio), watching the women actually bake their winning recipes within a time limit.

Arthur Godfrey (popular TV and radio personality) was brought in to do the final awards and make comments (and eat the winner's best efforts) while my father prepared press releases and wrote ads on the spot.

But loose as it was at times it was the genesis of an inspired public relations program.

Why did these two PR campaigns have such long term success? Because both Pillsbury's Bake Off and Maytag's Neptune campaigns had the ingredients for popularity inherent in the program.

–They were based on "down home" values (becoming a good cook/homemaker)
–They were respectful of the skills brought to the dinner table by women
–They correctly focused on the primary audience (the TA) for Pillsbury and Maytag's products–the homemaker.

A Definition

Now that you've seen two examples of successful public relations programs, both a little different–do they fit a pattern? Can they be defined? What exactly is public relations?
Here is a textbook definition.
Publicity is almost always associated with a news item, or editorial comments about a company's products. Publicity, like advertising, is non-personal communication to a mass audience, but unlike advertising, publicity is not directly paid for by the company that enjoys the publicity.
What does this mean?
The news item in question, or the editorial comments that relate to it, receive free print space or broadcast time because media representatives consider the information pertinent and newsworthy to their readers or listeners.
Does that mean that publicity is always random?
A happy accident?
Far from it. It is controlled and it is the job of a PR representative (of a client company for example) to solicit positive publicity for his/her client company or its brands. PR efforts are aimed primarily at customers, employees, suppliers, stockholders, governments, the general public, labor groups, and citizen action groups. Sometimes, to their sorrow, they have to confront, and blunt negative publicity.
But, there's a lot more to it than that simple definition would indicate.
Let's explore how, and where, public relations can work to the optimum.
According to K. Douglas Hoffman in his book *Marketing Principles & Best Practices*: there are two kinds of publicity. The two kinds are called "Proactive Marketing Public Relations (PMPR) and Reactive Marketing Public Relations (RMPR).

Proactive MPR

This is offensive publicity, intended, directed publicity. It is opportunity-seeking rather than problem solving. It is most commonly found in product introductions or product revisions and it strives for credability. Most consumers are skeptical of advertising claims–with good reason. When these same claims turn up as news, even though planted news, they have more credability and as such, are believed.

Burson·Marsteller

Burson-Marsteller is the fifth largest public relations firm in the world, with international clients and offices. Their range of services include: corporate/financial brand marketing, healthcare/public relations, crisis management, advertising/public relations and Internet development and integration. They are part of the Young & Rubicam affliliated group.

The tools PR firms have and use are: press releases, press conferences, happenings, personal appearances, events, including photographs, tapes, CDs and videos.

Reactive MPR

Reactive PR is undertaken when external pressures and challenges brought by competitive actions, changes in attitudes, government regulations, a crisis, create the potential for negative publicity. A good example would be when the government rates the safety factors of the newest automobiles, and those with less than high, positive ratings must counter this information. A typical one would be the problem the Ford Motor Company had a few years ago with its Explorer SUV and roll-over incidents. The problem was shared with Bridgestone/Firestone Tires.

Reactive MPR attempted to repair Ford's reputation, to prevent market erosion and regain lost sales. A public relations strategy can be focused on the corporate brand or on the product. PR departments usually manage the corporate image while marketing usually manages the brand image, although there is a lot of cross-over. Companies like Nike, Disney and Sony, and music promoters practice a kind of PR/Marketing mix that is hard to precisely define.

Brand Publicity

Brand publicity has become an integral and important part of the marketing communications mix. In fact a successful PR campaign often uses a mix of promotion, advertising and print design (see Chapter 11) to achieve its goals.

The goal is simple: to build a favorable impression with the public. How do they do this? With difficulty.

It is estimated that up to 70 percent of the PR effort goes toward brand publicity. Evidence of this can be found in the fact that of the fifteen largest public relations firms in the U.S., thirteen of them were acquired by the big ad agency holding companies (see Chapter 9).

McCormick Spice PR Program

One of the cleverest ongoing programs was devised by the PR firm of McCormick and Company, of Baltimore, the largest maker of spices in the U.S. Each year (since 1977) McCormick Spice has impregnated their annual report with a spice scent. They keep it a closely guarded secret until the annual report is sent out and the *Baltimore Sun* runs a pool inviting their readers to guess which scent is being used each year. This is PR at its best; the annual report gets attention for its novel aroma concept and the company generates media coverage through the contest in the newspaper.

The Process

Planning

Public relations must be planned, just like any other marketing endeavor. It should, as such, follow the traditional steps of 1) research (i.e. reviewing the situation), 2) setting realizable objectives, 3) developing strategies and tactics to achieve the objectives and 4) evaluating what has happened, and fix what hasn't worked.

First, understand and state your objectives.

Objectives

These are similar to advertising in that they seek to build brand awareness and brand knowledge.

> –Create or increase brand visibility
> –Create or change attitudes
> –Influence opinion leaders
> –Generate a sense of involvement

Often in a crowded, cluttered field direct efforts get lost. In situations like these the best one can try for is to create "Brand Buzz" or generate word of mouth. Word of mouth, when it happens, is powerful because of its high level of creativity. Guerrilla Marketing (see Chapter 7) is a useful method for generating buzz through the use of edgy and unconventional campaigns.

Research

It is the same as any marketing process for a consumer products company: doing background research, finding out about the company, its markets, its customers, and its competition. This is the place for a traditional SWOT analysis.

SWOT Analysis

It is a simple process for better understanding your brand's position in the marketplace.

S: stands for Strengths (What is my brand's most powerful quality?)

W: stands for Weaknesses (What is my brand's weak side?)

O: stands for Opportunities (Where might I take my brand?)

T: stands for Threats (What is my brand's competition? What might they try?)

Strategies and Tactics

The benefit of PR to achieve the objective of pushing brand awareness is that it usually can build brand credability faster than paid advertising. It can also attract hard to reach target audiences with articles in special interest and trade publications. These days there is a magazine for anything, any endeavor from sport fishing to home decorating. So, this strategy is devoted to careful, imaginative media placement.

Execution

Unlike traditional ad placement, publicity requires finesse with the media. It is critical to getting placement to generate good will, a comfortable relationship with editors and media buyers. These people are referred to by PR practitioners as "Gatekeepers."

And they are aptly named. For if you can't get into the paper, you're not getting through the "gate."

The best way to do this is to maintain a positive, professional relationship with the media avoiding the appearance of hype, or being blatantly dishonest. Over the top statements about the product seldom work ,just as obvious pandering doesn't. Bottom line, avoid being "sleazy."

Gatorade

Brand publicity is particularly useful for launching new products–and no better example exists than that of Gatorade. The use of on-camera consumption by athletes during a game, followed by the ritual of dumping the big Gatorade ice barrel over the head of the winning coach- is masterful. It is ubiquitous, free and believable and the viewing public loves it (but maybe not the coach).

And finally, along with imaginative usage in execution and media placement, other necessary and important parts of the strategy should include scheduling and budgeting.

Overall Advantages - When You Do it Right

1. You can build a climate of acceptance for a company or its brands.
2. You can increase the credability and believability of the brand.
3. You can break through the commercial message clutter.
4. You can have the potential to reach hard to attract audiences.
5. It can be very cost-efficient.

There are limitations, however.

Public relations, by its very nature, can only last so long. You can't get the same story in the paper weeks apart. Your message can become redundant, and the only way to counter this is to find ways to approach it from a different point of view, and to spread your message widely.

Placing the Story

This is the first priority, and there are many ways to do this. You should provide

–background information
–a point of view that makes it "unique"
–sometimes even writing the story
–press releases

News releases should follow certain criteria, such as:

–Ask who, what, why, where and when the story occurs.
–Organize paragraphs with the strongest point at the top.
–Write in short paragraphs, blurbs.
–Fit the story to the publication's audience.
–Be accurate and factual. Don't fudge an issue, you must always maintain the image of integrity.
–Provide News Kits.
–Fact Sheets, summaries, pitch letters (story proposal)

Overall you must maintain the following qualities in your presentation:

–Impact (What is the magnitude of the action, product or event?)
–Timeliness (Is your story breaking or a development?)
–Proximity (Is there a local story angle?)
–Prominence (Does the story affect a prominent person?)
–Conflict (Is there drama in the story?)
–Human Interest (How fun, entertaining or emotionally engaging is the story?)
–Novelty (Is our story unusual?)
These are the traditional methods of creating an effective public relations program. They are close to those for any well-crafted, well-thought-through marketing campaign.

The "Father of Public Relations"

Edward L. Bernays is considered by many to be the "Father of Public Relations," although this statement is open to question. It is more likely that there were several early practitioners of controlled information dissemination. But it does seem as if the practice began sometime after the turn of the twentieth century.

Whenever or whoever, Edward Bernays was an early pioneer and was responsible for some of the most innovative and effective public relations campaigns in history.

He was born in Vienna, November 22, 1891, the nephew of Sigmund Freud. Evidently Freud was a big influence on his life. As a boy and into early manhood he spent many days in Freud's company, sometimes hiking in the Swiss hills around Zurich with him.
His family moved to the United States when he was very young and they lived in Brooklyn. When he was of college age he went to Cornell and surprisingly majored in (and got a degree) in agriculture.

After college he became a press agent for some of the early Broadway productions and performers, including a concert tour for Enrico Caruso (1915), and another for the ballet impresario Diaghilev to promote the Ballet Russe troupe's U.S. tour (in 1917).

*In 1917, Bernays was able to sell ballet to the American public
with imagination and skill.*

His handling of the ballet troupe's publicity was masterful. There was an established stigma against women who showed as much leg as a ballet dancer would do, as well as a bias against the male dancers whom many considered sexual "deviates."

He overcame these obstacles by concentrating on the color, the costume, the interesting story lines of some of the ballets, and the history of Russia—a far-away country considered mysterious and "dangerous." When showing posters (and magazine ads) of certain female dancers in costume he had to retouch more skirt onto the dancer's costume to gain acceptance, especially when they appeared in cities in the Midwest.

He was one of the first to devise the press kit, which he sent to newspapers before the Ballet Russe came to town along with pictures and an eighty-two page publicity guide. These were used by advance men that Bernays employed to prepare the next city on the tour. He arranged for store windows in downtown Detroit and Chicago to have displays featuring Russian ballet costumes and reproductions from the stage sets. Ultimately it was a huge success and probably helped to change America's opinion about ballet forever. It also probably caused many young girls to dream of becoming ballerinas.

Some fifty years later both Adolf Hitler and his propaganda minister Josef Goebbels used the principles and lessons of Bernays' teachings (as published in Bernays' own book *Propaganda* in 1928) for the manipulation of public opinion in the lead up to and duration of World War II.

One of his early techniques was the use of third party (seemingly objective) endorsement. For one client (who made and packaged bacon) he conducted a survey of 5,000 physicians and asked them if they agreed that a healthy person should begin his or her day with a hearty breakfast. All agreed of course and so Bernays was then able to report, in publicity releases and ads, that 5,000 doctors recommended that people should eat hearty breakfasts which could include bacon and eggs.

Lucky Strike

In 1925 he received an assignment from the American Tobacco Company (makers of Lucky Strike). The goal of the project was to make cigarette smoking more acceptable with women, an as yet untapped market.

Bernays decided that the cigarette was symbolic of female emancipation, and slightly sugges-

tive of sexual gratification. So his idea was to send out a challenge in the form of an ad in *Vogue* which generally stated that "Holding a cigarette in one's hand was to hold a 'Torch of Freedom.' "
Furthermore, he challenged any female to make the highly visible, annual and upper-class promenade down Fifth Avenue on Easter Sunday morning, with a cigarette in hand. He also recruited a known feminist, Ruth Hale, to do the same. Bernays even sent the same challenge in a letter to the fifty debutantes who had "come out" that year. Ten women did do it, and the press went wild. Overnight it became a national sensation, and Lucky Strike became a symbol of freedom and emancipation.

Thomas Edison

Another less controversial project that Bernays tackled was to commemorate the 50th Anniversary of the invention of the light bulb-in 1929. It became known as the Light's Golden Jubilee, and it lasted six months. The grand climax was when President Herbert Hoover traveled to Dearborn, Michigan, to dedicate the Institute of Technology and to celebrate the achievements of Thomas Edison. In attendance were Henry Ford, Orville Wright, John D. Rockefeller, and, of course, Thomas Edison. The press lauded the half year PR campaign, and even the Post Master General brought out a special commemorative stamp.

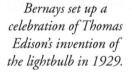

Bernays set up a celebration of Thomas Edison's invention of the lightbulb in 1929.

Bernays had a long and successful career, serving such clients as Procter and Gamble, CBS, American Tobacco, General Electric, Dodge cars, and American presidents: Calvin Coolidge, Herbert Hoover and Dwight Eisenhower.

Bernays wrote three books: *Crystallizing Public Opinion*-in 1925, *Propaganda* in 1928, and *Biography of an Idea* (his memoirs)- in1965.

He lived until 1995 and died at the age of 104.

He said that there were three main elements to public relations:

–Informing People

–Persuading People

–Integrating People with other People.

He said, "The engineering of consent is the very essence of the democratic process, the freedom to persuade and suggest."

There are those who feel strongly that Karl Rove studied Bernays' methods and used them in creating the politically successful persona of President George W. Bush. Rove positioned him as a "man of action, rugged and decisive."

"The use of words and pictures is not enough to persuade, it is in fact only one tool; you must touch a man or woman where they exist, in their core beliefs, which they have had and have carried with them from birth," said Bernays in 1950.

He extolled and exemplified Sigmund Freud's philosophy in his PR work all his long life.

The Growth of "Infomercials"

Clearly the most dynamic way one can advertise a product is on television.

Because of its ability to work with sound and moving visuals, and because it comes to you in your own home, it is the most powerful medium you can use. But its very popularity brings with it a negative–clutter. Almost one third of prime time is now being used for non-program content (commercials, etc.). A commercial pod, as they term it, is the commercial break in a TV program and often carries ten or more different brand messages.

Because of this condition and a certain watcher "ennui," infomercials came along.

An infomercial is generally a thirty-second commercial program that demonstrates a product, presents testimonial from satisfied users and usually offers viewers one or more ways to buy the product directly (a toll-free number, a website address, etc.). The weak point can be the call center because when the caller calls in, the manner in which he/she is treated makes a big difference between a sale and no sale. The rule of thumb is that for companies using infomercials to sell their products, they must generate $3 in sales for every $1 spent on TV time. If the product is also available locally in a retail store, the ratio can be less because infomercials can drive store sales as well as direct purchases.

Introducing New Products to the Public

When companies launch a new product line it generally combines a number of marketing techniques from packaging, to advertising campaigns, to public relations events. For maximum effect they should be coordinated and present a seamless message. The typical role of PR is to stage a press party.

Usually the CEO, or Marketing Vice President, hosts a luncheon and explains, even demonstrates the product to the press. We staged such a press party for the launch of a new Grey Poupon line of products.

The Nabisco Launch

When my firm designed the packaging for a new Nabisco line called "Grey Poupon Gourmet Foods" (see Chapter 5), the packaging and the advertising was all structured around the look of French and Italian Impressionism. We had, in fact, managed to gain permission to reproduce actual paintings by such artists as Monet or Van Gogh on the labels of a range of salad dressings, olive oil, cooking wine, etc. So the theme was "Impressionism." For that reason, and that the original advertising had prominently featured a white Rolls Royce, both were present and prominent at the press party which launched the new Nabisco/Grey Poupon product line. The press party was held on the terrace above Wollman Rink in New York's Central Park. Because it was summer we didn't have to contend with skaters and (with park permission) we were able to park a white Rolls Royce on the terrace. The Rolls had a painted mural on both doors–a floral scene in the style of an impressionist painting.

There was a chauffer in pearl-gray livery and a tuxedoed "pitch man" who spoke and served the press and public special salads and food items made or garnished with the new Nabisco Grey Poupon products.

After about forty-five minutes the white Rolls was packed up and driven away, off to tour twenty cities across the United States. We hoped and expected that this scene would be repeated to large crowds and an enthusiastic press from coast to coast.

I think the important ingredient here was that the publicity event grew out of the product's image. We had designed twelve products (salad dressings, Balsamic vinegar, Extra Virgin Olive Oil, cooking wines etc.) with scenes taken from actual impressionist painters. The theme of the press party echoed the image/theme of the packaging and, of course, the advertising which followed over the next six months.

The lesson to be learned is that the press event must emerge naturally and without strain out of the theme of the product, its advertising or in this case, the packaging. Consistency reflects honesty and the public respects it and remembers it.

If it isn't a new product, a product launch is much harder and invariably the company is tempted to slap a label "New" on the bottle. This never works, the press knows it, the public knows it and any credability disappears.

The best organized publicity campaigns succeed when the retail sales staff are included in the media.

Fact sheets should be distributed to the press and to the sales staff. Short, precise briefings should be held to bring the sales staff on board. Contests and sales incentives can be built-in to help launch the program.

But the human factor can still be the weak link. Many are reluctant to be trained, skeptical of the opportunity to be part of the team.

(There is more on the Nabisco Grey Poupon story in Chapter 5–Packaging)

Public Relations in the Twenty-first Century

Today the picture is much different than when Ed Bernays started practicing public relations. The interim 100 years has resulted in a nation that is shaped from all quarters by a deeply entrenched public relations industry augmented by new and very effective research methods. By the end of the twentieth century the machinery of research and ultimately the potential for manipulation got very sophisticated. The apparatus for reading the public mind and for appealing to the public eye has become increasingly pervasive. Economic mergers in the media and information industries (AOL-Time Warner, Comcast, etc.) made it possible to focus a PR pitch very precisely, at just the target audience you wish to reach.

Deep Knowledge

There is an organization in Little Rock, Arkansas, called the Acxion Corporation. It is not well known, but it isn't secret. Their business is to create and deliver customer and information solutions. They do this by blending data with technology to provide the most encompassing information infrastructure available. They divide their service into two categories, InfoBase and Personicx. They depend on each other. InfoBase is the biggest collection of U.S. consumer and telephone data in one place, in the nation, maybe the world. They have acres of the big IBM and Cray computers. Personicx divides this information into seventy distinctive segments and creates profiles (demographics) on consumer behavior, and they sell it to consumer products companies, or pollsters, or political parties.

They seek and gain legal access to public information, such as driver's license registration records, catalogs you take, what dogs or cats you have, customer records from credit card records, voting records, magazine subscriptions, education files, church affiliations, what you buy online, in short, ***everything.***

This information allows Acxion to deliver the right message to the right customer, in effect to custom fit a political presentation in the same city with one message for different parts of a city or town. A client (or a candidate) can advocate abortion rights on one side of town, right to life on the other side of town.

It is legal and it is accurate and it is, or can become, a powerful element of persuasion. They call it "Narrow-Casting."

The Power of Words

There is a political consultant named Frank Luntz, of the Luntz Research Companies, who conducts focus group sessions with a hand-held gauge that allows participants to measure reaction to words in a speech. Luntz is a big believer in word selection and is responsible (he says) for getting the Republican Party to substitute "Death Tax" for "Estate Tax" when he was pushing for tax reform. He knows that while they mean the same thing, one is more palatable than the other. Other switches included using "The War on Terror over The War in Iraq," or "Tax Relief over Tax Cuts," or "Climate Change over Global Warming."

Needless to say, Luntz is in great demand.

Kevin Roberts, CEO of Saatchi and Saatchi, agrees but from a different view point. He is striving to get new accounts for his agency. He believes passionately that brands can create loyalty beyond reason, that handled correctly, they can establish a bond with the consumer that is intimate, personal and iconic. He has even written a book on the subject, called *"Lovemarks."* He feels that advertising and PR practitioners must learn to build emotional branding–to equate the brand with a life style.

This has been done successfully with the iPod advertising and Nike. Roberts has done it successfully with such clients as Olay and Tide, where he equates the laundry soap with being an enabler, a liberator, and as such, has become the heart of the family.

It's a stretch, but it works.

A Kodak Moment
Kevin Roberts, CEO of Saatchi and Saatchi

By the mid 1990s a new force was about to start snapping pictures: Generation Y teens. Kodak, our client, wanted to be in the path of this movement but feared competition from Fuji, and the move to digital. We had to make the Kodak brand for teens fun and cool. We analyzed our position and realized we were already in the jargon with the expression, "Excuse me, can I have my Kodak moment back?" We built our PR program around that concept.

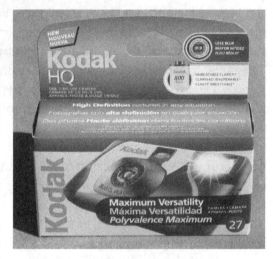

We staged a PR/Promotion event with a new (unknown and young) rock band called Youngstown. We put the band on a tour of twenty-two markets throughout the U.S., playing in malls. We had tie-in partners, like Sam Goody for record sales. And we had a Youngstown CD packed in with a Kodak one-time use camera as a premium. At each concert the boys in the band came running out snapping pictures of the audience, and then threw them out to the audience. It was a big success, for the band, for Sam Goody and for Kodak.

The Saturn Campaign

A wonderful example of emotional branding is exemplified in the Saturn campaign. This is the car that GM created in a very special way. In 1990 they realized that customers were turned off with GM and its cars, and Detroit in general. So they created a new car and a new way to reach customers. They built a plant in tiny Spring Hill, Tennessee. They worked hard to maintain good relations with the community and the union. They set up independent Saturn dealerships. They invited customers to watch their cars being built. They called everyone "Stakeholders," and this group included dealers, vendors, employees, suppliers, Spring Hill citizens and, of course, customers.

They hired Hal Riney & Associates to do the PR and advertising. He created the slogan, "A Different kind of Company, a Different kind of car."

And on the tenth anniversary of the company's founding (in 2000) they staged a giant reunion. 45,000 people (the original "Stakeholders") came to Spring Hill and they called it, appropriately, "The Saturn Homecoming." This giant PR campaign built emotional bonding, and thus branding that is real and

2007 Saturn Sky

is long term. It built on people's need to form a cult, to be part of a community based on simple values of quality, honesty and caring.

Another observation of Kevin Roberts (and it's not his alone) is that the newest crop of consumers is different from the ones preceding. They have been inculcated with the belief that they are "special, unique, should come first, have their desires fulfilled," in short, that they are empowered." We are experiencing a society that increasingly sees its own well-being as the central issue. The main problem is how to reach these new consumers, how to break through the clutter. Infomercials and clever public relations campaigns may be part of the answer.

There is no better example of the merger of public relations techniques with smart advertising and compelling sales promotion tactics than the transformation of New York's Bloomingdale's from a frumpy neighborhood store to one of the most cutting edge in the nation. It reshaped the retail business.

"Bloomingdale's... like no other store in the world."
By James S. Schoff, Former President of
Bloomingdale's, New York

Background on Bloomingdale's

Back in the 1930s and shortly after the Second World War, Bloomingdale's was just an ordinary promotional store on a par with Gimbel's or Macy's, slugging it out for volume on all the branded commodities. The transformation of the store into "Bloomies"–the trendiest store in New York," began in 1945 when new management arrived from Bamberger's Chicago store. They began to notice things. First, they noticed that their store (at 59th Street and Lexington) was smack in the middle of one of the highest concentrations of wealth in the world, the 19th precinct of the upper East Side. Next they noticed that the people who lived there weren't shopping there.

This unfortunate fact might have dawned on them when their newly-appointed treasurer went to a dinner party in the neighborhood shortly after arriving at his new job, and happened to mention to his dinner partner what he did and for whom. She responded, "Oh, that's very nice, my maid shops there all the time." It was known (and had been for some time) as having the best maid uniforms in the city!

Bloomingdale's management recognized the rich, potential market living beside them and set out to capture it. To do so meant refocusing the store to attract the neighborhood customers all around them. Little by little they created a store recognized for its assortments of fresh, exciting merchandise, some exclusive to the store, and all displayed in attractive, creative settings.

It was at about this time [1960] that I [Jim Schoff] joined the New York store, initially as a buyer. We started by altering (and reducing) the mix of the merchandise. Up until then Bloomingdale's carried everything, from refrigerators, to stoves to furniture. It was built on the principle of Gross Margin, not how many dresses you could sell as the result of an ad. Then we began to think about fashion and glamour in an effort to lure the young couples and singles who were moving into the area. Gradually, thanks to promotional efforts, publicity and advertising, people were beginning to think of shopping as entertainment–particularly at Bloomingdale's.

In the early 1960s we launched the model rooms program–a masterful public relations and promotional campaign.Twice a year the fifth floor (the furniture department) got itself completely torn up. We remodeled everything, from the walls to the ceiling. There was always a theme–usually a country or market area. The first such show was called "Casa Bello," in 1961, where the theme was the Italian home. This was followed by "Esprit de France" in 1962 (French homes), and our staff proved very imaginative at planning and showmanship–it was real theatre. We usually opened with a dinner and cocktails and a celebrity guest. This was the first appearance of international shows, and mostly it featured home furnishings, exclusive merchandise

252

from these countries. We also started buying merchandise overseas: England, France, Morocco, etc. Our buyers spent months on international buying trips. We also started taking designs overseas to be executed by foreign designers like Pierre Deux in Provence. Bloomingdale's was the first to do this, or at least people thought we were and that is what we wanted.

Both the *New York Times* and the *Wall Street Journal* did major stories on us in 1974. Italian and French film stars like Marcello Mastroianni and Catherine Deneuve bought sheets and pillowcases there. Socialite Gloria Vanderbilt designed a bed and bath collection for us, and Jackie Onassis' favorite dressmaker, Valentino, presided at a fall fashion show that same year. Perhaps our biggest publicity moment happened when Queen Elizabeth and Prince Philip paid the store a visit in 1976, when we did an England show. Our promotional and public relations efforts paid off. We were getting talked about, and of course our neighborhood customers took note, and came in themselves.The

Bloomingdale's created an imaginative series of shopping bags which became "walking billboards" along 5th Avenue.

transformation of our neighborhood store into the hottest, trendiest in town was the result of the efforts of successive managements and took close to 50 years to achieve.

The Shifting Role of the Department Store

Today Bloomingdale's is one of only 2 "brand names" in the Federated portfolio. From now on Federated (who owns Bloomingdale's and now The May Company stores) will only sell under two brands: Macy's and Bloomingdale's, a total of more than 960 stores. They will compete with Sears Holdings, which has about the same number of stores, and annual sales of over $30 billion. Federated will forsake the names and legacies they own with such famous stores as Burdine's in Florida, Rich's in Atlanta, Marshall Field's in Chicago, Wanamaker's in Philadelphia, Hudson's in Detroit and a lot more.

bloomingdale's
LIKE NO OTHER STORE IN THE WORLD

★macy's
way to shop!®

Saul Bass

Saul Bass is one of the most celebrated and successful graphic designers of the middle twentieth century. Like Paul Rand he was a native of New York City (born in May of 1920) and studied at The Art Student's League in Manhattan as well as Brooklyn College. Unlike Paul Rand he became famous for his work in Hollywood (in 1954) with filmmaker Otto Preminger. He devised a unique method of designing animated motion picture title sequences that enhanced the meaning and excitement of the picture to follow and won an Academy Award for his work on *Why Man Creates* in 1968.

Bass was responsible for some of the best-remembered, most iconic logos in North America, including: Celanese (1965), Continental Airlines (1968), Bell Telephone (in 1969), United Airlines (1974), General Foods and AT&T (1983).

In the course of his forty-year career he designed title sequences for films as diverse as *Man With the Golden Arm, Spartacus, Psycho, North by Northwest, Vertigo, Exodus, Advise & Consent* and *West Side Story.* He worked for such directors as Alfred Hitchcock, Stanley Kubrick, Preminger and Martin Scorsese. His work is held in the permanent collections of the Museum of Modern Art in NY and the Library of Congress. He lived a long time, and died at 76 in April of 1996.

"[His] combination of intellect and emotion came through in everything he touched…a packaging program, a poster for a film festival, an extensive corporate identity program or a gasoline station in South America."

- Lou Dorfsman (graphic designer)

Movie posters and logos
(in the center)

11

PRINT

Design in Publications

There is a vast and largely unexamined, unappreciated world of design that deals only with the printed word; the printed word as manifested in brochures, catalogs, annual reports, books and magazines. Some are well-designed, highly sophisticated brochures (like the catalogs of *Sharper Image* or *Restoration Hardware),* some are clumsy and unappealing, like gardening catalogs, some are heavy with financial facts and figures (like most annual reports), some are thin, slim and understated. Whatever, the published (printed) annual report, catalog or brochure is a vital link in the chain of marketing communications that is the comprehensive subject of this book.

It is safe to say that they are all marketing something: a product, a service or even simply entertainment.

Typography

It would not have existed if one invention about 600 years ago hadn't caught on–the invention of printing with moveable type. The year was 1454 and Johannes Gutenberg gets the credit for this invention. Gutenberg only printed 300 copies of his famous bible and forty-five still exist. The pages of the Gutenberg bible are highly decorated, much in the style of hand-drawn early illuminated manuscripts. The type (in Latin) is also decorative, gothic and the pages contain illustrations which flow between the two columns. Naturally attention quickly turned to the craft of type design, and some of the earliest designers of type are still popular today. The Italians were printing with moveable type in Rome and Venice by 1469, the French by 1470 and Great Britain by 1476.

Matthew Carter is a contemporary type designer in great demand.

A contemporary type designer is an Englishman named Matthew Carter, who designed a typeface (font) for Microsoft called "Verdana." (See Chapter 3 for more on type.)

Essentially type is offered to publication's designers in two ways, with serifs and without serifs. A serif is the small "foot" found at the bottom of a vertical stroke of a letter form.

A (Bookman-serif face)
A (Garamond-serif face)
A (Futura-sans serif)
A (Verdana-sans serif)

There are other stylistic techniques that good type designers use.

Linkages. This is when the type is touching or almost touching–*intentionally*, so that you notice it as a single idea, or linked word.

Stacking. Another is stacking–where the letters, and whole words are placed unnaturally close, even on top of each other, again to make an intended impression.

It's really all about "spacing" – how do the individual letters relate to those next to them, or below or above and then what is the visual impression this creates?

Part I: The Printed Word

Generally speaking, there are three types of brochures:
1. Annual Reports
2. Capability Brochures
3. Catalogs

Let's begin this examination with the largest group, Annual Reports.

1. The Annual Report

There are approximately 5,500 common and preferred stock issues from (about) the same number of companies, traded on the New York Stock Exchange, American Stock Exchange and NASDAQ. Additionally, there are approximately 450 more from non-U.S. companies.

All these companies must, by law, issue a 10K once a year–commonly known as the Annual Report. The statutes that dictate this are known as Federal Trade Commission Act of 1914 and The Securities and Exchange Laws of 1933 and updated in 1934. This was an important issue back in the mid 1930s when many companies were not being honest with their shareholders and investors–a contributing factor to the stock market crash of 1929. The laws, as stated, require full financial disclosure in the form of a 10K, annually and quarterly. Many companies use the occasion to project a marketing and public relations opportunity to make their annual report more attractive.

Clockwise from top: ExxonMobil, Nike, Heinz, P&G

This means that the front thirty (approximate) pages can become "promotional." They are (often) liberally sprinkled with full color photos and well designed graphics.

257

No one knows for certain precisely how many annual reports (as opposed to 10Ks) are produced each year, at least those that involve a graphic designer's skills. It is estimated that approximately 2,800 companies are publicly traded at the New York Stock Exchange daily and another 800 at the American Stock Exchange, and about 2,000 on the NASDAQ. There are also approximately 4,500 Mutual Funds listed separately, and some of them issue a promotional annual report. It comes to about 10,000 in total.

This is fertile territory for graphic designers.

The Layout

The typical layout of an illustrated, promotional annual report is as follows:
- **First:** cover and back cover, full color picture of the company or its products in action.
- **Second:** Financial Highlights of the year at a glance.
- **Third:** The Chairman's or CEO's (sometimes both) message to shareholders, written as a letter.
- **Fourth:** the promotion section, advantageous business highlights; approximately eight pages with pictures of the operations of the company in the year being reported.
- A picture of the Board of Directors and a listing or picture of the corporate officers.
- **Fifth:** Analysis and Consolidated Financial Statements–in depth
- Statement of Assets
- Statement of Profit and Loss
- Notes and details

A typical annual report is about 80-100 pages plus cover and back cover.

Graphic Design firms like working on these brochures. The fees are good (around $250,000 for a Fortune 500 company) but the deadlines can be brutal, especially in the last days before printing the Financials. The numbers get moved around a great deal and there is intense pressure to not make mistakes. The ultimate, unmovable deadline is the annual meeting of stockholders, which is publicly announced and unchangeable.

2. Capability Brochures

There are two types:
- Those which explain or glorify a **product**
- Those which explain or glorify a **service**

There are many, many types, for many sorts of companies. They can be brochures to explain and sell the virtues of a consulting company, a hospital, a law firm, a medical group, or a college or university, to name a few.

The advantage of a capability brochure over an advertisement is that it represents a well-thought out message about the company and its people, gets passed around and often provides the stimulus for a new project.

The sequence of the context of a capability brochure also usually follows a set pattern.

The Georgia-Pacific papermill in Crossett, Arkansas

Upper left: Cover;
Middle: Page 1;
Lower left: Back Cover

Cover: to glorify the service or product being discussed in the brochure, with often a full-sized photograph. The goal of the cover is simple and direct – to entice someone to open it and read.

First Page: reveal the lead into the central message, cogently but compellingly.

Inside Spread: reveal the main message. The critical relationship is the headline to the picture and the picture to the text.

Back Cover: a final reminder of the subject, with the company logo and address.

Good examples are the brochures for Georgia-Pacific which promote their products or one of their papermills.

3. Catalogs

They come in all sizes and shapes in an endless variety of items. Their mission is simplest of all, sell their products.

The variety of products are almost endless, or seem so.

Clothing is perhaps the largest category: Lands End, J. Crew, J. Jill, etc.

Tools are also a large group: like Brookstone and Sharp Electronic.

Sports items: LL Bean, Cabela's for fishing and hunting, etc.

Artistic collectables: The Metropolitan Museum Gift Store

Home Furnishings: Restoration Hardware, Crate & Barrel, etc.

Three catalogs: (counter-clockwise from left) Chico's, Land's End and Crate & Barrel (with one inside page)

They are usually seasonal and try to evoke an aesthetic mood linked to the season. Fall in New England, Christmas anywhere, etc. Often these days the printed catalog works in smooth tandem with an Internet pitch and customers can be attracted with the dual approach.

Statistics put out by the DMA (Direct Marketing Association) tell us that the primary target for consumer catalogs is women; about 62 percent of adult women buy one or more items a year from catalogs. Most catalog marketers have adapted their brochures to work on their websites and can easily be kept up to date.

Today it is possible to work in tandem with a printed catalog and the Internet. A potential customer can read about it in the brochure and then go online to learn about its availability. The final step in the process (and hard to resist when you find your desired item) is to make the purchase online with a credit card. The sequence is similar to that of the capability brochure in this regard.

The Catalog's Aesthetic Thrust

The copy can be very flowery. Here is a bit of copy describing products from the store, Pottery Barn.

" ...Visions of a more durable, hand-hewn past, a horsy old leather scent of an America that may be apocryphal." Pottery Barn's copy lies in its ability to convince customers that it is possible to market authenticity in a catalog as well as in a shopping mall.

Of course, the granddaddy catalogs (in the early twentieth century) were the famous and massive tomes like those of Sears Roebuck or Montgomery Ward. Everything was available in these big books, from farm equipment to clothing. In rural areas they usually finished their days doing important work in the outhouse.

There is a fourth category of brochure, the Promotional Brochure. These tend to be less well designed, sacrificing restraint and taste for impact. They strive to grab attention, at any cost. Promotion brochures related to sales are the most blatant, although sometimes the automobile companies will design an upscale brochure for their more expensive models.

Perhaps the most vital ingredient/tool in the design of brochures (and print advertising for that matter) is the photograph. Commercial photography became much in demand in the mid twentieth century when it was possible to reproduce good photography in print. Two genres attracted the best: still life photography (for food shots) and fashion (of models, on location and in studios). Some of the photographers of this period became rich and famous—the most celebrated possibly being Richard Avedon.

Birth and Growth of the American Magazine

The years between 1865 and 1917 represent an exciting period for publishing. It was a dramatic time of expansion. Previously the publishing industry had been made up of a collection of small enterprises, but as soon as the Civil War ended hundreds of new publications were launched. The growth in the next thirty-five years was prodigious, and so was its influence on the American reader.

Previously, publications consisted (mostly) of newspapers, from which most everyone got their news. There were magazines, such as *Scribner's* and *Harpers'*, available as weeklies or monthlies, but the methods of reproduction were limited, particularly for illustrations. All such artwork had to be transferred to a woodblock, on which the image was engraved and finally printed.

But grow it did!

In 1865: 700 periodicals existed

In 1900: 5,700 periodicals now competed for readership and ad dollars.

Like many things, the growth of the publishing industry directly corresponded with the ability of the population to buy the things advertised – and magazines and newspapers were the chief source for advertising revenue then.

The expansion of publishing matched the growth of the cities. The necessary ingredients were:

–a sufficiently large market

–an economical method of manufacture

–an efficient means of distribution

All of these ingredients were in place by 1890.

Advertising in Demand

Publishing periodicals needed revenue and that required advertising sales, and that demanded goods to sell. With the post-war expansion of industry, Americans got a proliferation of goods to be sold. *Scribner's* is credited with being the first magazine to carry pages of advertising (in 1887).

Printing advances in technology naturally followed in an effort to produce a better, clearer publication. Near the end of the nineteenth century the rotary press was introduced, allowing publishers to print faster and in more volume, and even cheaper.

Perhaps the single most important technological advance was the ability to reproduce pictures by means other than wood engraving.

Publishing Houses Flourish

The aspirations of America's citizenry seemed to be influenced by what they read in the pages of these new publications.

There were many periodicals, but only a few endured and were widely read. Two of the most influential newsweeklies were *Frank Leslie's Illustrated Newspaper,* and *Harper's Weekly.*

Clockwise from top:
Life - 1921, McClure's - 1900,
Saturday Evening Post - 1911,
Ladies' Home Journal - 1928

Harper's grew out of a book publishing firm (of the same name), founded in the early 1800s. They launched their first magazine in 1850 with *Harper's* new monthly magazine, and *Harper's Weekly* in 1857, and it was a primary source for news of the Civil War. For many years. The House of Harper was the most prominent, successful publisher in the northeast. Other publishing houses started, noting the success of the publications of The House of Harper. Among them, the *Atlantic Monthly* in 1859, *Putnam's Monthly Magazine* and *Scribner's* and *The Century Illustrated,* all started up and flourished. As successful as these magazines were, they were considered a little "high-brow" for the average American taste. The public wanted more entertainment and craved good reading matter. From this need grew what were to become known as "Family Magazines."

Family magazine orientation led to the establishment of: **Ladies' Home Journal** (in 1883), and the **Saturday Evening Post** (in 1897). **Ladies Home Journal** was the creation of Cyrus H.K. Curtis, one of the first businessman/publishers.

Curtis pitched **The Saturday Evening Post** directly at a "middle-class" American audience, meaning a combination of stories, home-maker advice and good art. Another great publisher of those early years was P. F. Collier, who launched the magazine, **Collier's Weekly** in 1895. This magazine grew to rival the **Post,** but never surpassed it. Well into the twentieth century saw the establishment of *Time Magazine* in 1923, Life (the name was purchased from the original publication of 1883) around 1936 and *Look* magazine in 1937.

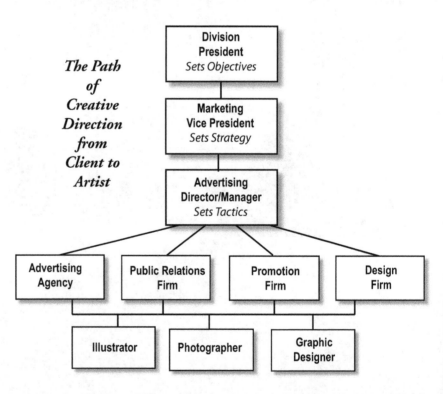

The Path of Creative Direction from Client to Artist

Part II
The Painted Image

Before there was commercial photography, before there was photo engraving, before there was the offset or rotogravure press, before there was the half-tone screen, there was illustration. Illustration, the art of illustrating contemporary life, goes back, at least, to the Dutch painters like Vermeer and Frans Hals. They were the illustrators of life in the seventeenth century. The Dutch painters were able to translate into paint the very things that depicted life in Holland at that time: the space, the light, atmosphere and air which envelop ordinary people in kitchens, courtyards, or under vast skies.

Because seventeenth century Dutch artists were preoccupied with showing what was at hand, they have been called realists. This is an unfair and perhaps pejorative term hinting at portraying them as nothing more than early photographers. They brought to their realistic scenes much more, like human interest emanating from the simple things of everyday life.

Like Norman Rockwell 300 years later, Frans Hals celebrated the faces of his countrymen. He painted single and group portraits, and genre scenes of freshness and joy. He championed the common man.

*Lady with a Turban,
by Jan Vermeer*

What is the difference between Fine Art and Illustration?
–In illustration (Commercial Art) the artist finds out how much he's going to be paid, and then the artist does the work.
–In fine art it's the other way around.
Generally speaking, illustration is art that is commissioned and is directed by an art director representing the client, who might be a brand manager from Procter & Gamble, or the Story Editor at *The Saturday Evening Post.*
Sometimes fine art seems to be illustration, either because of its realism, or because of its story-making quality. Some of Claude Monet's country scenes look like illustrations. The poignancy of a Mary Cassatt painting showing a mother with child at bath time also seems like an illustration. It is not, both are genre paintings. Illustrators were doing the same thing a century later in America.

The Golden Age of American Illustration
In June of the year 1900, twenty-nine nations submitted their best artists to represent them at the Exposition Universelle in Paris. It was a world's fair, one of the first.
America was represented, and ten of the artists in the total pantheon were American. And one of them was an illustrator.

They were: Mary Cassatt, William Merritt Chase, Thomas Wilmer Dewing, Thomas Eakins, Frederick Childe Hassam, Robert Henri, Winslow Homer, John Singer Sargent, John Sloan and James Abbott Whistler.

Winslow Homer was the illustrator, a regular staff artist for *Harper's Magazine,* the weekly and the monthly editions. There were other excellent illustrators at this time, men like Howard Pyle, Frederic Remington, NC Wyeth, Maxfield Parrish, James Leyendecker, Charles Dana Gibson, Rockwell Kent, as well as Norman Rockwell. If these men and the art community in New York had embraced what they were doing, it would also have been a golden age of fine art painting. It is hard to find an era during which the sheer quality of the painting, of draughtsmanship, of composition – reached such a level of excellence.

Most were easterners, born in the New York or Philadelphia area, trained in such fine schools as The Art Students League, or the National Academy of Design, exhibited at the Salma-gundi Club on 12th Street in New York or the National Academy of Design on upper Fifth Avenue.

If their presence in the art scene hadn't coincided with the birth of a number of weekly and monthly full-color magazines *(Colliers, Saturday Evening Post, Look)* and if advertising hadn't boomed in the 1920s with associated fat budgets for the commissioning of illustrations for ads for Lucky Strike or Coca-Cola, America would never have experienced the birth of a golden age art movement of such unprecedented imagination and skill.

For sheer picture making it was a Mount Olympus!

Winslow Homer

It all started for him, and for illustration in America, in the middle of the nineteenth century.

In 1862 Winslow Homer was assigned by *Harper's Weekly* to the Army of the Potomac, under the command of Major General George McClelland.

Homer first experienced the Civil War directly in mid-October 1861 when *Harper's Weekly* sent him to the front as a combat illustrator. His mission was "to go with the skirmishers into the next battle." The front at that time did not extend much beyond Washington, DC. He made his camp in Arlington, Virginia with the troops. Homer submitted his first wood engraving called "A Night Reconnaissance," and it was published on October 26, 1861. His next visit was a little more lively. Six months later he was with the 61st New York Volunteer Infantry (2nd Corps of the Army of the Potomac), and witnessed the siege of Yorktown. This visit, and ones that followed, showed the change in his personality. He covered the war for the next two years, and his method was to make sketches in a sketch-book at the front, then transfer them to illustrations-done in oil or as wood engravings. His most prolific year was 1862 when he sent in twelve illustrations.

He worked in a variety of ways. One was when he translated a sketch directly into an engraving. In others, his sketches supplemented an overall narrative of a moment in the war. In some situations, his sketches were collaged together by Homer or the engraver back in New York into complete illustrations ready for printing.

Perhaps his most profound illustration was "The Sharpshooter on Picket Duty."

A sharp-shooter on picket duty. *Harper's Monthly,* Nov. 1862

He painted (as well as drew) this illustration and it was the first time he broke with the tradition of military art. The scene depicts a single soldier sitting in the branches of a tree, taking aim at a Confederate target well out of sight beyond the right edge of the illustration.

It is a breakthrough painting and illustration. The message behind it is powerful–the instrument of death in the top of a healthy, pine tree.

It was published in *Harper's Weekly* in the November 1862 issue.

Many Americans were affected by the character of this war, with its intimations of modern warfare and bloodshed.

Homer stayed with the Union Army, sporadically, and witnessed the Battle of the Wilderness in the spring of 1864 and the Siege of Petersburg in late 1864/65. His paintings from this period were insightful, as always.

The painting that rivals the Sharpshooter for integrated meaning, is "The Veteran in a New Field," painted in 1865. In this painting we see a soldier, newly returned from the war, cutting down his wheat with a sythe. The painting is simple and powerful. The wheat field fills the background, left to right, with the solitary figure of a man cutting the wheat with his sythe. The painting is loaded with symbolism: Homer's veteran, still wearing his campaign hat and uniform pants is mimicking death as a reaper, only recently returned from the harvest of war.

In the ensuing years after the war he developed as a painter and gradually stopped doing illustrations (but never totally). His reputation grew, his assignments and commissions proliferated and he was now making a handsome living as a fine art painter.

His early years as an illustrator were very instrumental in his development later as a fine artist.

Homer painted "The Veteran in a New Field" in 1865

At the age of forty-seven, he moved to the property that his brother, Arthur, had purchased at Prout's Neck (near Scarborough), Maine. His brother built a studio for Winslow and he lived in Maine for the next twenty-seven years, painting the seacoast, waves and rocks. He exhibited widely and was much in demand by the 1890s. But the center of his life was Maine and his brother and his brother's family. Eventually he died there in 1910, at age 64.

Winslow Homer was the first illustrator, initiating what was to become A Golden Age of Illustration. It lasted about 100 years, from the middle of the nineteenth century to the middle of the twentieth and included some of America's greatest illustrators and fine artists. The stories of two more of the finest, follow.

Charles Dana Gibson

Charles Dana Gibson was a city person—urbane and sophisticated. It is reflected in his art—perhaps the most developed body of work dealing with the upper classes at play in New York, Boston or Philadelphia.

Charles Dana Gibson (related to Richard Henry Dana, the author of the celebrated sea novel *Two Years Before the Mast* -1840) was born in September of 1867. He was the descendant of a line of New Englanders and he inherited the Yankee practicality and reverence for hard work and diligence to duty. Although not rich, his parents were very supportive and realizing that he was artistic, sent him (at high school age) to the Art Students League in New York City. He had to live on a tight budget, but he got the art training he craved. He worked at his craft alongside Frederic Remington for a short period. Unlike Remington, who loved to paint, Gibson concentrated on pen and ink drawings.

In 1885 he entered the commercial world as a line illustrator; he was only eighteen years old.

Like all young, unknown illustrators, he peddled his samples (drawings) around New York, concentrating on the art buyers at the weekly and monthly maga-

Charles Dana Gibson, circa 1910

zines (like *Harper's*). In his biography he recalled visiting every publishing house, photoengraving establishment and lithographer in the city of New York and getting rejected regularly. The first magazine to recognize his talent and buy his work, was *Life*. This magazine was not the photographic journal of *Time* magazine fifty years later–but was a humor magazine, competing with *Puck* and *Judge*.

In 1889 he went to Europe and studied at the Academie Julian in Paris where he developed a vigorous new pen and ink style.

When he returned to New York, his work was very much in vogue, and he illustrated for the biggest magazines of the times: *The Century, Harper's Monthly, Bazaar* and *Scribner's*. By 1890 Gibson was well established as a successful illustrator–and this was even before his "Gibson Girl" was introduced.

The Gibson Girl

The Gibson Girl was an idealized female figure that Charles Dana Gibson dreamed up. She embodied many qualities that were current and popular, qualities of independence, spirit, gallantry, courage and self-reliance. She was also beautiful. She arrived just in time. American women hungered for an identity that could counter the attitude of superiority practiced

269

by their European rivals. **The Gibson Girl** represented the independent spirit in spades. Gibson showed her active in sports: golf, bicycle riding, tennis and horseback riding. Each week Americans eagerly awaited the appearance of their ideal woman in the pages of *Life*. And her influence was wider than the printed page. Her image was reproduced on ashtrays, teacups and saucers, spoons, pillow covers, chairbacks, table tops, matchboxes, screens, silk handkerchiefs, ceramic tiles, calendars and even wallpaper. There was a hit song in 1906 called "Why do they call me the Gibson Girl?" Waltzes and fox trots were named after her, as well as a play called, "A Night with a Gibson."

He placed his Gibson girl in the life he found in front of him: the elegant Fifth Avenue chateaus, the balls and cotillions at Delmonico's and the Waldorf-Astoria, the opera at the Metropolitan, not to mention summertime in Newport, Rhode Island.

His drawings were often gently sarcastic, targeting the hypocrisy of Americans trying to acquire the condescension of the English upper classes. As harsh as they sometimes were, the public loved them.

Murder at Madison Square Garden!

One of Gibson's models was a woman named Evelyn Nesbit.

Gibson did a portrait of Evelyn for the *Collier's* centerfold in 1901. As a result of this, she became the most sought after model of the day and caught the attention of famed architect Stanford White. Shortly thereafter she became his mistress. The problem was that Nesbit was married to Harry Thaw. One night in 1906, Thaw was dining with his wife on the roof of Madison Square Garden (located then at 26th Street between Broadway and Fifth Avenue). Unfortunately Stanford White was there too, and alone. Harry Thaw noticed him, approached White's table and shot him dead–right at the table. There was a scandal, a trial, the newspapers had a field day, and Thaw was acquitted for reasons of temporary insanity. He did serve a little easy time in an upstate mental hospital but society revered his act.

In 1917 Gibson helped form the Society of Illustrators, which still exists today on 68th Street in New York. He was the first president of the Society. America joined the British and the French at this time in opposing the Germans in World War I. Gibson rallied his fellow artists in the society providing patriotic pictures to push the war effort. From this effort came the famous "Uncle Sam–I Want You" poster by James Montgomery Flagg.

Gibson was awarded the Legion of Honor from France for his work in this effort.

After the war ended America turned to other images, and the Gibson Girl was not one of them. The American woman now identified with the "flapper" and the Charleston. He never had the popularity in this medium, even though he was good at it. He died in 1944.

Norman Rockwell

The most famous of them all was Norman Rockwell. He saw and painted an idealized world, and it was a world that Americans embraced. Rockwell was as much a part of the publishing/illustration world as his colleagues James Montgomery Flagg or Charles Dana Gibson. He, like the others, called on the same art buyers, peddled his samples to the publishing houses and agencies. He socialized with the illustrators who lived around New York, was popular and influential and until he moved upstate, did so for thirty years.

Rockwell was born in 1894, in Manhattan, to a family of modest means.

The restless young artist found the art training he was looking for in the newly founded Art Students League, on 57th Street. Here he could study with one of the top artists of the time, who was also an instructor at the school, Frank Bridgeman.

Following art school he began to get regular illustration work for *Boy's Life* but the magazine he really wanted to work for was *The Saturday Evening Post.* This Philadelphia magazine had become famous and popular for its depiction of basic, middle-class American life.

Rockwell commented in his biography, "In those days the cover of the *Post* was the greatest show window in America for an illustrator. If you did a cover for the *Post* you had arrived."

In the spring of 1916 he summoned his courage and took a train to Philadelphia. Under his arm he had a bulky case which contained two finished paintings and three sketches. His appointment was with the editor and publisher of the magazine, who instantly liked Norman's work and bought all he had brought. Norman had arrived as an artist, and particularly on the covers of the *Post* ! Rockwell depicted Americans at work and play in a gentle, sympathetic manner. Furthermore, his painting style reflected his own personality, one of basic uncertainty, vulnerability and a genuine innocence. He was diligent in searching out the

Norman Rockwell at his easel.

Illustration for
Mark Twain's Tom Sawyer

perfect piece of furniture, or costume for an illustration. This even extended (sometimes) to visiting the site of a story. One time he traveled to Hannibal, Missouri, to get the feel of the area, preliminary to painting illustrations for Tom Sawyer and Huckleberry Finn, by Mark Twain.

The subjects of Rockwell's illustrations range widely, from cheerleaders to paper boys, to boy scouts, to soldiers and sailors. His subjects ran the gamut from prosperity to poverty. The common denominator has always been, "ordinary people in everyday situations..."

Perhaps Rockwell's most ambitious series of paintings were the Four Freedoms, which he completed in February of 1943. They were commissioned by the U.S. Treasury Department and *The Saturday Evening Post* and depicted the four freedoms expressed by President Franklin Roosevelt in 1942: "Freedom from Want, Freedom from Fear, Freedom of Worship and Freedom of Speech." They were large and difficult for the artist to complete–taking seven months. Immediately after their publication the four paintings went on a tour of sixteen cities where over a million people saw them, and they raised an estimated $133 million in war bonds.

In his lifetime, Rockwell painted 322 covers for the *Post*, not to mention many calendars and illustrations for *Collier's, Life, Country Gentleman, Look* magazine, war posters, books and advertisements.

Norman Rockwell died in 1978 at age 84. Today his work is just beginning to be accepted as fine art,

"Freedom from Want," painted in
1943 for the U.S. government

for its depiction of a certain period of American history—not altogether different from the position that Vermeer and Frans Hals enjoy. A sizeable and comprehensive museum to his work has been built just outside of Stockbridge, Massachusetts, not far from where he lived the last twenty years of his life.

Illustration Today

The illustration world began to change in the 1960s, becoming less realistic and more "interpretive." Norman Rockwell, (and others) had created a world of romantic realism which bordered on cliché—often over sentimentalized and lacking freshness. To some extent the same was happening in the fine art world. Abstract expressionism emerged in the early 1960s, championed by such artists as Mark Rothko and Robert Motherwell.

The Saturday Evening Post cover, August 11, 1945

At the same time, photography got so good, along with the printers' and engravers' ability to reproduce it in four colors, that illustrators started to lose business. A few illustrators (like Robert Weaver and Andrew Parker) began to experiment, to try more interpretive pictures. It seemed that a door had been opened for greater exploration and illustration started to "loosen up" to make social commentary on many subjects that comprised America in the last quarter of the century.

A dozen years later another change was evident when illustrations became more designed, merging interesting typography with the picture area. European surrealism merged with parody and humor. But the most powerful trend was to surrealism—influenced by Rene Magritte. *The New York Times* Op-Ed page became a platform for modern illustration. Artists like Saul Steinberg began to get commissions for advertisements or journals. The art began to take on new importance as an interpretative device to deepen the meaning of an article or a subject. The effect of Op-Ed art in newspapers was profound. Illustrators had to become the creators of their own ideas and language.

Some were often, frankly, difficult to comprehend. Illustrator Tom Ungerer's work was enigmatic, often visual puzzles.

Gerald Scarf's highly satirical drawings of British royalty often appeared on the Op-Ed pages of the *London Observer* and it was noticed and enjoyed.

Best among them were illustrators like Seymour Chwast and Milton Glaser who founded a hot new studio in California called Push Pin.

By the 1980s illustration had evolved from Op-Ed art into a style that included surrealism, cartoon and interpretation. It was basically a new way of perceiving subject matter and interpreting it as narrative art. The new trend in illustration has been called "New Pop." It

Seymour Chwast

appears to be a mix of everything, but far more interpretative and far more central to the idea of the article or story being illustrated. Fifty years back the illustration market demanded realism and skilled painting.

Poster for Mobil Masterpiece Theater, circa 1995

Media diversity has opened the field up to many interpretations, styles and methods. The illustrator has become as much the source of the idea as he has the painter of it.

The Colorful World of Milton Glaser

He is as much a graphic designer as an illustrator, his work

bridging both disciplines with style, verve and imagination. Like many of his colleagues (Paul Rand, Saul Bass) he is a product of New York City, both by birth and schooling. His early art training began in high school, then Cooper Union, graduating in 1951. Later, via a Fulbright scholarship he studied engraving at the Academy of Fine Arts in Bologna, Italy. In 1968 he founded

New York Magazine with Clay Felker. His work embraces posters, book jackets, album covers, posters for theatre and film, advertisements and magazine illustrations. Among his most famous creations are: The "I Love NY" logo, and an illustration of Bob Dylan for one of his album covers. His work is in the permanent collection of the Museum of Modern Art and the Smithsonian, to name a few. He lives today in New York City.

Illustrating for the Movies
By Bruce Macdonald

One day in June of 1966, I got a call from an artist's agent. His name was Virgil.
"I say, Bruce, if you're free tomorrow I might have something for you."
Virgil wore a bowler hat, always carried a furled black umbrella and went to Eton. He was very British.
Virgil picked me up the next morning in his little black Morris car. We drove for about an hour west of London, to the town of Elstree. Virgil had picked up an assignment for me from a movie production company.
It began with an interview in an office adjacent to the big movie studio. An American movie-man was in charge of publicity and promotion; he was short, burly and smoked a big cigar.
He said, " Okay, here's the deal. Wander at will, for a week. Go anywhere you damn please-but be sure to draw these big things on the set-these space things. You bring me your work on Friday. If I like 'em, you stay, if not, you go. I'll pay you 80 guineas (about $120) per day until Friday. Deal?"
I accepted, and Virgil took off quickly (He was always uncomfortable around Americans). So, I wandered, with camera and sketchbook. I had never been on a film set before and it was fascinating. I felt this one was very unusual. There were big space wheels, space ships with big, white futuristic interiors. Everything seemed arranged in circles around the camera, the director and the actors. Outer circles contained the script girl, makeup people, costume designers and carpenters. At the center of it all was (I later learned) director Stanley Kubrick and the film he was making was the classic, *2001- A Space Odyssey.*
I did my week's work, not without a number of false starts, and even won a second week. My illustrations (along with others) were put in a fancy magazine that was sold at the movie's premiere in London and New York. The assignment led to more jobs, from more traditional sources, and we stayed in London a full four years.

I seldom saw Virgil again.

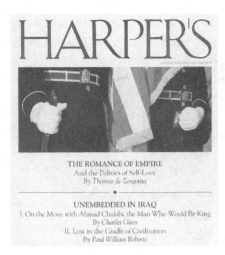

THE ROMANCE OF EMPIRE
And the Politics of Self-Love
By Thomas de Zengotita

UNEMBEDDED IN IRAQ
I. On the Move with Ahmad Chalabi, the Man Who Would Be King
By Charles Glass
II. Lost in the Cradle of Civilization
By Paul William Roberts

Harper's magazine has had an unbroken run from the middle of the 19th century into the 21st.

For all of its new, fresh directions, illustration today is more of a side show—appearing infrequently in specialty magazines or newspapers. It is unlikely to ever recapture the popularity and affection of the American people as did the illustrators of the golden age.

The Modern Magazine

We are in a period of magazine popularity and proliferation. Seemingly there is a magazine for every interest, from golf to gardening. They are popular with advertisers because they are able to reach one of the most affluent, informed audiences in the nation.

Here are a few, randomly selected magazines. *Better Homes & Gardens:* circulation: 7,603 million, *Harper's:* circ.: 597,000, *Esquire:* circ.: 721,000, *Golf Digest:* circ.: 1, 578 million, *Guns & Ammo:* circ.: 528,000, *Martha Stewart Living:* circ.: 2,323 million, *New Yorker:* circ.: 925,000, *Playboy:* circ.: 3,217 million, *Rolling Stone:* circ.: 1,254 million, *People:* circ.: 3,617,000, *Vogue:* circ.: 1,245 million. The variety is wide and special interests flourish.

In the *Mediaweek Marketer's Guide to Media,* a potential space buyer can get media circulation trends for any of these magazines, magazine audience profiles, and demographic trends.

The growth in magazine circulation from 1970 to 2000 was prodigious. In 1970 there was paid circulation for all magazines of 244 million for a U.S. adult population of 134 million, while today it is 3.75 million (circulation) for a U.S. population of over 300 million persons—or more than 63 percent growth in 30 years. From 1991 to 2002 there was a growth of 3,063 new magazines in eleven years, from 14,256 to 17,321!

People magazine was created in the middle of the 20th century by Time-Life, Inc.

Newspapers

The situation with newspapers is not such a happy tale. There were, in fact, many more daily newspapers in the major American cities 100 years ago than today.

There are about 1,400 daily newspapers in the United States, representing a circulation of 55.6 million.

Of that group, 52 percent are morning papers, 48 percent evening papers. But remember that newspers are passed around, in fact (national average) statistics reveal that each paper is read by 1.88 or more readers. Of these, the most read by the most readers is: 1- *The New York Times,* 2- *USA Today,* 3- *The Wall Street Journal.*

People tend to rely on the daily newspaper for opinion, but rely on television programs for daily and breaking news. There is a growing trend to rely more and more on the Internet for news. A selection of five top U.S. papers reveals the following.

1. *The NY Times:* circulation: 650,000.
2. *The Los Angeles Times:* circulation: 840,000.
3. *Chicago Tribune:* circulation: 679,000.
4. *Boston Globe:* circulation: 468,000.
5. *Dallas-Ft. Worth Morning News:* circulation: 506,000.

Newspapers are more general, possessing a less defined readership. Magazines are more precise, offering a measured rifle shot to your audience.

Conclusion

The oldest method is still the biggest. Communication through the means of print and picture still dominates the marketing world. From Johannes Gutenberg's marvelous invention 600 years ago to a current issue of *People* magazine, Americans are still responding to creativity in word, artwork and excellent graphic design.

12

THE BRIDGE TO THE FUTURE

Looking Back, Looking Forward

The evolution of design and advertising in the past sixty years has been both rapid and diverse. This is not surprising in this business. The audience has grown, the ad spending has grown, the number of consumer products has grown and the methods of reaching them (the consumers) has grown. And, of course, the money has grown. We now seem to be on the cusp of yet another growth spurt, that of a new delivery system for getting advertising messages before our eyes–electronically.

When I first entered the marketing communications world, it was in the late 1950s and it was in Chicago. At that time camera-ready final art (called mechanicals) was created on hot press mount board with set type. Large proof sheets were delivered daily, if not hourly from typography houses to the art studios and agencies up and down Michigan Avenue. The next step was for the mechanical artist to "butter" the back with a brush from a rubber cement pot, let it dry, and cut the type strips into copy headlines or text-blocks with a steel T-square and triangle. The finished product (called a "Key-Line") went on to a printer or publisher where it might become next month's Marlboro ad. Today, of course, all of this is done on a computer, cleanly and quickly. The fifties also saw the rise of TV, of research, of the concept known as the "Unique Selling Point" and sixty-second commercials for such clients as the Ajax White Knight.

Our positive image of advertising and its lifestyle was personified by Gregory Peck in Sloan Wilson's popular book (and movie), *The Man in the Gray Flannel Suit*.

In the previous eleven chapters we have examined the role of design in its many forms of marketing communications, from early symbols to modern logos, early and contemporary packaging, the retail space, sales promotion, advertising, public relations and print design. Here in the last chapter, the observations of the men who made things happen in that same half century will be explored. At least half of my contributors are still making things happen: in design studios, advertising agencies or classrooms. Their observations, anecdotes or just funny reminiscences, follow.

We've covered a lot of ground in this book, crossed a lot of bridges. Let's review what we have learned from the beginning (more than 1000 years ago) to today.

1000 A.D.	- Symbols influence early man, circles, stars, triangles, animals.
	- Symbols become heraldic designs, appearing on the battlefield (at Hastings, Agincourt) and on shields, banners, flags and crests, representing kingdoms and dynasties.
1100-1600	
	- The era of exploration, colonies in the New World, Williamsburg, VA, Mystic, CT; symbols become signage.
	- Symbols morph into modern logos, critical to the marketing and identification of packages, companies and brands.
1750-1850	- Cities develop, commerce becomes widely practiced, trading companies, institutions, newspapers start, as well as early magazines.
	- Packaging emerges with the development of tin cans, paper bags and plastic bottles.
1870-1910	- Retail life expands, first with country stores, then supermarkets, then big department stores, leading to specialization - chain stores and malls.
	- Consumer products compete for brand share, Coke vs. Pepsi, Altria vs. P&G. Sales Promotion becomes popular and widely
1920-1950	used.
	- Advertising begins, modestly then more grandly. Media opportunities present themselves for radio and television. TV
1955-2000	audiences of 100 million for Super Bowl commercials become possible along with big bucks.
	- And now the Internet.

In the 1960s

American business was looking with increasing frequency beyond its borders, sensing and seeking new markets for its products. If "New Blue Cheer" sold well in New Jersey, why not sell it to housewives in Holland or Frankfurt? To facilitate this, corporations were establishing offices in overseas cities like London, Paris and Milan. Procter & Gamble led the way with an office complex in Brussels to serve European markets (soon to become the Common Market countries). Creative centers for graphic design and packaging soon followed, set up to service the needs of P&G's brands like Ariel and Tide.

In this decade we saw the beginnings of a creative revolution, thanks to graphic designers like Paul Rand, Saul Bass, and Herb Lubalin. It was a time of modernizing old trademarks in order to let them better express the magnitude and forcefulness of new, expanding businesses. Logos were turning up on tails of airplanes, on tops of buildings, even matchbook covers. Design firms were specializing in "corporate identity systems," a new buzz word of the time. In 1963, Tom Geismar of Chermayeff and Geismar designed the spare and imaginative Chase Manhattan symbol. Many insurance companies, banks and financial organizations followed suit, sensing that a sophisticated and memorable logo (like Chase's) represented their intangible product perfectly. Ad men like Rosser Reeves, Jock Elliott, Bill Bernbach and his agency DDB were also active. Bernbach's ground-breaking and still classic Volkswagen ad campaign demonstrated the benefit derived from having art directors and writers working together. Bernbach's creative art directors and writers also introduced humor into advertising–maybe not for the first time but certainly with a first-time freshness and wit.

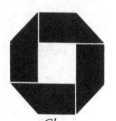

Chase Manhattan Bank logo

In 1965 I moved to London to join colleagues from Cincinnati, Ohio, who were establishing a design firm to service these large expanding U.S. corporations. Once a week someone from my office made the "milk run" to Procter and Gamble's office in Brussels. Usually we simply delivered artwork or received a briefing for a new design project and were home in our London flats by dinner time, sometimes with a loaf of fresh French bread.

Our small design office (established in an old apartment just off Piccadilly) grew rapidly, more than doubling its size in the first five years. Other American firms were doing the very same thing. Package designer Donald Desky set up a successful London office to service Unilever's needs. P&G moved an American and his family to Belgium on a permanent basis to oversee and direct their European packaging needs. The management consulting firm McKinsey & Company established a sizable office in London. The McCormick Spice Company sent a young man with promise to run their European office in the town of Croydon, just south of London. They picked well, he grew the business and that man became a Vice President and later corporate board member.

Chicago's Leo Burnett Agency sent two of its best and brightest young executives, one a Creative Director, one a young Account Executive to expand their modest office in that city. It, too, expanded rapidly.

The Beatles came back from a tour in Hamburg to capture public adulation in London, and soon the world. Cosmetics designer Mary Quant and dress designer "Biba" established their own original styles in fashion, which I have always thought was the precursor for the Annie Hall look of Diane Keaton fifteen years later. They were exciting times.

On Coke and McDonald's
By John Gillin, Division Director
and Sr.VP, The Coca-Cola Company

In the '60s, I was what they call, "an account guy," meaning I represented an advertising agency to the client and vice-versa. In this case, my client was Procter & Gamble. In those days it was the practice for the agency to help the P&G brand manager build the annual marketing plan and then present it to P&G senior management. It was considered the best and toughest marketing training in its day and it appealed to me. By the end of the decade I was made one of the youngest VPs of a major NY advertising agency. Those were very exciting but very long days.

A P&G executive, who later became Vice-Chairman, suggested I move to the client side of the business. I liked the idea and decided I wanted to go to work for the Coca-Cola Company because they had the strongest trademark in the world, were marketing dependent and often hired from their advertising agency. Being young and bold at the time, I went to Coca-Cola's agency in NY and suggested they hire me and send me to Atlanta and in a year Coke would hire me. They told me I was crazy but they hired me anyway and it worked! That was 1969 and I've been with Coca-Cola ever since. I started as a vice-president in charge of new product development for a newly formed division, The Coca-Cola Foods Division.

In a few more years Coke asked me to take over management of the relationship we had with McDonald's. This was an unusual assignment, but in the end, rewarding and fun. In the next twenty years the McDonald's business grew to well over half a billion unit cases annually and I was running a division of over 150 employees, managing our business with McDonald's in over 120 countries.

Coke and McDonald's were (and are) kindred spirits. If you look closely, these two companies are very similar. Both are in the food business. Both are franchise businesses and both are public companies committed to international as well as domestic growth. Both are leading global brands requiring first rate marketing support. Both do business in well over a hundred countries and derive over half their sizable sales and profits from overseas markets.

All good relationships are built on trust–beginning with personal trust. Amazingly, there has never been a contract between McDonald's Corporation and The Coca-Cola Company. Business is conducted and investments are always made on a handshake. Personal relationships at all levels of these two companies have always been carefully cultivated and maintained through constant organizational change over many years.

In the 1970s

In 1973 Raymond Loewy designed a new logo for Exxon, which replaced Esso in the U.S. It was heralded as a name change with "saturation advertising" from coast to coast. It had a lot of influence and as a result, monograms and abstract symbols became popular. Others followed, like Xerox, Met Life, Chubb Corporation, and Westinghouse. It became harder to differentiate between the logo of a bank and that of a utility. There was a brief flirtation with embellishment but it was replaced by a return to strong, no-frills trademarks. Sperry Rand became Sperry, Mobil Gas became Mobil, The American Stock Exchange became AMEX. The American Tobacco company, fearing pressure on smoking, became American Brands. Advertising was affected by a period of tighter budgets, the result of an economic recession. There also was some pull-back in creativity. Research was beginning to stifle new ideas as clients tested, and retested, and tested them again - often to death.

Westinghouse   *Chubb*   *Kimberly-Clark*

It was a time of caution but for some like super agency Young and Rubicam, it was a time of new accounts and fierce competition. Management brought a man out of Amsterdam to head up their new business effort, to great effect. Over seventy-two million dollars was added to the books by him and his team in 1978. Y&R had a stable of all blue-ribbon accounts, some for decades. Among these were: Eastern Airlines, Sears, General Electric, Sony, General Foods (now Kraft), Lincoln Mercury, Procter & Gamble and the U.S. Post Office. It was also a time of new thinking–at Y&R and certainly at the other big five agencies.

Ed Ney, who became President and CEO in 1970, started to think about offering clients a wider spectrum of services. This concept became the matrix for a kind of "super-agency" that could provide sales promotion planning and execution, package design, logo design and medical advertising as a separate entity. Ney wanted to offer his clients all these services under one roof, his roof. It was the genesis of the "Whole Egg" concept.

On the "Whole Egg"
By Edward N. Ney, Chairman Emeritus,
Young and Rubicam Advertising, New York

Here's what I remember of those times.

At the beginning of 1970 Young & Rubicam was not the large agency it was to become, and we had some problems. Our clients included: Procter & Gamble, Goodyear Tire, JELLO (acquired in 1951), Remington Shaver (acquired in 1954), and Dr. Pepper (in 1969). But despite a good client list, there was dissension in the agency, and unrest outside the agency. Some of our mainstream creative work was over the top, too much so, and it was disturbing our big clients like P&G. Tension was in the air, in the halls. One day I even witnessed a fist fight at the agency between creative and account service people.

At this time I was President of Y&R International (which was comprised of 35 offices outside the United States), and I was deeply troubled by the internal atmosphere. I decided to have a talk with the CEO (Ed Bond) to tell him that I was thinking of leaving. He invited me to lunch.

Some lunch! He asked me what was wrong with the agency and what could be done to fix it. I had some ideas jotted down and we explored them for more than two hours. Finally at the end of lunch he paid the bill, we stood up and walked back to his office. Upstairs he wrote out a press release and to my surprise he made me head of the agency. I was only forty-five years of age!

The reaction to this news was mixed- four top creative group heads resigned and not many cheered. I expected it and was ready with new leaders. Over the next year we worked very hard, and internally I named three Y&R groups to study and recommend new thinking re: a) U.S. operations, b) International development, c) New Plans/ideas/exploratory work all aimed at creating a "New Agency for the 1970s. After nearly a year of planning and hard work I called a meeting in Jamaica of the fifty top Y&R people and presented the plan to them. I'm happy to say that it was received with enthusiasm and starting in 1972 we began to execute it. We called it **"The Whole Egg"** concept.

Vital to the basic idea was a new, expanding agency with many creative services under one roof.

The idea for the Whole Egg probably first occurred to me one Monday when I picked up the *New York Daily News* to get the sports scores from the weekend. I checked ads in the back and one in particular caught my eye. It read something like this: "Buy Four Goodyear Tires for $99.00 at... etc. It was poorly designed, poorly written and bold without emphasizing anything except price. Subconsciously I began comparing these ads with what we'd been doing for Goodyear on N.F.L. TV, a marvelous campaign called "No Man Around." It featured a woman driving in the rain, with one or two children in the back, and she had had to pull over to the side of the road, in trouble with a tire. Our message was that Goodyear tires were so reliable they would never fail you or your loved ones. It was a powerful campaign and we knew it was working. I viewed it against this poorly conceived, poorly executed, all price-off ad for a dealer in Brooklyn. First I thought, "What a pitiful mess this ad is–too bad for Goodyear." Then (I thought) "Why don't we do  this ad, and for that matter, all the related marketing communications (public relations, posters, collateral materials, promotion programs, full international resources etc.) that Goodyear did each year in the marketing of their tires?"

The response was mixed at first. The client liked it but the dealers fought to retain their right to publish price-off ads–probably because the client was supplying Coop money for this effort. We realized that to do a proper job, we needed: a) a great PR company, b) direct marketing capabilities, c) a very good (sales) promotion company – and on it went.

Once applied to Goodyear, we felt we needed to offer it to our other accounts. It seemed fair and it made economic sense.

And we realized something else–we needed experts in this kind of marketing communications to do the job right. That is when we started looking at outsider companies who knew and practiced sales promotion, or public relations, graphic design etc. So progressively we started buying successful outside firms and bringing them into the Y&R family. There were many, each adding their special skills to the mix and soon we were able to offer our clients **"The Whole Egg"** company, and the name stuck.

Over the years we've discovered two things: the concept is still sound- and secondly, it works best for our large clients, like Colgate, Ford, Kraft and Sony. We call this our KCA group (Key Corporate Accounts), of which there are more than 15-20 major worldwide "KCAs" in the company.

I'm glad to say that **The Whole Egg** concept lives on–some forty years later–and flourishes!

In the 1980s

The '80s saw an improvement in creativity, perhaps due to the optimism engendered by President Reagan. There was a spirit of anything goes in ad making and design. New packaging stimulated new ideas, one being the brand new concept called the aseptic package, which was unveiled at the Knoxville World's Fair in 1982. This was also the "Me" era–typified by such headlines as "You deserve a break today," or "I'm Worth it" headlines. It was an egotistical social period and advertising, naturally, mirrored it.

On the positive side, we began to see integrated marketing take root. Clients were now able to utilize a graphic designer, public relations, promotion or direct response programs, as well as their advertising often from the same overall source. It was Ney's Whole Egg concept, expanding. It was also the beginning of mergers and consolidations.

In the middle of this decade Coke lost its nerve and changed its formula, thanks to a relentless bombardment of taste test battles, compliments of Pepsi. Seventy-seven days later Coke changed back, realizing, finally, that Americans valued Coke more than as a beverage but as a national treasure, not to be tampered with.

On Ford
By Ralph Rydholm, Chairman Emeritus
for TLK/Euro RSCG, Chicago

It was never dull on the Ford Branding business. I was fifteen years with J. Walter Thompson, but not always directly on the Ford Account. I was creative director of JWT for Chicago, and overall for the US.

The Ford dealers were a tough bunch. Many of them carried guns, and once I walked into the men's room of a hotel where the Ford Dealers Association was meeting, and two of them had drawn their guns and were threatening to shoot. It was scary and it was a small men's room, too.

Another time I was on the top of the Ferris Wheel of Kings Island Resorts in Dayton, Ohio, testing out the rides (as ordered) of our newest account–when I heard my name announced on the loudspeaker (this was before cell phones). We descended and I called in. It was Dan Seymour, Ford's CEO, calling from NYC. He said, "We have some damn fine middles for the new Ford Granada car, but we lack openings and closings. He asked me to come, right then, to NY and complete the commercials with "darn fine middles but no heads or tails." So, being a good soldier (and loving the adventure) I did it; flew to NY buying clothing along the way. Their middles consisted of just (about) twelve words, the only twelve words that had been approved by the Board. I managed to get the fronts and backs written and finally got to go home.

On another Ford project we needed a song, and I was able to buy the Chicago Bears Fight Song, "Bear Down, Chicago Team." It was, and remains a very popular song. The fans loved to sing it at games. And since we owned the song and knew it was popular in Chicago, we changed the words to adapt to a current Ford promotional theme, "Buy Down, its bargain time. At the end of a particular bad season the Chicago Bears fans showed their disgust (in Soldier Field) by singing the fight song with our lyrics. Imagine, 70 thousand fans singing, "Buy Down, its Bargain Time." In the aftermath the Bears Team management was furious and insisted that we sell them back the rights to the song–in order to kill forever our lyrics–which drove them nuts.

On Beauty vs. Comfort
By Paul Rand, from a lecture given at Yale University in 1987

A company's reputation is very much affected by how it looks and how its products work. A beautiful object that doesn't work is a reflection on the company's integrity. In the long run it may lose not only its customers but also its good will. Good design will no longer function as the harbinger of good business but as the herald of hypocrisy. Beauty is a by-product of needs and functions. A Lazy-Boy chair is extremely comfortable but it is an example of beauty gone astray. A consumer survey that would find such furniture comfortable might, most likely, find it to be beautiful as well. If it works, it must also be beautiful. Not true.

Paul Rand at home in the 1970s.

On the Package as a Reflection of Lifestyle

By Richard Shear, CEO of LMS Design, Inc.,
Norwalk, CT

Think of the brands you buy in the supermarket, for example picture Coca-Cola, or Chanel No.5, or Campbell's Soup and the appearance of the bottle or can is what immediately comes to mind. The package has become the most important visual icon of modern brand identity. Its shapes, colors, materials and graphics all contribute to a single impression that consumers rely on when making purchase decisions. Increasingly, package designers recognize that these purchase decisions represent a lifestyle choice and a reflection of an intimate relationship between product and consumer. The package has come a very long way in the last 150 years.

In theory, a package must play three simple roles. It protects the product during shipping, storage and use, it acts as the user interface to dispense the product, and lastly to identify the contents within. While these seem like straightforward functions, keep in mind that the package has a fourth role of being a brand icon in advertising and other marketing media. In the simplest terms, it is the face of the brand. The package is the only marketing tool that combines both the mundane necessities of product protection and identification with the magic of creating a meaningful, and often lifelong relationship with consumers. Because this relationship is long term, the package is also the most stable of all marketing media.

Today's designer is distinctly aware of their role in creating products that will have the same long-term ability as Coca Cola, Campbell's Soup or Chanel No. 5 to capture the imagination and build lifetime relationships with brands. Packages are part of our lifestyle. What began in the late 19th century has now become inextricably linked to the personality of the brand–a critical link in the marketing chain–the path from market to table.

In the 1990s

The '90s was the decade of new media–essentially the computer. Websites and interactive companies were springing up everywhere and the Internet began to grow. Microsoft took off. Any illustrators who were still trying to make a living drawing and painting had to switch to computer-generated artwork, as did commercial photographers. Many left the business altogether.

It was also the fruition of global marketing. Procter & Gamble was reaping the rewards of its expansion into the global arena thirty years earlier (the '60s) and was now selling its products all over the world. At least ten of their brands were each now contributing $1 billion annual sales to their bottom line.

It was also the decade of consolidation. Advertising agencies were being bought- up by holding companies and five big ones now emerged, controlling all but 16 percent of the existing ad agencies. Eventually there were six holding companies, each made up of advertising agencies, public relations agencies, sale promotion firms , graphic design, etc. There were odd new names and new personalities we had to learn, names like: Publicis, Interpublic, WPP Group, Omnicom, Dentsu and Havas.

Within the next few years media companies followed suit, spinning off of the big advertising agencies to offer an independent source for buying and placing ads. Again there were, and remain, five large dominant agencies.

 Logos arrived after a long journey that brought them from the time of symbols and imagery like: anchors, clipper ships, animals and heraldic devices to the sleek modernity of IBM, Altria or L'Oreal. Graphic designers were still using symbolism but it was buried inside a new symbolism of shapes, themes, abstractions and calligraphy. Typography became more popular than ever in helping marketers achieve a desired effect through manipulation of lines and solid forms and space. Perhaps the most important element in modern design today is how the designer uses space. Today's identity designers play with shapes against solids, large against small, space and non-space. And the public, (for the most part) gets it, they recognize and appreciate the often very complex public and private meanings inherent in modern graphic marks.

On The Roots of Good Design
By Paul Rand, at Yale in 1987

The roots of good design are in aesthetics: in painting, drawing and architecture, while those of business and market research are in demographics and statistics – disciplines traditionally incompatible with each other. They are not speaking the same language.

To many designers, art/design is a cultural mission, in which life and work are inseparable. Clean surfaces, simple materials, and economy of means are the designer's articles of faith. Asceticism, rather than "the good life," motivates good designers.

Advertising, especially broadcast advertising (traditional media), was becoming prohibitively expensive and led to the emergence and proliferation of non-traditional media. One of the most popular is the so-called "Guerrilla" media meaning employing methods of reaching consumers in unconventional ways, often in the open air, and in unexpected places. What they are trying to do is create "Brand Buzz," which is another way of saying, "Word of Mouth."

On Being a Guerrilla
By Jay Conrad Levinson,
author and former creative director

The best Guerrilla marketing concepts usually employ the use of "Memes" (pronounced "meemz").

What are Memes? Memes in marketing are a whole new idea. The word meme (first coined in 1976 by Oxford biologist Richard Dawkins in his book, *The Selfish Gene)* has been a term for human behavior since the beginning of time.

The wheel was maybe the first meme (along with fire).

There are three things you should know about memes:

1. It's the lowest common denominator of an idea, a basic unit of communication

2. It has the ability to alter human behavior

3. It is energized with emotion

For guerrillas, a meme is a concept that has been so simplified that anybody can understand it instantly and easily. To use a meme in Guerrilla marketing you must convey who you are, why someone should buy from you instead of a competitor, trigger an emotional response and generate a desire–all within the first two seconds. Not easy.

Words put together as slogans, can become Memes. Here are several.

Got milk?, Intel Inside, Drivers Wanted (VW), A Diamond is Forever (DeBeers), Things Go Better With Coke, M&Ms Melt in Your Mouth, Not in Your Hand.

"Intel Inside" is a meme.

Sometimes it is a mental picture Meme: Gatorade poured on the winning coach at the end of a game, Burger King's luscious flame-broiled hamburger.

Sometimes it is a sound Meme: the "Ho,Ho,Ho" of the Jolly Green Giant.

"Ho-ho-ho,"
is a meme.

Keep in mind that in marketing, a meme is an idea or concept that has been refined, distilled, stripped down to its bare essentials, then super-simplified in such a way that anybody can grasp its meaning instantly and effortlessly.

Memes have an enormous impact on our lives. They invade our minds without either our knowledge or our permission, and initiate a chain reaction. They create an involuntary shift in perception, which in turn creates a shift in attitude, which creates a shift in behavior – and that is the ultimate goal of all marketing.

With the telecommunications wars being waged with ferocity and non-stop telemarketing, all the phone companies have been striving for a point of difference. Research showed that one of the benefits that could be offered by a phone company was clarity of sound. That quest led to one of the best...a Meme that does it with (implied) sound, image and words.

"So quiet, you could hear a pin drop," is its core idea and that spurred the birth of Sprint's meme, a graphic depiction of a pin dropping and bouncing next to a telephone receiver.

Since that time, Sprint (now called "Embarq") has been using its meme wisely, carefully and consistently, in true guerrilla fashion. Ideally, they'll be able to stay with it for a long time, or at least until research shows that clear sound is now taken for granted. The pin drop-ping can be a meme with longevity – the best and most pow-erful kind.

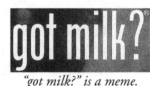

"got milk?" is a meme.

On Stressing the Benefit
By Ralph Rydholm, Chairman Emeritus,
TLK/Euro RSCG, Chicago

One day, in a pointless and fruitless creative strategy meeting for our client, Phila-delphia Cream Cheese, our heavy-set account guy came in the room and said, "Well I'm finally on a diet, and I learned recently that ounce for ounce, Cream Cheese has fewer calories than butter or margarine."

We all looked at each other–no one had ever said this before, had realized this fact before. I said, "Good God, let's go with that!"

A few days later at the client's office we presented our concept.

We immediately got resistance from the Brand Manager who claimed that it was a category benefit–not a brand benefit. I was annoyed and wouldn't give up. I asked for and got a meeting with the CEO of Kraft. In a second he realized that the idea was pure gold and ordered us to create ads around that promise. And on reflection we realized that Kraft had about 90 percent of the market–so we owned the category anyway. I believe this story illustrates the wisdom of stressing the benefit of the brand over petty differences between our brand and the competition. And that's what the best of the British and American agency guys do.

Here's another way to look at it.

1. Don't spend too much time worrying about the new lemony scent of our cleaning agent, as opposed to, "We clean better than our competition."

2. Never shortchange the benefit of a great execution. You can preempt competition through the execution.

No matter how brilliant the strategy, no matter how well tested it is, in the last analysis, the execution is the only thing that matters. That's the only thing the consumer will see, anyway.

FOOTE CONE & BELDING

Ten Observations About Advertising - from a guy who writes the stuff.
By Rob White, Vice President
and Associate Creative Director at FCB in Chicago.

1. When you're on the creative end of things you have to be well versed in popular culture because ideas can come from anywhere. For instance, a creative team may be discussing the Raveonettes' latest CD one minute and then move on to the subtle differences of Burt Reynold's mustache in *Cannonball Run I* versus *Cannonball Run II*. On the surface, that may seem like a tremendous waste of time. But that's how we get to the solutions that sell more toilet bowl cleaner.

2. Many people think advertising is glamorous. But then I tell them about focus groups and quantitative testing and that changes their tune pretty quick.

3. Writer's block is nothing. The hardest part about ideas isn't coming up with them. It's getting them sold, keeping them sold and then producing them the way you intended.

4. The worst place to think about advertising ideas is in an advertising agency. Working offsite stimulates creativity. So when you're in the concept phase, go spend the afternoon at a coffee house, browse the bookstore or visit the monkey cages at the zoo. You can't think outside the box if you're always sitting in one.

5. Sure, I often wear jeans to work. But there are days I dress casually, too.

6. If you have to set up a concept by describing how simple it is, it probably isn't. Besides, clients expect you to bring simple ideas. The complicated ones tend to take the air out of the room.

7. Using your spelling and grammar check ain't a bad idea. Apparently it isn't a bad idea either.

8. To be a good creative person you don't have to dress all in black, be the loudest person in the room or have a monstrous ego. Of course, if that works for you... super.

9. Never walk around the office empty handed. That sends people the message you're not very busy. So make sure you're at least clutching a pad of paper or even tuck some ancient storyboards under your arm. And walk briskly. That says you're adding value!

10. The best part about being in advertising is I get paid to laugh every day with very funny people. I'm thinking that's got to be better than working at the bank.

In the Twenty-first Century

We're more than halfway into the first decade of the twenty-first century. It is perhaps a little hard to have the perspective to judge this decade yet, but one thing is certain. It has gotten a lot more expensive to advertise or to do anything in the creative arts. When you consider that the average prime time commercial can cost around $2 million, that buying time on the Super Bowl cost(s) over $90,000 per second, that advertisers have to get their message into a thirty-second spot, sometimes fifteen seconds, you are seeing the effect of escalating costs. Marketing in this new world of proliferation and endless variety (500 channels) is more difficult than ever. "Trying to break through with consumers is definitely tougher and it's definitely a challenge." So said the chief marketing officer at PepsiCo Inc.'s North America division.

On Clutter!
John Geoghegan, Managing Partner
of MarketingPlus, Thousand Oaks, CA

To excel and stand out in this environment is becoming more and more difficult. Clutter abounds and it is becoming increasingly difficult to get through to the consumer. Art and design have become so common in the commercial marketplace that they have become the wallpaper of our world. Statistics reveal that there are about 500,000 commercials aired every year–adding up to about 1600 messages each day. The average viewer can't possibly retain it all. In today's downsized business world, it will probably fall to men and women who are not experts in these functions to make decisions that require a new perspective about art and design; through instinct and common sense they will restore a sense of balance and proportion in their future marketing decisions.

They must begin by asking themselves, "Is my campaign communication or wallpaper?"

Two Quick Questions
So, can a bad product executed with great branding and great design do anything but fail? Likewise, can a terrific product that is poorly executed be rescued along the way?

Two Quick Answers
The answers to the questions posed above are: a) No, to the first. A bad idea executed with style and focus will, in most cases, *still* fail. You can't save an Edsel with chrome and a two-tone paint job. b) Yes, to the second–but a great business

idea without a persuasive and visually compelling brand identity will almost always develop much more slowly, often to the point where it doesn't pay for itself and is withdrawn from the marketplace. The power of art and design in the marketplace will accelerate the success of a brilliant idea, and surely expose the weaknesses of a bad one.

Bridging the gap between product and image.

The marketing universe abounds with practical rules for product introductions, customer retention, brand extensions and loyalty building strategies. Graduate schools produce business professionals who can apply these rules to everything from farm equipment to frozen dinners. But, for the most part, this avalanche of words based on sound thinking has one critical piece missing—how to manage the visual components.

It is becoming necessary for marketing managers and product specialists to understand the elements of style and quality that eventually define the ethos of a brand for its purchasers and end users.

In the end, what a brand looks, sounds and feels like at the emotional level influences perceptions about taste and aroma, service and time. These communicate the critical elements that drive consumer choice and loyalty. All the brand theory, business planning and profit analysis in the world is just a pile of paper unless somebody knows how to create and evaluate compelling brand imagery and packaging that generates trial and builds loyalty from consumers. This is the way to break through the clutter- to avoid becoming wallpaper in today's marketing arena.

On the Internet

Marketers seeking an alternative, a better way to today's cluttered media universe are increasingly turning to the Internet to get their messages across.

The Internet evolved not from a single idea, or person but as the natural outgrowth of the computer. It developed out of the many interconnected computer networks and by 1982 was well established. The World Wide Web on the other hand, *was invented*–and by one man, an Englishman named Tim Berners-Lee. The year was 1989 and Berners-Lee was spending six months as a software engineer at CERN, a particle physics laboratory in Geneva, Switzerland. His invention was deceptively simple and consisted of computer software that could "keep track of all the random associations one comes

Sir Tim Berners-Lee

across in real life," as he put it. He envisioned a platform on which anyone anywhere could communicate on an equal basis.

Beginnings

He called it Enquire, short for "Enquire Within Upon Everything." Furthermore, the coding system he created for gaining access was relatively easy to learn, it is the well-known HTML (Hyper Text Mark-up Language). He also wrote a set of rules that permitted documents on the web to be linked together on computers all across the Internet and these became known as HTTP (Hyper Text Transfer Protocol). What is amazing and very praiseworthy is that he declared that it should be open to all who want to use it, without restriction or fee. He wanted no central manager and no central database. He wanted it to grow, open-ended and infinite. And grow it did!

Berners-Lee debuted his invention (the World Wide Web), in 1991 and it caught on instantly. The growth rate was incredible: in five years the number of users grew from 600,000 to 40 million and at one point it was doubling every 53 days.

Tim Berners-Lee and his invention changed lives and influenced the world. Ironically, he never got rich from his invention (although he was knighted by the Queen of England). He now teaches and does research at the Massachusetts Institute of Technology in Boston.

The Internet is really a delivery vehicle. It brings us information and it provides us with the means to connect to the sources of that information. It has an insidious side, though. It knows us by our hits on various websites or banner ads, or purchases and it uses this information to carefully (and repeatedly) direct marketing messages to us.

As far as marketing a product on the Internet, it utilizes three methods: banner ads, pop-ups and websites. Only websites market well, are respected by the public, and are having a big influence.

There are two essential and related entities connected and integral to the Internet: the web browser and the search engine.

Browsers

Netscape is a good example of a web browser. It began in 1995 and is a superb facilitator. AOL is another first class web browser. If you want to know something, Netscape or AOL are the primary paths to finding it.

Search Engines

Yahoo is a good example of a search engine and it too was established in 1995. Google is another example of a search engine. Both firms, Yahoo and Google, are huge, perhaps unfathomable. Here's an example of both at work.

Recently my AOL site announced an offer to "Find the 101 best places to live in the USA." I clicked on this site and was immediately connected to Google and then deluged with opportunities to find a moving company, find a real estate broker to sell my existing home, find financing to buy a new home, find deals on furniture, decorating and house repairs." Ironically, the only thing it didn't tell me was where were the 101 best places to live.

The Web can level the playing field for all business. And it is vast, in November of 1995 there were 100,000 websites. That was more than ten years ago and it has doubled every three months since. No one knows the size for sure but estimates are 250 million people are online around the world, and growing. No one disagrees that it is big–AOL alone claims twenty-one million subscribers.

The Search Engine is a most amazing vehicle. The groupings that the search engine seeks and finds have been described as "villages" and the individual entering the Web is in fact entering a world of connections to the many, many villages.

How do you navigate around in such a vast universe?

It is a lot easier if the Website is well designed. Here are some parameters of good websites.

–A good website entices the visitor to respond to questions, thus initiating a dialogue. A bad website is one that is nothing more than scanned brochures that are static and boring.

–A good website provides an environment of curiosity, a stimulus to explore, a sense of security (i.e. assurance of anonymity) and a sense of excitement (as in, "What's in here? Let's look around").

–Provides benefits, like information that has a clear association to your interests.

–Reveals brands (current ads, headlines, taglines, like "Just Do It" for Nike or "Generation Next" for Pepsi) related to the website, with subheads that show places where you can click to move deeper. These are often: "Our Mission, our products, our financials, recent news about us, and importantly, how to contact us."

–Has aesthetics, reveals the experience of using the product or service. These can work effectively at automobile company websites. Audi gives us a good example.

Audi's Website

Under a picture of their future automobile (The R8) is their current advertising tagline, "Never Follow." Then there are special offers, such as " Build your Audi," Streets of Tomorrow Events, all the models individually available, the home page, financial services and how to locate a dealer in your area. Finally there is an opportunity to "Experience the driving of our Audi," which requires a Flash Player accessory on your computer and plays a tiny, short movie of the experience of driving an Audi. As the Audi website demonstrates, website marketing can be the best, most effective method for advertising online.

2009 Audi R8 Cabrio

The Audi website is dramatic and compelling. There is a lot of business generated in less dramatic ways, however, as on Amazon.com, CDNow.com, LandsEnd. com, Kmart.com, LLBean. com, The SportsAuthority.com and many more. In these websites customers are simply using the website as a means to order products or services. Most popular items ordered are: online sales of electronics, books, CDs, software, apparel, toys and games, and ticketing (to airlines or even the theatre).

Measuring results for website ads is dependent on four factors: Lift (meaning transactions of visitors to the site), Conversion (customers who buy something), Frequency (number of visits) and Duration (how long does a customer remain on the site).

Who creates these website ads? There are many sources and in the forefront are all the major ad agencies with divisions devoted to this service. At Y&R it is a group called "Brand Dialogue." One of the current non-affiliated agencies is "DoubleClick." They claim to place 1.5 billion ads on the Internet every day, and they pledge these benefits: Interactivity (ability for the website viewer to respond), flexibility, precise targeting, quick results and measurable hits. Another is R/GA. a digital ad agency owned by the Interpublic Group of Companies.

Banner Ads and Pop-Ups

Besides website advertising, there are three other kinds: Banner Ads, Intertitials (a form of pop-up ad) and Pop-Ups.

Banner ads are the most popular (next to website advertising), and here are some tips for creating effective banner ads: (1) keep the banner ad simple, (2) maximize the size of the logo and (3) use with frequency.

As opposed to websites, banner ads are not as effective and pop-ups do little more than annoy. They do have one advantage–they are not expensive.

Typical costs for banner ads are as follows:

–$1.00 for each 1,000 impressions

–$55.00 if a "click through" is achieved

For Pop-Ups: $3.85 for 1,000 impressions.

Banner ads do not have a high response rate: 3/10 to 5/10 of 1 percent, or 3-5 responses for every 1,000 people. As far as those who "click through," the average is worse, one person out of every twenty-thousand who sees the banner ad will actually respond. (Source: *Principles of Advertising & IMC,* by Tom Duncan, McGraw-Hill Irwin, 2005)

It's a Wireless World
The cutting edge of this business is yet to be achieved but all indications are that it will be related to Broadband capability, and wireless. Broadband has expanded rapidly in recent years and is now offering online hookup through portable and small computers, like Black-Berries, and soon, cell phones. MTV is in the forefront of this business representing a huge television network with all revenue generated on the sale of ad space. The ad space they are

selling online is digital space and they offer many methods to be integrated. They offer whole packages of on air-advertising, driven by the popularity of mobile devices (BlackBerries or iPods etc.). The key to catching and staying on this bandwagon is engagement planning. Engagement planning will soon allow these facilitators to direct a sales pitch straight at a defined target audience or small group. They do this by understanding their target audience's behavior, best time of day to reach them etc. Google is working on this capability (engagement planning) as is Microsoft.

And then there are Blogs. Blogs are becoming more and more organized, offering websites of their own for the dissemination of similar information. Many call it the "Democratization of the Internet."

Some of the mainstream ad agencies, like Crispin Porter + Bogusky in Miami, are already creating websites that are truly interactive. Their most celebrated is "The Subservient Chicken" for Burger King. Those who visit the site can command the chicken to do things (like stand on its head, jump over a chair, etc.) and it will do it. It is preprogrammed to do something like fifty actions and responds to voice commands, and can only do those commands.

The Future is Now
The future of all of this is forming as we read this. MTV is convinced, as are others, that Broadband will provide TV entertainment, interactive shopping, interactive information and search all combined. It will be broadband TV, which MTV calls "Overdrive." Exciting new websites are forming with names like: Coolhunting.com or Comcastic.com or Myspace.com.

Both Yahoo and MTV are already very client-directed, although Yahoo is also linking itself to Ebay and its auction/sales services. One day (not far away) everything will be digital through a mobile hand-set, like a telephone. It will be a more sophisticated BlackBerry-which will also be a camera by the way.

The audience will use technology in a holistic way as a digital component that incorporates all the technology that affects people's lives.

Clearly the media landscape is changing and the three popular TV networks are not the dominant media force of old. Now marketers have many new media choices, most of them electronic. There are hundreds of TV channels and many services offering video on demand, as well as videogames, and of course, the Internet.

Internet Offerings

Advertisers can place video ads alongside newsclips, which can't be skipped; they can use the Internet to present an advertisement as a rifle shot approach, specific to a certain viewer's interests. Car companies can have their ads appear on search engines when people are hunting for information; websites have become ideal methods for creating buzz about a product, using email to tell people about a product or service. Marketers are using Web logs to push

products and treating bloggers as a regular outlet for ads–even sending them press releases. Apple Computer is selling ads for Time Warner's HBO, on podcasts for their iPod. The Internet has become one of the fastest growing forums for advertising with increases in ad revenue up 30 percent from last year to approximately $12 billion. Other forms of media that are growing too: outdoor advertising (posters) up 9.8 percent to $3.5 billion, and consumer magazines.

There is growth in Guerrilla advertising as well. Kellogg's has been placing stickers on supermarket coffee grinders to pitch its new Special K Vanilla Almond cereal.

"Our landscape is clearly changing at a rapid pace," says Andy Jung, Kellogg's senior director of advertising and media. "Advertisers and agencies must both assess the viability of the myriad of new communications options available as well as the near term and long term value."

On Achieving Digital Relevancy
(with Young Adults)
By Mark Barker, former Account Executive
with McCann Erickson, NY

The half-life of "cool" (young adult shorthand for relevancy) is constantly diminishing. In the time it used to take to resonate with the earliest of adopters, a brand can now have hit the Internet and matured across a global market. Consequently, there are an infinite and ever-changing number of trends, behaviors and activities vying for the attention of young adults.

While a great deal of hype surrounds identifying "what" those trends are, we see our job at McCann as uncovering the "why's." Why are these trends happening? What need are they serving? By uncovering these underlying motivations and leveraging them for marketing communications and activities, brands can tap into something that matters and endures.

As the channels through which young adults receive information continually become more varied and complex, a meaningful idea or message is only as good as the vehicle by which it is communicated. All points of contact must be considered potential media to drive and motivate young adults. Every minute of their lives young adults employ tools (such as e-mail, text, and instant messaging–to name only a few) that help them to communicate and share with unprecedented speed. These are powerful new marketing channels for delivering messages in a fast, cost-effective and impactful way. And, if a brand can offer young adults something they like, they'll pass it on to their friends and brand messages can spread like wildfire.

The message (is) has become the medium
(with apologies to Marshall McLuhan)

We have reached a situation where the effect of the message (whether it is for a marketing purpose or strictly informational) is more dependent on the way it is said, than what it says. Among these is speed. Young consumers are hooked on the speed and convenience, and the sheer "cool" of what can be done today.

The Future is Now
Advertising in the 21st Century
By Harry Jacobs, Chairman Emeritus,
and John B. Adams, CEO
The Martin Agency, Richmond, VA

How companies talk with consumers is becoming far more important than what they say. It's not logical, but it's true. We are experiencing an evolution in advertising that illustrates the changes in advertising campaigns and reflects the new schools of thought in a new world of marketing products and services.

Parity products are now so plentiful and similar that marketing strategies themselves have come under fire. So, for better or worse, these changing times have fostered new ways of presenting product messages. Simpler, quicker, and more interesting ways of creating effective work are now commonplace. Computer technology is allowing us to create images never before thought possible. This new form of advertising is just the beginning of what's ahead. Everything is up for grabs, and everything is certain to change.

For one thing, advertising will move from a presentation to a conversation. This will require some severe changes in the way we advertisers think. Information is becoming a commodity, it is everywhere and all the time–so we must find new ways to generate thought. It is, in many ways, an age of anti-logic.

In both industries, the real substantive differences between service and product are disappearing.

A classic example, one that is held up time and time again, is the advertising for Nike.

Nike was one of the first of the advertisers to move dramatically, radically to this method of new advertising as a conversation about style. If you look at Nike advertising, there are no Nike advertisements that are broadly seen in the public domain that have anything to do with substantive differences between their shoes, and their competitor's shoes.

None.

All of the (Nike) communication is about style and attitude. If we are going to be approaching communications differently, approaching business strategy differently, we must deal with profound change. It is such a profound change that it almost suggests that we need to un-train ourselves from a consistent insistence on approaching things rationally, logically, with a fixed input in mind. We've got to retrain ourselves to think laterally, non-sequentially, and to do it quickly–jumping the tracks of logic, if you will.

It is hard to predict how it will play out or what it will look like. I do believe that it will be characterized by, and be built around, a single, phenomenally important difference in the way communication is going to be done going forward, versus the way it has been done. And that is that marketing communication will no longer be a presentation, which it is today. A television commercial or a print ad in a magazine are both one- way communications. Thanks to the Internet that is simply going to change, and rapidly, The process of marketing, the process of selling–the process of putting products before the consumer, is going to become a conversation.

EVOLUTION

And so the last bridge is in many ways, the first.

It still is a conversation, transferring information–shaping it to achieve a desired end.

The intent remains the same, for an invading army in the eleventh century, a king consolidating his nation in the sixteenth, a glassmaker in Venice in the seventeenth, a retailer in Virginia in the eighteenth, a ship builder in Connecticut or a soup maker in Philadelphia in the nineteenth, a car maker in Detroit, a magazine publisher in New York, a meatpacker in Chicago, a software inventor from Seattle, an Internet designer from Palo Alto. The intent is still the same–to inform, to convince, to persuade.

Only the tools are different. Instead of a logo on a shield or a flag, a sign in front of a pub or a general store, a package in a supermarket or an ad in a magazine or on television, new methods of communication keep coming. They evolve and change; some get more far-reaching, some get quicker, some become prettier, some go wireless. Today it is the Internet, a lightning-fast electronic tool connecting unknown millions to each other, growing in size to unimaginable proportions. The ageless need to communicate, to market something, never goes away.

NOTES

Cover photo: Verazzano Bridge, taken by Gerard Sioen, Boulbon, France (used with permission), originally published in 2002 in a book by Bernhard Graf, and entitled, *Bridges That changed the World*, Prestel Publishing, Munich, 2002.
Author's photo: taken by Lloyd Goad, on the campus of Washington and Lee University, Lexington, VA.

Chapter 1. Marketing – The Essential Bridge

1. Charles Lamb Jr., Joseph Hair Jr., Carl McDaniel, *Essentials of Marketing*, Thompson/Southwestern, 2005, Part I-Page 6-26.
2. The differences in companies (Product-Centered, Sales-Centered, etc.) was drawn from: K. Douglas Hoffman, *Marketing Principles and Best Practices*, published by Thompson/Southwestern, Mason, Ohio in 2006. Particular reference was found in Chapter 1, Introduction to Marketing: pages 4 –20.
3. The history behind the Campbell's Soup logo, package and early advertising efforts came from two sources: Thomas Hine's, *The Total Package*, published by Little Brown & Company, Boston, 1995 and an interview in 2005 with the manager of public affairs (Beth Jolly) at that company.
4. From "Leo," a privately printed compilation of the thoughts, writing and wisdom of Leo Burnett, prepared and printed by the Burnett Agency, 1971.
5. "Lasting Loyalty and Positioning" came from an article in *Advertising Age* in 2005, as noted.
6. K. Douglas Hoffman (as noted above in 1) pages 240 – 255.
7. General thoughts on the creative process came from Jay Levinson-from varous emails he sent me on the subject of Guerrilla Marketing and his experiences as a creative writer with J. Walter Thompson and the Leo Burnett agency when we were in London.
8. The Six Stages/Bridges of Marketing is original but based (in part) on an expanded interpretation of the traditional 4 Ps concept expressed in many marketing textbooks.
9. Tom Friedman, *The World is Flat*, Farrar, Straus & Giroux, NY, 2005, pp. 516-518.
10. Helen Vaid, *Branding*, Watson-Guptill Publications, NY, 2003.
11. The profile of Paul Rand came from two sources: Allen Hurlburt, Paul Rand,

Communications Arts (CA) magazine, March/April 1999, published by Coyne & Blanchard, Palo Alto, CA, Volume 41, Number 1: pages 119-135. Used with permission. and Paul Rand, Good Design is Good Will, Yale University, School of Art, New Haven, 1987. These are excerpts from some of Paul Rand's lectures.

12. The Toyota Store, Noel Capon, *The Marketing Mavens*, Crown Business Press, New York 2007.

13. Brooks Brothers and the Golden Fleece, Wikipedia Foundation, 2008.

14. Procter & Gamble Sets the Standard, and Neil McElroy, Wikipedia Foundation, 2008.

15. Howard Schultz, *Pour Your Heart into It,* Hyperion Press, NY 1977.

Chapter 2: A Bridge Back - The History of the Logo

1. The early influences of the logo: symbolism, mythology etc. came from several books on the subject: these are:

David Fontana, *The Secret Language of Symbols*, Chronicle Books, San Francisco, 1993, pp. 20-40, and 64-93 and Jack Tresidder, *Symbols & Their Meanings*, by Duncan Baird Publishers, London, 2000, pp. 42-72 and 142-156.

2. References on Heraldry and the development of the logo of Great Britain came from:

Michel Pastoureau, *Heraldry*, Harry N. Abrams, NY 1996, pp. 16-60, and

Peter Spurrier, *The Heraldic Art Source Book*, Cassel Press, London, 1997, pp. 11-46 and Plantagenet Somerset Fry, *The Kings & Queens of England and Scotland*, Grove Press, NY 1990, pp. 24-109.

3. The Diners Club Story came from my own experience with this account in the late 1970s.

4. The Bayeux Tapestry research was greatly augmented by conversations and correspondence with J. Bard McNulty, Professor and English Department Head-Emeritus at Trinity College, Connecticut. Professor McNulty has written several books on this fascinating subject and made impressive and original discoveries related to the symbolism and legends found along the borders of the tapestry. Among these:

5. J.Bard McNulty, *The Narrative Art of the Bayeux Tapestry Master*, AMS Press, New York, 1989.

6. Reference to Harold's logo and flag came from *Rulers of Britain* by Plantagenet Somerset Fry, f.r.s.a., Paul Hamlin Press, London 1967.

7. Reference to Harold and William's relationship to Edward came from *The Saxon and Norman Kings* by Christopher Brooke, Collins Clear-type Press, London, 1963 (pg. 25).

8. The other sources I used for this event (The Battle of Hastings) and life and commerce in the middle ages of Great Britain (Wessex) came (in part) from Winston Churchill's, *A History of the English-Speaking Peoples*, Volume 1, Cassell & Company, London, 1956, pp. 121-140.

9. The Hundred Years War (1337-1453) was sourced (in part) from Andre Maurois, *A His-*

tory of England, Bodley Head, London, 1962, pp. 180-189,

10. "Aftermath and The Stubborn Scots" was researched, in part, from James Webb's excellent book, *Born Fighting*, Broadway Books, 2004. pp. 37-63.

11. Life and retailing in the colonies was researched from several sources: Michael Olmert, *Official Guide to Colonial Williamsburg*, by The Colonial Williamsburg Foundation, 1985, pp. 52-111. and Mary Goodwin, *The Colonial Store*, Colonial Williamsburg Foundation Library.

12. References to early trademarks and logos was researched from Per Mollerup, *The Marks of Excellence*, Phaidon Press, London, 1997, pp. 31-201.

Chapter 3: The Bridge Forward - The Logo Today

1. Reference to The Growth of Stores came in large part from Thomas Hine, *The Total Package*, Little Brown & Co., 1995.pp. 110-303.

2. Design's Growing Importance came, in part, from several articles in *Business Week* magazine: "The Power of Design," May 17, 2004 and the 2006 Procter & Gamble Annual report's statements made by their CEO, A.G. Lafley–headlined "First & Second Moments of Truth".

3. K. Douglas Hoffman, *Marketing Principles and Best Practices*, chapter 6.

4. "Segmenting and Targeting": Tom Duncan, *Advertising & IMC*, McGraw-Hill Irwin, New York, 2005, Chapter 7.

5. Bernd Schmitt and Alex Simonson discuss the concept of market targeting also in their excellent book, *Marketing Aesthetics*, Free Press, New York, 1997.

6. Design briefs and company goals are discussed at length in Clive Chajet's, *Image by Design*, Addison-Wesley Publishing, NY, 1991, Chapter 1 and Chapter 12.

7. The Pepsi-Cola International Design Standards Manual (known as the "Look Book") was the reference for graphic design applications to their products and brands. These books were written by my firm and were published by Pepsi-Cola International, Purchase, NY in the mid 1990s. The actual identity design was primarily the work of Peterson Blyth, NY.

8. Reference to the different types of identities comes from: Per Mollerup, *Marks of Excellence*, Phaidon Press, London, 1997, pp. 50-175.

9. Restyling Logos in Mainstream America was written for this book by Arthur Congdon, CEO and founder of Congdon and Company, Greenwich, CT, 2005. I suspect that some of his own influences come from his years as a graduate student at Yale University, where he earned a masters Degree.

10. The Story of the Black Dog Café and its unique and special logo came from interviews I conducted with some company officers, Robert Douglas Jr. in particular in 2004.

12. Naomi Klein, *No Logo*, "The Brand Expands" was gleaned from her book, published by Picador Press, New York in 2000.

13. The many faces of AT&T came from two sources: A) Wikipedia Foundation, 2008; and B) *The Telephone Book* by H. M. Boettinger, Stearn Publishing, NY, 1977.

Chapter 4: Preferences, Prejudices and Persuasion

1. "Season of Desire" is from *The Chicago Tribune*, editorial page, Christmas, 2005.
2. Aesthetics and Product Design, Spatial Design and Style was referenced from:
Schmitt and Simonson, *Marketing Aesthetics*, Free Press, New York, 1997, pp. 80-119.
3. The Absolut Story came from two sources: the book referred to above and the book that the parent company published: Richard W. Lewis, *Absolut Book*, by Journey Editions, Boston, 1996.
4. Creating a Marketing Plan comes from my own experience and marketing plans from past projects, as well as from the following two books:
David A. Aker: *Managing Brand Equity*, The Free Press, Toronto, 1991, pp. 104-130 and David A. Aker, *Brand Portfolio Strategy*, same publisher, but published in 2006, pp. 3-88.
5. John Berendt, "The Venice Effect," comes from an excellent book called *The City of Falling Angels*, published by The Penguin Press in 2005.
6. "Synesthesia" Size, angularity, proportion, dimensions of style etc.: Schmitt and Simonson, *Marketing Aesthetics*, The Free Press, NY, 1987, pp. 105-107, also comes from
7. Ibid, pages 120-158, for Themes.
8. Ibid. 150-153 for the Xerox Story, augmented by personal knowledge and from graphic designer Don Ervin.
9. Ibid for Attitudes: past, contemporary and futuristic.
10. The Rango Story comes from personal experience.
11. The Marlboro Story comes from: Thomas Hine, *The Total Package*, published by Little Brown, Boston, 1995.
12. Doing research on the target audience comes from an essay written by Robert Lauterborn, Professor of Advertising and University of North Carolina/Chapel Hill.
13. Vance Packard, *The Hidden Persuaders* published by David McKay Company, New York, in 1957.
14. Lawrence Vincent, *Legendary Brands*, Dearborn Trade Publishing, Chicago 2002
15. In addition, one article form the *New Yorker* in September of 2004: entitled "Wine by the Numbers" (how people are influenced by wine copywriting), by Adam Gopnik.

Chapter Five: The Package As the Brand Bridge

1. Thomas Hine, *The Total Package*, Little Brown & Company, "In the Beginning," Boston, 1995.

2. "The Golden Age, and origins of glass in packaging came, in large part from Encyclopedia Britannica (1946 Edition), volume 10, pages 398-420.

3. Thomas Hine, "Early Brands, the Kikapoo Indians" etc. came from *The Total Package* (referenced also in Chapter 4).

4. Ibid, "Then Along Came Uneeda."

5. Smuckers and Arm and Hammer came from the Internet-the websites of these two firms, which list the history and early development of the companies.

6. Thomas Hine, *The Total Package*, "The Tin Can That Went to the North Pole."

7. Ibid, "The Quaker Oats Story."

8. The Nabisco Story, came from personal experience

9. Pepperidge Farm same as 8 above.

10. Packaging Innovations, came from Thomas Hine, Ibid

11. Richard Shear, "Packaging has become a reflection of lifestyle," CEO of LMS Design in 2005

Chapter 6: The Arena

1. Lamb, Hair and McDaniel, *Essentials of Marketing*, Fourth Edition, published by Thompson/Southwestern, Mason, Ohio, 2005- "The Supermarket," reference material, Part 3, Chapter 11, pp. 354-384.

2. "The Top 10 Supermarkets", figures came from the Internet and *Advertising Age* magazine, Crain Communications, NY

3. Store intelligence, regarding layout and product distribution, and profit margins came from personal observation and from interviews with store managers (Kroger and Wal-Mart).

4. Lamb, Hair and McDaniel, from *Essentials of Marketing*, "The psychology of store layout", Part 3, Chapter 10, and "The Science of Shopping" narrated by Paco Underhill, Today Show (TV), October, 2006.

5. "Meet the Gladiators", comes from the Internet or annual reports from the public companies cited in the chapter.

6. "The Ocean Spray Story" came from personal experience.

7. Lamb, Hair and McDaniel, pp. 328-365.

8. Schmitt and Simonson, *Marketing Aesthetics*, Free Press, New York, 1997, pp. 7-10: The Gap story.

9. Lamb, Hair and McDaniel, pp. 357-364: Types of stores, format and categories

10. Marketing Space was written by Gerald Postlethwaite, at my request.

11. Howard Schultz, *Pour Your Heart Into It*, Hyperion Press, NY, 1997. The Starbucks Story was also augmented by telephone interviews in 2005 with Harry Roberts (interior designer and marketing consultant for the Starbucks Company).

12. Part II, "Early Retailing" was researched in the J.D. Rockefeller Jr. Library at Colonial Williamsburg, VA in 2004, as well as from two books:

T.H. Breen, *Marketplace of the Revolution*, Oxford University Press, NY, 2004.

and Thomas Dionysius Clark, *Southern Country Stores: Pills, Petticoats and Ploughs*, published by Norman: University of Oklahoma Press, 1989.

13. Further research into early retailing came from: Henry Boley, *Lexington in Old Virginia*, published by Garrett and Massie, Richmond, VA, 1936 and Mary Goodwin, *Colonial Store*, by Colonial Williamsburg Foundation Library, Research Report Series (also part of the J.D. Rockefeller Jr. Library).

14. IKEA, from Wikipedia Foundation, 2008

Chapter 7: Advertising's not so little sister-Sales Promotion

1. Louis Boone and David Kurtz, *Contemporary Marketing*, by Thompson Corporation/ Southwestern, 2005, Chapter 18.

2. "Early Days in Promotion" was researched from personal experience as well as from the book, *Direct Marketing*, Wunderman Ricotta & Klein (NY) and published by their parent organization, Young & Rubicam Advertising, in the 1970s.

3. Lamb, Hair and McDaniel, *Essentials of Marketing*, by Thompson/Southwestern, 2005, Chapter 13, pp. 472-473.

4. "Couponing, Sweepstakes and Contests", was researched from The Holiday Inn Promotion in the 1970s, and from personal experience.

5. "Scratchcards" and other Pepsi related promotion information came from personal experience as (acting) International Promotion Manager for Pepsi-Cola International for a year in the mid 1980s.

6. "Promotion at Pepsi-Cola" as written by Pedro Vergara, who succeeded me as (official) International Promotion Manager for Pepsi-Cola International (see Chapter 8).

7. "Choosing the Right Promotion Technique" came from The Promotion Resource Book, written for Pepsi-Cola in the 1980s.

8. "Guerrilla Marketing" was researched by me and augmented by information supplied by Jay Conrad Levinson, co-author (with Seth Godin) of *Guerrilla Marketing Handbook*, published by Houghton Mifflin Company, Boston, 1994.

9. Boone and Kurtz, *Contemporary Marketing*, (see No. 1 above), on Ethics.

10. Extra background information was gleaned from three sources: *Documents of American History*, edited by Henry Steele Commager, Appleton-Century Croft, Inc., NY. 1949, *Marketer's Guide to Media*, volume 26, VNU Business Publications, NY, 2003, and the *Sales Promotion Handbook*, edited by Ovid Risso, The Dartnell Corporation, Chicago, 1979.

11. Saul Bass researched from two sources: A) *Six Chapters in Design*, Philip B. Meggs, Chronicle Books, CA, 1997 and B) Wikipedia Foundation

Chapter 8: The Cola Wars

1. J. C. Lewis and Harvey Yazijian, *The Cola Wars*, Everest House, NY, 1980.

2. Frederick Allen, *Secret Formula*, by, Harper Collins Publishers Inc., NY, 1994. Early history of Coca-Cola: from "Bottles make the Scene".

3. Constance L. Hays, *The Real Thing, Truth & Power at the Coca-Cola Company* by, Random House Publishing, NY 2004.

4. Thomas Hine, *The Total Package*, by Little Brown & Company, Boston, 1995.

5. "Pepsi Comes Onstage" was referenced, in part, from J.C. Louis and Harvey Yazijian, *The Cola Wars*, published by Beaverbooks, Ontario, Canada, 1980.

6. Frederick Allen, (see one above)"Twelve Full Ounces'.

7. "Moscow Trade Fair" came from a Pepsi-cola International company magazine, *Panorama,* published in June of 1986.

8. "Coke/Pepsi Marketing Strategies: comes from personal experience as well as *Advertising Age* magazine, Crain Communications, Inc. and each company's website.

9. "Taste Tests" comes from personal experience while working at and for Pepsi, and the Pepsi corporate magazine *Panorama,* February 1987 issue.

10. "New Coke and Formula change" came (with permission) from Sergio Zyman, *The End of Marketing as We Know It,* by Harper Collins Publishers, NY, 1994, and Pepsi"s Panorama magazine, February 1986 issue.

11. Ibid.

12. Frederick Allen, pp. 368, 400-401.

13. Constance L. Hays, "Gatorade", as well as the Pepsi-Cola Inc. annual reports of 2002 and 2004.

14. "It Never Ends" comes in part from *Beverage Digest* magazine -an article on market share slippage in 2002, Sergio Zyman quotes and the annual reports of both companies for 2005.

15. New Logo is Born, came from personal experience, and Peterson Blyth, NY.

16. Keeping Up with Coca-Cola, written by Pedro Vergera, International Promotion manager for Pepsi-Cola, in 1982-85.

Chapter 9: Advertising-the Image Makers

1. Marshall Loeb, "Advertising, The Visible Persuaders," *Time* magazine cover story, October 12, 1962,

2. "Consolidation" comes in part from information from Fact Pack–a supplement to *Advertising Age*–the *3rd Annual Guide to Advertising & Marketing,* published by Crain Communications, 2005.

3. "The Whole Egg at Work" comes, in part, from Young & Rubicam promotional literature on the firm and its structure as well as personal interviews with Ed Ney in 2004.

4. Tom Duncan, *Advertising & IMC*, by published by McGraw Hill Irwin, NY 2005, pp. 419-455. The process of advertising comes in part from this book.

5. Lamb, Hair and McDaniel, Chapter 13, pp. 446-466: Types of advertising.

6. George and Michael Belch, *Advertising and Promotion*, fifth edition, by published by McGraw–Hill Irwin, New York, 2001, Chapters 8 and 9 in particular, pp. 132-149, pp. 304-329 (on Media).

7. Ibid. Advertising headlines and creating strategy references comes in part from: George and Michael Belch, as well as interviews within Y&R in 2003, for the roles and the functions of persons within a typical advertising agency.

8. Ibid, Chapter 9.

9. Jay Levinson, Strategic Advertising Planning Guide, came from and his *Guerrilla Marketing Handbook*, published by Houghton Mifflin Company, Boston, 1994.

10. Reflections on the creative person came from The Martin Agency literature and a speech by the president of the agency, Mike Hughes.

11. Jon Steel, *Truth, Lies & Advertising*, published by John Wiley & Sons, New York, 1998, chapter 7 on the role research played in the "Got Milk" campaign.

12. Jack Sissons and Roger Baron, *Advertising Media Planning* by McGraw-Hill, 2002, pp. 397-434.

13. David Ogilvy, *Ogilvy on Advertising*, published by Atheneum Books, NY, 1983. How to Make TV commercials that Sell, etc.

14. Marshall Loeb, "The Mammoth Mirror" (item one above), Time magazine cover story, October 12, 1962.

15. Phillipe Lorin, *Five Giants of Advertising*, Assontine Publishing, Paris, 2001, Three Memorable Ad Campaigns and Three Memorable Ad men, and the 50th Advertising Hall of Fame, published by American Advertising Federation, New York, 1999.

16. David Ogilvy, *Confessions of an Advertising Man*, by Atheneum Books, 1952: "Ogilvy had Opinions," pp. 56-81.

17. Phillipe Lorin: "Profiles of Leo Burnett and Bill Bernbach,"pp. 96-140.

18. "Bernbach and his creative crocess" came from an article in *CA (Communications Arts)* magazine, by Dick Coyne, Coyne & Blanchard, Inc, March/April 1999 issue.

19. Ibid, the background of designer Paul Rand.

20. Kevin Roberts, *Lovemarks*, published by Powerhouse Books, NY 2004: Time and Tide, pp. 196-200.

21. The Advertising/Communications timeline came from *Advertising Through the Ages, Advertising Age,* March 28th, 2005.

Additional information for this chapter came from: Don Schultz, Stanley Tannenbaum and Robert F. Lauterborn, *Integrated Marketing Communications*, NTC Business Books, Lincolnwood, IL, 1994, Chapter 1.

Chapter 10: Spin, or the Craft of Public Relations

1. Tom Duncan, *Principles of Advertising and IMC* by McGraw Hill Irwin, NY, 2004: Maytag and Pillsbury promotions, Chapter 17, pp. 543-556.

2. "More About MS&L" came from the firm's (Manning, Selvidge and Lee) website.

3. Tom Duncan, ibid, Chapter 17: "Types of Public Relations programs."

4. "The Father of Public Relations" was researched from two books: L. Roy Blumenthal, *The Practice of Public Relations*, by The Macmillan Company, NY, 1972, and
Edward L. Bernays, *Biography of an Idea* (Memoirs) by Simon & Schuster, NY, 1965.

5. "The Nabisco Launch" came from personal experience.

6. "Deep Knowledge" came from a PBS television program aired in 2004 entitled The Persuaders, and the Internet.

7. Kevin Roberts, "A Kodak Moment," pp. 150-152.

8. Stuart Ewen, *P.R! A Social History of Spin*, by Basic Books (Harper Collins), NY, 1996.

9. Tom Duncan, Chapter 17.

10. "The Bloomingdale's Story" came, in the main, from an essay written by James S. Schoff, past president of that store and partially from articles in the *New York Times* September 8, 1974, the *Wall Street Journal* September 24, 1974, and *Barron's*, September 19, 2005.

11. Additionally, some information for this chapter came from K. Douglas Hoffman *Marketing Principles and Best Practices*, pp. 465-467.

Chapter 11: Print, or Design in Publications

1. The history of typography came, in part from Encyclopedia Britannica (1946 edition), Volume 22, pages 650-651 and an article in the *New Yorker* magazine on type design and Mathew Carter, December 5, 2005.

2. Annual reports research on the Securities and Exchange Laws of 1933 and 1934 came from *Documents of American History*, edited by Henry Steele Commager, Appleton-Century Croft, New York, 1949.

3. Seymour Chwast and D. K. Holland, editors, *Illustration: America*, Twenty-five outstanding portfolios, Rockport Publishers, Rockport, MA, 1996, pp. 11-15.

4. The Painted Image was researched in *Illustration: America*, and Susan E. Meyer, Harry N. Abrams *America's Great Illustrators*, by Publishing, NY 1978.

5. Two books on Winslow Homer were used: Nicolai Cikovsky Jr, and Franklin Kelly, *Winslow Homer*, by National Gallery of Art/Washington, Yale University Press, 1995, and
Philip C. Beam, *Winslow Homer in the 1890s, Prout's Neck Observed*, by Hudson Hills Press, NY, 1990.

6. Two Books on Norman Rockwell were used: Seymour Chwast and D.K. Holland, *Illustration: America*, and Laura Claridge, *Norman Rockwell, A Life*, by Random house, NY, 2000.

7. Charles Dana Gibson was researched from several sources: *Illustration: America.*
Paul R. Baker, Stanny: *The Gilded Life of Stanford White,* by Free Press/Macmillan, NY, 1989.
8. The Modern Magazine came, in part, from *Marketers Guide to Media,* VNU Press, NY, 2003.
9. *The Lively World of Milton Glaser,* from Wikipedia Foundation and *Milton Glaser Graphic Design,* The Overlook Press, Woodstock, NY, 1973.

Chapter 12: The Bridge to the Future

1. This chapter is made up in the main by personal reminiscences and anecdotes from men in the world of advertising, graphic design, retailing, public relations, and sales promotion. Each of their contributions are clearly marked by author.
2. In addition, some research was done from *Image by Design,* by Clive Chajet, and *Business Week* magazine, a cover story called the "Power of Design," May 17, 2004.
3. Research on the Internet came from:
4. *Advertising & IMC,* by Tom Duncan, chapter 12, pp. 388-413.
5. Lamb, Hair, McDaniel, *Essentials of Marketing,* pp. 479, 488-490.
6. "The Marketing Maze," a special supplement on current methods of reaching potential customers, from the *Wall Street Journal,* July 10, 2006.
Additionally, other (general) references were:
–Charles and Mary Beard, *Beard's Basic History of the United States,* by Doubleday, NY, 1944.
–*Communications Arts* magazine, "40 Years of Creative Excellence", March/April 1999, Coyne & Blanchard Inc, Palo Alto, CA.
–Ed Gold, *The Business of Graphic Design,* by Watson-Guptill Publications, NY, 1985, pp. 126-129 and the Introduction.

Absolut bottle design and calligraphy are trademarks owned by V&S, Vin & Spirit AB© 1995.

CONTRIBUTORS

The following men (in alphabetical order) have given generously of their time to share their experiences and wisdom for the students who read this book.

John B. Adams is Chairman and CEO of the Martin Agency–the south's hottest advertising agency, located in Richmond, Virginia. Their reputation for creativity is considerable, evidenced by their work on United Parcel Service, Geico and now Wal-Mart. The agency has won numerous awards.

Mark Barker: after graduating from Washington and Lee University, went on to become an Account Executive with McCann Erickson Agency, where he worked with a team devoted to finding the right words and media to appeal to today's youth markets. He is presently a free-lance writer in Austin, Texas.

Bruce Bendinger is a man of many talents and interests. He has been a writer and creative director at J. Walter Thompson, a publisher and author of several books on advertising. *The Copy Workshop* is very popular and is now in its third edition.

Arthur Congdon is the founder and president of Congdon & Company LLC, his own identity/logo firm in Greenwich, CT. His clients include Mercury Marine, Pepsi-Cola, and Burger Chef, to name a few, and he has a BFA degree in Advertising Design from Boston University and an MFA degree in Graphic Design from Yale University.

Barbara Crawford is a popular, celebrated fine artist, is also the director of the Fine Arts Department at Southern Virginia University in Buena Vista, Virginia. In 1995 she co-authored a book entitled "Rockbridge County Artists and Artisans."

John Geoghegan is founder and principal of MarketingPlus, a busy consulting firm in Thousand Oaks, CA. His clients include Swedish Match, DjEEP, and Target Marketing Group, among others. Prior to his current activities he was Vice President of Strategic Planning and Brand Development at the General Cigar Company. He also enjoyed an eleven year career in the Young & Rubicam organization. John is presently working as Vice President of Market Development with a specialty tobacco importer in Los Angeles.

John Gillin: Division President Emeritus and corporate Senior Vice President of the Coca-Cola Company in Atlanta, still serves as consultant to his former firm. Until recently he was Chairman of Boys (and now also Girls) Town, USA.

Harry Jacobs was Chairman and CEO of the Martin Agency in Richmond, VA from 1977 to 1997. He has been featured in numerous articles on advertising in the *Wall Street Journal* and *Adweek,* as well as being a member of New York's One Club Creative Hall of Fame. During his term in office he did much to bring his agency into the front ranks of American Advertising. For this, and a lifetime of achievement, Mr. Jacobs was recently inducted into Advertising's Hall of Fame.

Robert Lauterborn: Professor of Advertising at the University of North Carolina, at Chapel Hill, NC, teaches and writes topical books on marketing communications. Prior to entering the academic world he served for ten years as Director of Marketing Communication and Corporate Advertising for the International Paper Company in New York, and sixteen years with General Electric in various corporate communications positions.

Jay Levinson is a former writer and creative director with both the Leo Burnett agency in London, and Senior Vice President at J.Walter Thompson. He is also the author of many books on Guerrilla Marketing, many of which have sold in excess of 14 million copies worldwide and in forty-one languages. He has become the primary authority on the subject, and is referred to as the "Father of Guerrilla Marketing."

Mort Libby is Chairman Emeritus of Libby Perszyk Kathman, headquartered in Cincinnati, Ohio. Under his leadership in the 1980s and 1990s LPK became one of the largest and most successful graphic design firms in the nation.

J. Bard McNulty is an authority on the Bayeux Tapestry and the author of several books on the subject. His most recent is *Visual Meaning in the Bayeux Tapestry.* He is also Chairman Emeritus of the English Department at Trinity College, Connecticut and has been a consultant to the BBC on the subject of the Bayeux Tapestry.

Edward N. Ney is Chairman Emeritus at Young & Rubicam, New York, and served as Chairman, President and CEO at that agency from 1970 until 1985. After leaving Y&R he served as U.S. Ambassador to Canada until 1992. In addition he is a Trustee at the Museum of TV and Radio in NY, Amherst College, a Fellow on the Council of Foreign Relations, a member of the Advertising Hall of Fame and has been named Advertising Man of the Year numerous times by *U.S. News and World Report.* Today Mr. Ney continues as a consultant to Y&R/worldwide and as a director of the Ney Conference Center in New York.

Gerald Postlethwaite has worked in senior management positions for more than forty years, primarily in the communications industry, covering such disciplines as: advertising, packaging, direct marketing and retail strategy and design. Until 2000 he served as Chairman and Managing Director of RPA, Ltd, London, planning and executing retail marketing operations for diverse clients throughout Europe, Asia and South America.

Ralph Rydholm is former Chairman of TLK/EuroRSCG and former president of the American Association of Advertising Agencies. He began his career in advertising as a creative writer and became, ultimately, the Worldwide Creative Director for J. Walter Thompson.

James S. Schoff is former president of Bloomingdale's from 1978 to 1984, joined the store as assistant buyer in the Upholstered Furniture Department in 1960. During his many years at the store he saw, and helped direct Bloomingdale's growth from a strictly New York metropolitan-area store into an extremely popular place to be seen and to shop. With recent mergers "Bloomies" will soon become a national retail business.

Richard Shear is a principal and creative director of LMS Design, a package design and brand identity firm established to focus on strategic design excellence and "hands-on" management of the creative process. Richard, a graduate of Temple University's Tyler School of Art, has written and lectured widely on the role of design and the creative process. To "relax" he has become a competitive bicycle racer and is now ranked nationally.

Pedro Vergara is chairman emeritus of Promos SA (in Santiago, Chile) and was formerly the Pepsi-Cola International Promotions Director. During his Pepsi years he did much to put the firm's international promotion effort on a disciplined and effective basis. He owns a sizeable sailboat and loves to sail in the challenging waters off Chile's southern coast.

Rob White is a vice president, associate creative director and seasoned copywriter with Foote Cone & Belding Advertising in Chicago. Some of his television commercials have won national recognition for excellence and creativity.

And two men who graciously allowed me to excerpt their own books or lectures:

Sergio Zyman was chief marketing officer for the Coca-Cola Company during some of its most dramatic years. He is credited with having restructured the worldwide marketing organization and strengthened Coke's global marketing leadership position. As such Sergio is responsible for the introduction of Diet Coke and the New Coke initiative in the mid 1980s, and for many of their most creative advertisements.

Kevin Roberts is CEO Worldwide for Saatchi & Saatchi Advertising, New York. In that capacity he oversees the agency's more than 7,000 creative people in eighty-two countries. When he has the time he also teaches at Cambridge University's Judge Institute of Management, the University of Limerick in Ireland and the University of Waikato (the management school) in New Zealand.

Also included: **Paul Rand,** preeminent graphic designer of many of the nation's best identities and a veteran of advertising life, partly with Doyle Dane Bernbach. After Madison Avenue he went on to teach in the School of Art at Yale University in New Haven, Connecticut. Some of his observations are excerpted from a group of lectures he gave at that college in 1987. They remain as fresh today as when he delivered them to his students twenty years ago.

Picture Credits

Chapter 2: Shield with Crow and Bayeux Tapestry: Michael Pastoreau, *Heraldry*, Harry Abrams Publisher, 1997.

Chapter 3: Absolut Bottle: Richard W. Lewis *Absolut Book*, Journey Editions, Boston, 1996

Chapter 4: Ibid: Absolut Ad

Chapter 8: Taste test in Germany photo, Pepsi *Panorama* magazine, PepsiCo, Inc. 1985; Two cans of Coke photo: Pepsi *Panorama* magazine, PepsiCo, Inc., June of 1986 The Moscow Trade Fair in 1959: from Pepsi *Panorama* magazine, June of 1986

Chapter 9: Pie Chart on Media Placement, Two Pie Charts on Advertising Holding Companies, One Pie Chart on Advertising Expenditures.
All of the above from *Advertising Age's* Agency of Family Trees, and Fact Pack, Crain Communications, Fall 2005.
Absolut Ads, Richard Lewis, *Absolut Book,* Journey Editions, Boston, 1996.
Ogilvy Photo: from *Ogilvy on Advertising*, Vintage Books, New York, 1985
Levy's Rye Ad: from *Communication Arts* magazine, March/April, 1999
Ibid, VW Ad, Got Milk? Ad from Jay Schulberg, *The Milk Mustache Book*, Ballantine Books, NY, 1998.

Chapter 11: Mathew Carter photo from *New Yorker* magazine, December 5, 2005
Catalogs: Chicos, Lands End, Crate and Barrel.
Illustration for Masterpiece Theater poster and Seymour Chwast, from:
Illustration: America, Edited by S. Chwast and K. K. Holland, Rockport Publishers, Rockport, MA, 1996. Illustration of Bob Dylan, by Milton Glaser, The Overlook Press, NY, 1973.

Chapter 12: Paul Rand Photo from *CA* magazine, March/April 1999.

INDEX

ABOUT THE AUTHOR

Bruce Macdonald is an Adjunct Lecturer and Executive in Residence at the Williams School of Commerce, Economics, and Politics at Washington and Lee University in Lexington, Virginia. Every spring and fall Professor Macdonald teaches a popular course called "Art in Business" and has sparked the interest of many of his students to the world of marketing communications. Prior to coming to Virginia he and his family lived in London, where he illustrated for a number of advertising agencies and publishing firms. They moved to Connecticut in 1970, and he commuted daily to New York City, first to work at Young & Rubicam Advertising, later for his own graphic design firm, Congdon Macdonald & Shear. He has taught marketing communications at Trinity College, Hartford (his alma mater), Southern Virginia University, ECLA (the European College of Liberal Arts) in Berlin, as well as W&L. He and his wife Sunny live in a 1775 house (lovingly restored) on a farm just outside of Lexington.

CPSIA information can be obtained
at www.ICGtesting.com
Printed in the USA
BVHW011316061219
565855BV00008B/435/P

9 781600 374463